MISSION IN A BOTTLE

MISSION IN A BOTTLE

THE HONEST GUIDE TO DOING BUSINESS DIFFERENTLY— AND SUCCEEDING

SETH GOLDMAN AND BARRY NALEBUFF

ILLUSTRATED BY SUNGYOON CHOI

CROWN
BUSINESS

NEW YORK

Published in the United States by Crown Business, an imprint of the Crown Publishing Group, a division of Random House, Inc., New York.
www.crownpublishing.com

CROWN BUSINESS is a trademark and CROWN and the Rising Sun colophon are registered trademarks of Random House, Inc.

Crown Business books are available at special discounts for bulk purchases for sales promotions or corporate use. Special editions, including personalized covers, excerpts of existing books, or books with corporate logos, can be created in large quantities for special needs. For more information, contact Premium Sales at (212) 572-2232 or e-mail specialmarkets@randomhouse.com.

Library of Congress Cataloging-in-Publication Data
Goldman, Seth.
Mission in a bottle / Seth Goldman and Barry Nalebuff. — First edition.
    p. cm
1. Honest Tea (Firm)—History—Comic books, strips, etc. 2. Tea trade—United States—Comic books, strips, etc. 3. Soft drink industry—United States—Comic books, strips, etc. 4. Iced tea—United States—Comic books, strips, etc. 5. Graphic novels. I. Nalebuff, Barry. II. Title.
HD9198.U54H654 2013
338.7'663940973—dc23
                            2013004799

ISBN 978-0-7704-3749-7
eISBN 978-0-7704-3750-3

Printed in the United States of America

Book design and illustrations by Sungyoon Choi
Jacket design by Jessie Sayward Bright
Jacket illustration by Sungyoon Choi

10 9 8 7 6 5 4 3 2 1
First Edition

To the past and present
employees of Honest Tea—
the superheroes who made
our dream come true

CONTENTS

Those who say it cannot be done should not interrupt the people doing it.

—Chinese proverb

Sign at the entrance to Honest Tea world headquarters

We were thirsty. We couldn't find anything we wanted to drink, so we started a company to make bottled iced tea that actually tasted like tea. Given all the beverages out there, you might think this was a recipe for disaster. You've got a professor and his former student, neither of whom had ever done anything like this. If it was such a good idea, why hadn't someone—someone who actually knew something about the beverage industry—already done it? The truth is, we stumbled quite a bit but ultimately succeeded because of, and in spite of, our ignorance.

We trusted our gut—in more ways than one. Seth started out in the nonprofit and government sectors because he wanted to change the world. Over time, he came to realize that business can be an even more powerful tool for change. And you don't have to sacrifice your ideals to succeed.

Of course, if the business doesn't thrive, you won't have any impact. We wrote this book to help you learn from our mistakes and our successes.

And we want to prepare you for what's to come. We experienced countless rejections, sleepless nights, and close shaves with our life savings—and even Seth's life. While this is a story about building a brand, it's also a story about life getting in the way. We'll share some of the personal struggles any entrepreneur will inevitably face while trying to balance the demands of raising a company and a family simultaneously.

One reason we survived is we had the big picture right. That wasn't an accident. We'll take some trips to Barry's MBA classroom at the Yale School of Management to illustrate how economic principles helped guide our decisions.

Another reason we persisted is that we had passion. It's easy to be passionate when you build your company around a mission you believe in—especially one that improves people's lives. We wanted to create a beverage unlike anything on the market, and we stuck to what we believed in, even when there was a lot of pressure to conform.

MAKE YOUR DRINKS SWEETER!

MAKE THEM CHEAPER!

This isn't rocket science. Honest Tea didn't require a fancy computer or even a garage, just a kettle and some counter space. While the technical part of the tea business is pretty simple, figuring out how to build and finance a fast-growing company is more complicated.

Does the world need another business book? Well, did it need another beverage? (Can you answer a question with a question?) We wrote this book for much the same reason we founded Honest Tea: we wanted a book that we wish we could've read before we started out.

We'd like to think this isn't your typical "How I Built My Business" book. For starters, it looks like a comic book. Seth fell in love with graphic novels while reading them with his three boys. We designed the book this way because we wanted the story to come alive. You get to share in our journey, meet some colorful characters, and not take us too seriously.

Again, we trusted our gut. And we didn't do it alone. We got invaluable help from our fabulous illustrator, Sungyoon Choi, whose artwork in the book *American Widow* inspired us to collaborate with her.

Honestly yours,

Seth + Barry

1. START-UP: 1997–1999

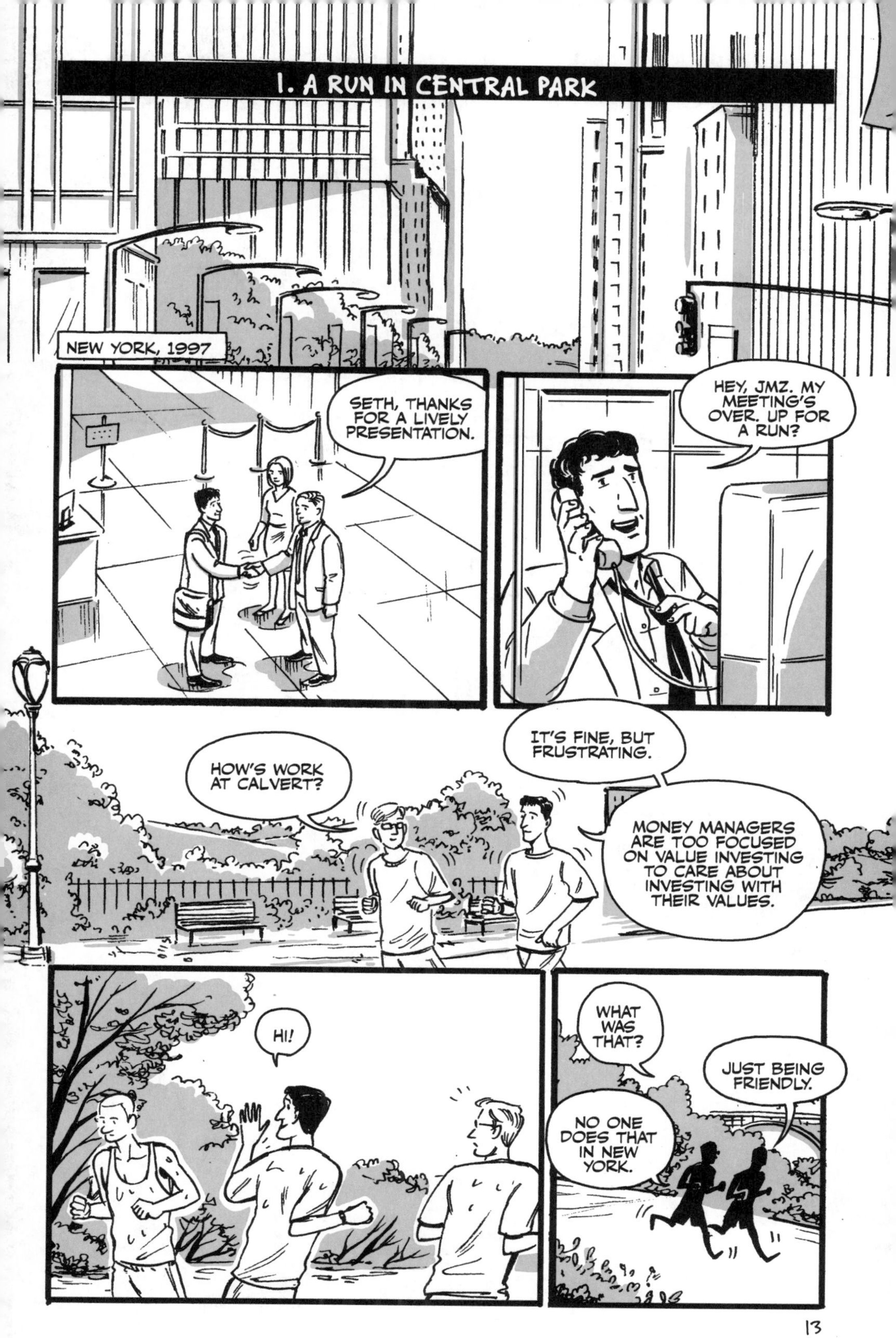
1. A RUN IN CENTRAL PARK
NEW YORK, 1997
SETH, THANKS FOR A LIVELY PRESENTATION.
HEY, JMZ. MY MEETING'S OVER. UP FOR A RUN?
HOW'S WORK AT CALVERT?
IT'S FINE, BUT FRUSTRATING.
MONEY MANAGERS ARE TOO FOCUSED ON VALUE INVESTING TO CARE ABOUT INVESTING WITH THEIR VALUES.
HI!
WHAT WAS THAT?
JUST BEING FRIENDLY.
NO ONE DOES THAT IN NEW YORK.

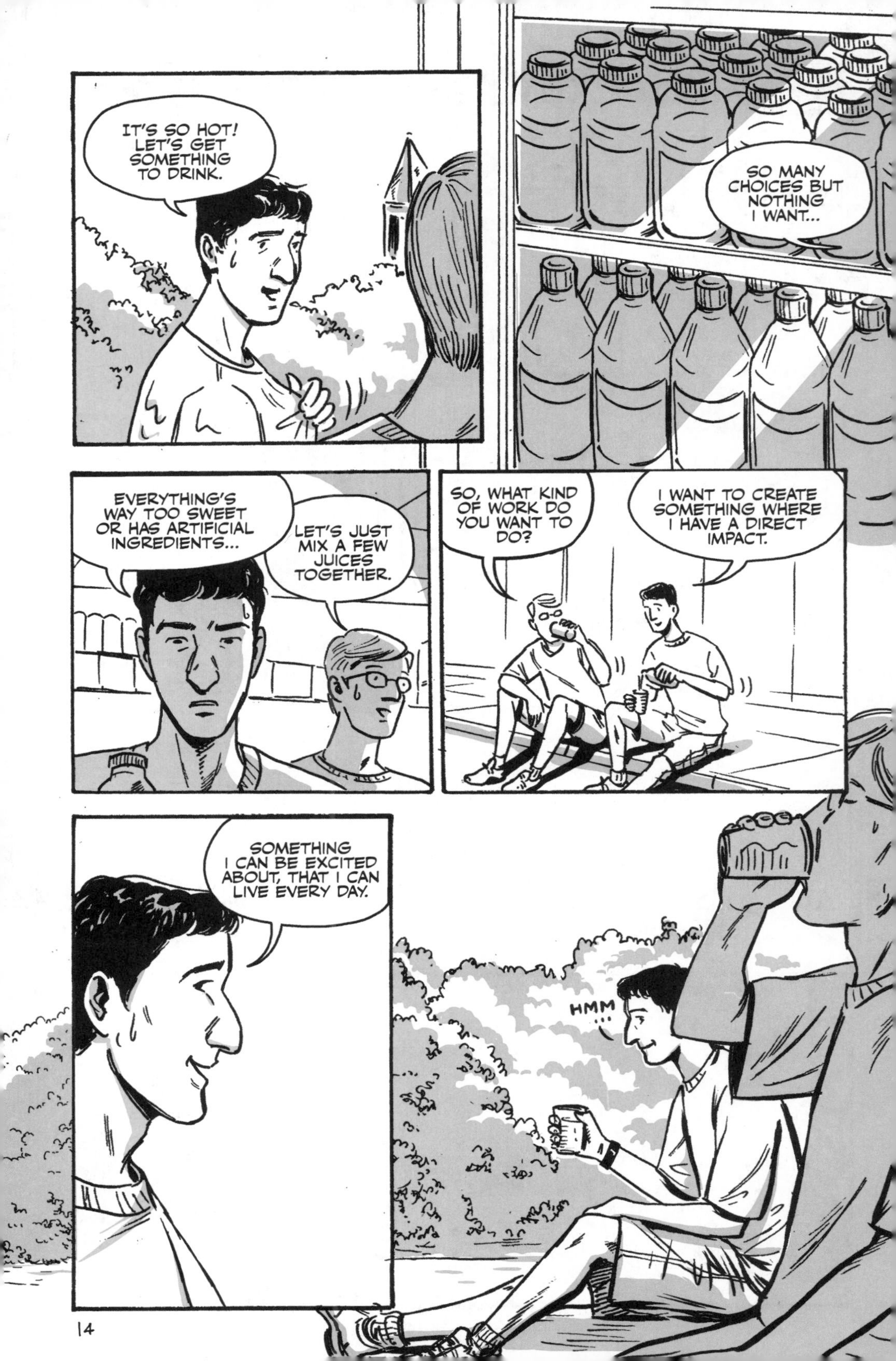
IT'S SO HOT! LET'S GET SOMETHING TO DRINK.
SO MANY CHOICES BUT NOTHING I WANT...
EVERYTHING'S WAY TOO SWEET OR HAS ARTIFICIAL INGREDIENTS...
LET'S JUST MIX A FEW JUICES TOGETHER.
SO, WHAT KIND OF WORK DO YOU WANT TO DO?
I WANT TO CREATE SOMETHING WHERE I HAVE A DIRECT IMPACT.
SOMETHING I CAN BE EXCITED ABOUT, THAT I CAN LIVE EVERY DAY.
HMM...

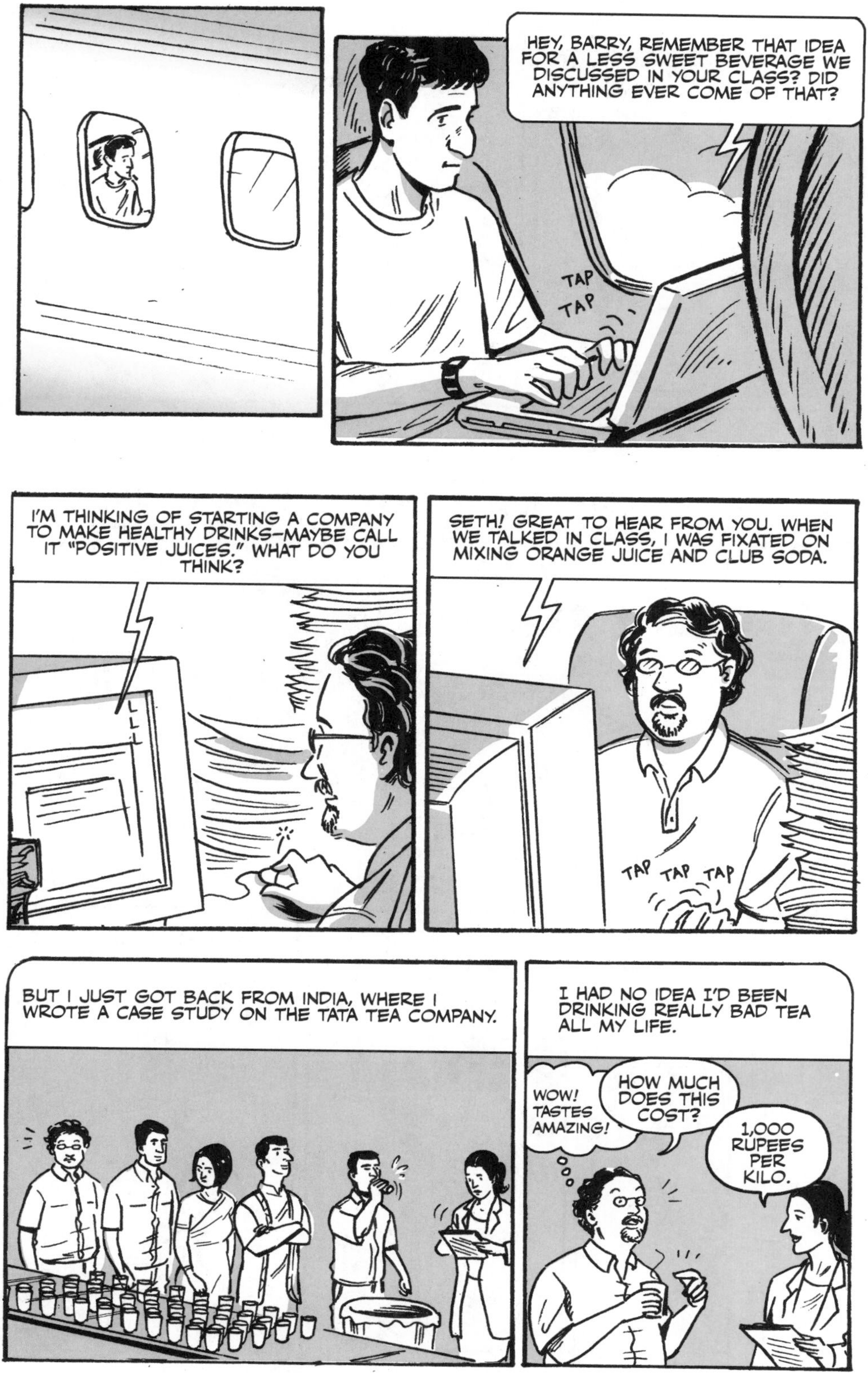
HEY, BARRY, REMEMBER THAT IDEA FOR A LESS SWEET BEVERAGE WE DISCUSSED IN YOUR CLASS? DID ANYTHING EVER COME OF THAT?
TAP TAP
I'M THINKING OF STARTING A COMPANY TO MAKE HEALTHY DRINKS—MAYBE CALL IT "POSITIVE JUICES." WHAT DO YOU THINK?
SETH! GREAT TO HEAR FROM YOU. WHEN WE TALKED IN CLASS, I WAS FIXATED ON MIXING ORANGE JUICE AND CLUB SODA.
TAP TAP TAP
BUT I JUST GOT BACK FROM INDIA, WHERE I WROTE A CASE STUDY ON THE TATA TEA COMPANY.
I HAD NO IDEA I'D BEEN DRINKING REALLY BAD TEA ALL MY LIFE.
WOW! TASTES AMAZING!
HOW MUCH DOES THIS COST?
1,000 RUPEES PER KILO.

I REALIZED SOMEONE COULD DO FOR TEA WHAT STARBUCKS DID FOR COFFEE.

THE WORLD'S CHEAPEST LUXURY GOOD—

ONLY A NICKEL A CUP!

5¢

$$$$

$$$$

I EVEN CAME UP WITH A NAME FOR THE BUSINESS.

HOW CAN TATA TEA EXPORT MORE TEA TO THE U.S.?

WHILE THE TATA BRAND IS ESTEEMED IN INDIA, AMERICANS DON'T KNOW IT. PICK A NAME THAT CONVEYS WHAT YOU STAND FOR: HONESTEA!

I THINK THE TATA NAME IS PERFECTLY FINE.

GOOD POINT, MR. TATA.

WELL, I THINK HONESTEA IS A GREAT NAME!

ME, TOO. THE TRADEMARK IS AVAILABLE, AND I CAN REGISTER IT ONLINE FOR ONLY $245.

A FEW WEEKS LATER

THIS IS TO INFORM YOU THAT YOUR PROPOSED TRADEMARK REGISTRATION IS IN VIOLATION OF THE NESTEA® MARK.

WHO KNEW THAT HONESTEA WAS "HO NESTEA"? HO, HO, HO!

ANY OTHER NAMES? HOW ABOUT THIRSTEA, PURITEA, VITALITEA, HONES TEA...

LET'S JUST MAKE IT TWO WORDS: HONEST TEA!

2. THE CASE FOR A NEW BEVERAGE

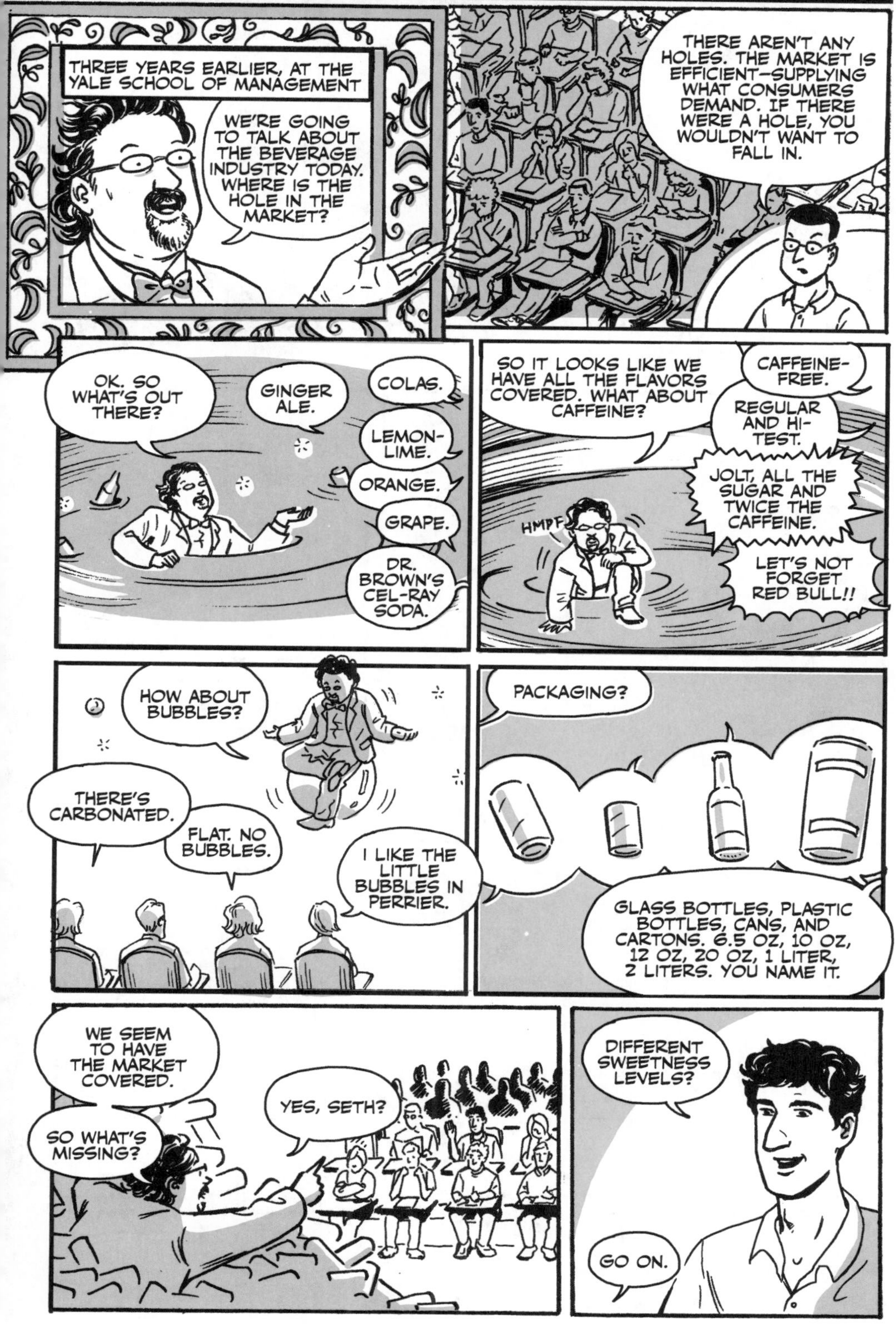
THREE YEARS EARLIER, AT THE YALE SCHOOL OF MANAGEMENT
WE'RE GOING TO TALK ABOUT THE BEVERAGE INDUSTRY TODAY. WHERE IS THE HOLE IN THE MARKET?
THERE AREN'T ANY HOLES. THE MARKET IS EFFICIENT—SUPPLYING WHAT CONSUMERS DEMAND. IF THERE WERE A HOLE, YOU WOULDN'T WANT TO FALL IN.
OK. SO WHAT'S OUT THERE?
GINGER ALE.
COLAS.
LEMON-LIME.
ORANGE.
GRAPE.
DR. BROWN'S CEL-RAY SODA.
SO IT LOOKS LIKE WE HAVE ALL THE FLAVORS COVERED. WHAT ABOUT CAFFEINE?
CAFFEINE-FREE.
REGULAR AND HI-TEST.
JOLT, ALL THE SUGAR AND TWICE THE CAFFEINE.
HMPF
LET'S NOT FORGET RED BULL!!
HOW ABOUT BUBBLES?
THERE'S CARBONATED.
FLAT. NO BUBBLES.
I LIKE THE LITTLE BUBBLES IN PERRIER.
PACKAGING?
GLASS BOTTLES, PLASTIC BOTTLES, CANS, AND CARTONS. 6.5 OZ, 10 OZ, 12 OZ, 20 OZ, 1 LITER, 2 LITERS. YOU NAME IT.
WE SEEM TO HAVE THE MARKET COVERED.
SO WHAT'S MISSING?
YES, SETH?
DIFFERENT SWEETNESS LEVELS?
GO ON.

YOU CAN HAVE 0 OR 140 CALORIES, BUT NOTHING IN BETWEEN.

0 cal ··· 140 cal

CONSUMERS WANT FULL FLAVOR OR DIET.

THEY DON'T WANT COMPROMISE.

NOT ME. I THINK ALL THE DRINKS OUT THERE ARE TOO SWEET. I CUT MY CRANBERRY JUICE WITH CLUB SODA.

ME, TOO!

HOW MANY OF YOU WOULD LIKE A BEVERAGE WITH 20 TO 50 CALORIES?

HMM... ABOUT A THIRD OF YOU.

LET'S SEE HOW MANY TEASPOONS OF SUGAR YOU MIX IN YOUR ICED TEA.

0 — 7

1 — 20

2 — 15

3 OR MORE — 4

I'M FROM THE SOUTH, WHERE WE PUT IN 5 OR 6.

MOST OF YOU ARE AT TWO TEASPOONS OR LESS. HOW MANY TEASPOONS OF SUGAR DO YOU THINK THERE ARE IN A TYPICAL BOTTLE OF ICED TEA?

ONE... TWO... THREE... FOUR... FIVE...

KEEP GOING.

SIX... SEVEN... EIGHT...

KEEP GOING.

NINE... TEN... ELEVEN?

WORLD HEALTH ORGANIZATION

CONSUME NO MORE THAN 10 TEASPOONS OF ADDED SUGAR PER DAY.

TWELVE TEASPOONS IN ONE 16-OZ BOTTLE!

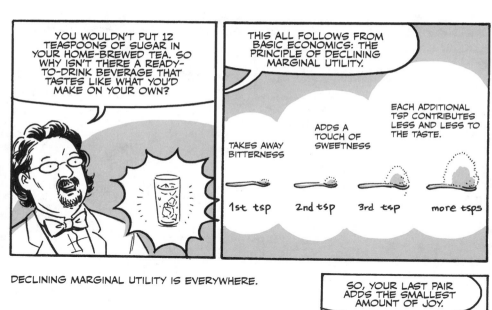

DECLINING MARGINAL UTILITY IS EVERYWHERE.

3. ALL IN

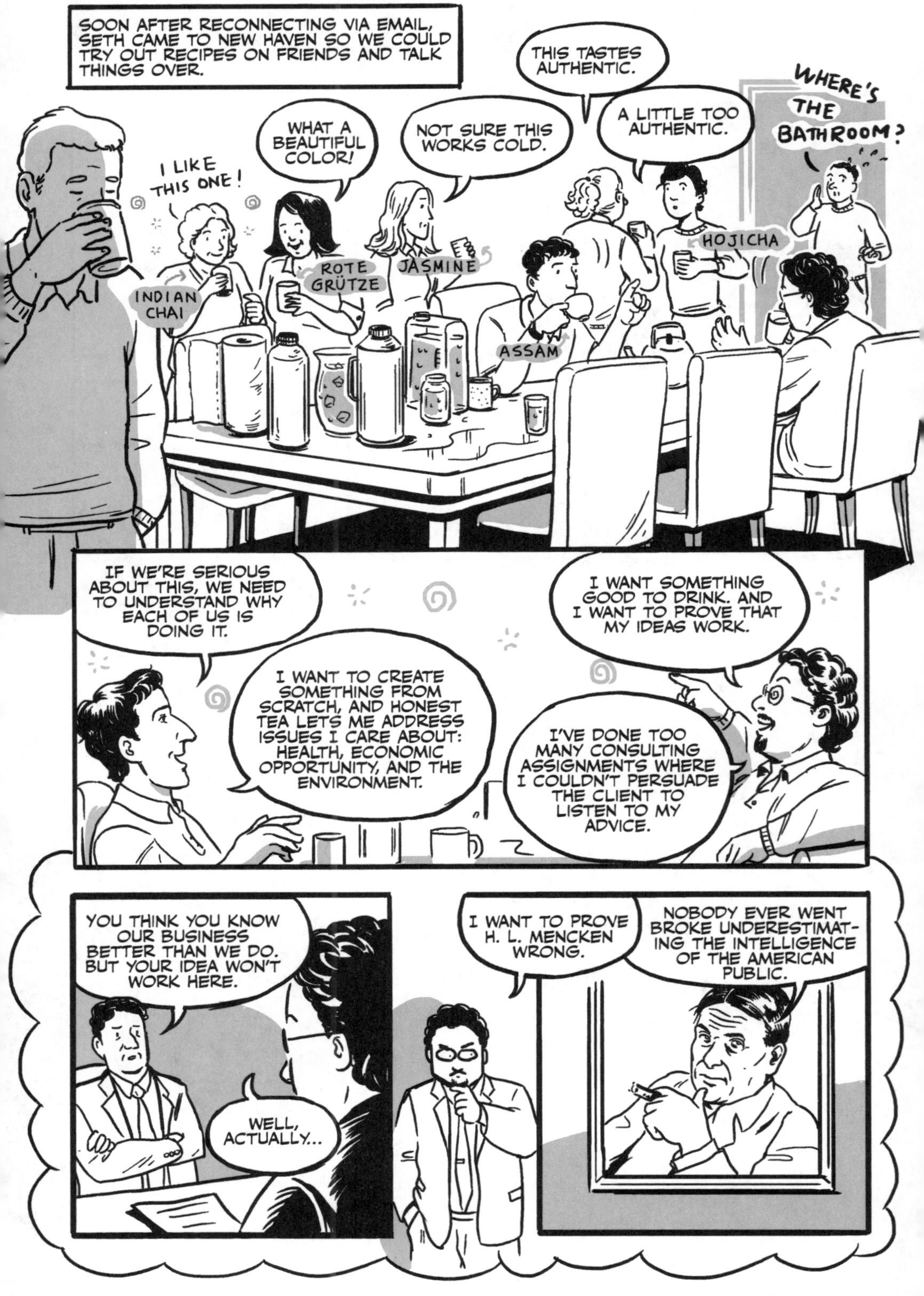
SOON AFTER RECONNECTING VIA EMAIL, SETH CAME TO NEW HAVEN SO WE COULD TRY OUT RECIPES ON FRIENDS AND TALK THINGS OVER.
I LIKE THIS ONE!
WHAT A BEAUTIFUL COLOR!
NOT SURE THIS WORKS COLD.
THIS TASTES AUTHENTIC.
A LITTLE TOO AUTHENTIC.
WHERE'S THE BATHROOM?
INDIAN CHAI
ROTE GRÜTZE
JASMINE
ASSAM
HOJICHA
IF WE'RE SERIOUS ABOUT THIS, WE NEED TO UNDERSTAND WHY EACH OF US IS DOING IT.
I WANT TO CREATE SOMETHING FROM SCRATCH, AND HONEST TEA LETS ME ADDRESS ISSUES I CARE ABOUT: HEALTH, ECONOMIC OPPORTUNITY, AND THE ENVIRONMENT.
I WANT SOMETHING GOOD TO DRINK. AND I WANT TO PROVE THAT MY IDEAS WORK.
I'VE DONE TOO MANY CONSULTING ASSIGNMENTS WHERE I COULDN'T PERSUADE THE CLIENT TO LISTEN TO MY ADVICE.
YOU THINK YOU KNOW OUR BUSINESS BETTER THAN WE DO. BUT YOUR IDEA WON'T WORK HERE.
WELL, ACTUALLY...
I WANT TO PROVE H. L. MENCKEN WRONG.
NOBODY EVER WENT BROKE UNDERESTIMATING THE INTELLIGENCE OF THE AMERICAN PUBLIC.

THERE ARE PLENTY OF CONSUMERS LIKE US WHO READ LABELS AND CARE ABOUT WHAT THEY PUT IN THEIR BODIES. IF WE CAN MAKE A GREAT ICED TEA WITHOUT LOADS OF SUGAR, I'M CONFIDENT WE CAN SELL IT.

I ALSO WANT TO MAKE SURE THAT HONEST TEA HAS A COMMITMENT TO BEING A SOCIALLY RESPONSIBLE BUSINESS.

AND HERE I WAS HOPING TO CREATE A SOCIALLY IRRESPONSIBLE BUSINESS.

THAT'S NOT FUNNY.

THIS COMPANY'S MISSION SHOULD REFLECT OUR VALUES. WE WON'T BE PERFECT, BUT WE SHOULD DO OUR BEST TO LIVE UP TO IT.

SETH, I GET IT, AND I AGREE. I LOVE THAT TEA IS ONE OF THE HEALTHIEST FOODS ON THE PLANET.

THE MORE TEA WE SELL, THE MORE GOOD WE DO. WE'RE PRACTICALLY STEEPED IN SOCIAL RESPONSIBILITY.

OK, OK.

LOOK, YOU HAVE A FULL-TIME JOB AT YALE. I'LL BE THE CEO... OR, SHOULD I SAY, *TEA-EO*. AND YOU CAN BE THE CHAIRMAN.

PERFECT. MY JOB WILL BE TO HELP YOU BE SUCCESSFUL.

CEOS GET DISTRACTED BY HAVING TO SPEND TOO MUCH TIME RAISING MONEY.

I CAN TAKE THE LEAD ON THAT JOB. AND I CAN BE THE BAD COP WHEN YOU NEED ONE.

THAT'S A PERFECT ROLE FOR YOU.

21

WHAT'S YOUR TIME FRAME ON THIS? WHAT DOES SUCCESS LOOK LIKE TO YOU?

I DON'T KNOW HOW LONG IT WILL TAKE, BUT MY GOAL IS TO CREATE A NATIONAL BRAND THAT BECOMES A MODEL FOR CHANGE.

WELL, I HAVE NO INTEREST IN CREATING SOMETHING SMALL, SO THAT WORKS FOR ME.

BIG BIG BIG

I'M ABOUT TO GO TO THE PRESIDENT OF CALVERT AND TELL HER I'M LEAVING A GREAT JOB AT A GREAT COMPANY TO LAUNCH... A TEA BUSINESS.

ARE YOU SURE WE CAN PULL THIS OFF? CAN WE REALLY MAKE THE TEA, AND WILL PEOPLE BUY IT?

HOW HARD CAN IT BE TO ADD TEA LEAVES TO BOILING WATER?

JUST TAKE THE RECIPE FROM OUR KITCHEN AND MULTIPLY BY 10,000.

THAT'S EASY FOR YOU TO SAY. YOU'RE NOT LEAVING YOUR JOB.

ARE YOU SURE WE CAN RAISE THE MONEY WE NEED?

WHAT IF YOU ASK CALVERT FOR A SABBATICAL? YOU'RE A RISING STAR; I BET THEY'D GO FOR THAT.

NOT EXACTLY THE WORDS OF ENCOURAGEMENT I WAS HOPING TO HEAR.

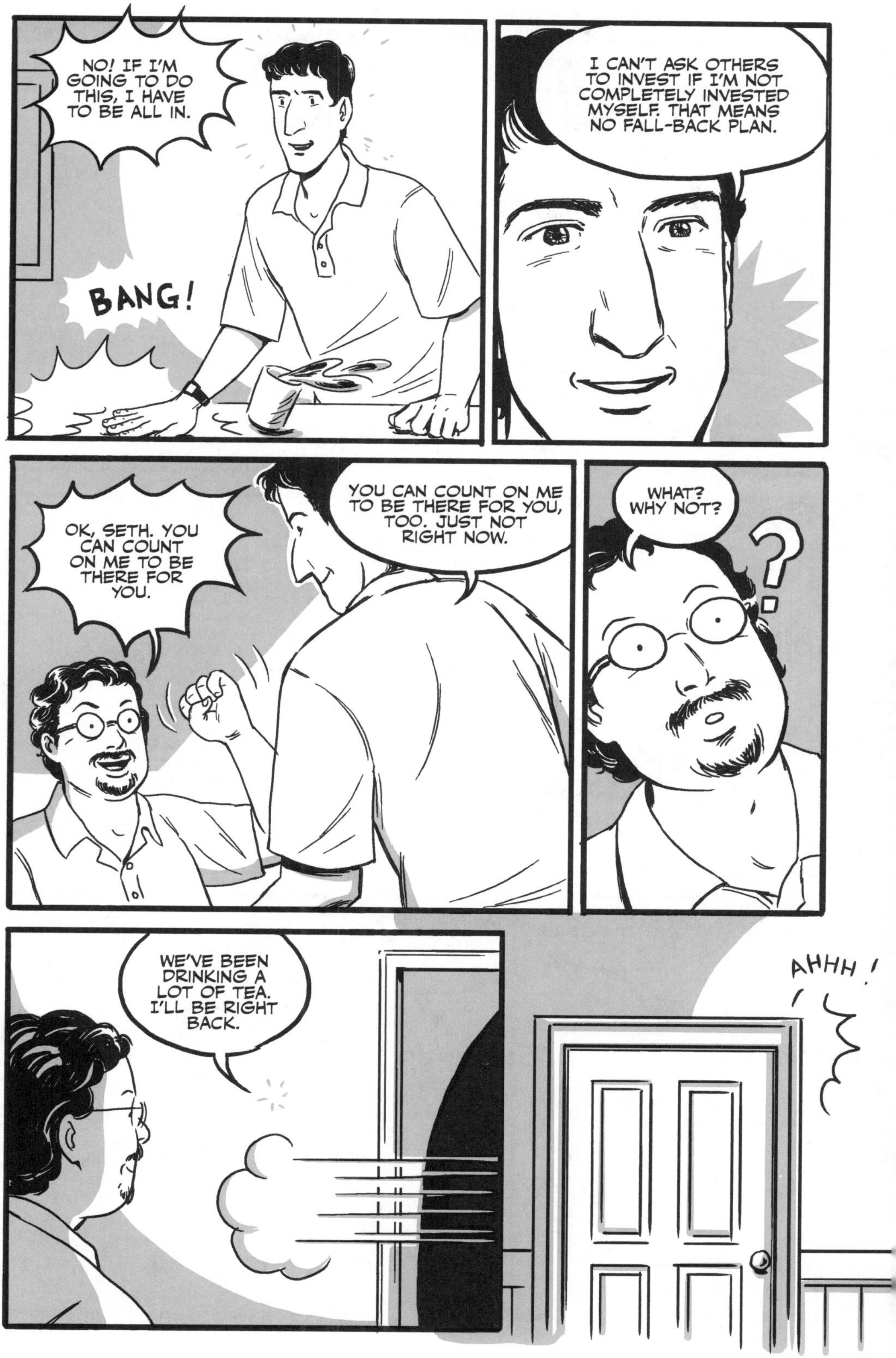
NO! IF I'M GOING TO DO THIS, I HAVE TO BE ALL IN.
BANG!
I CAN'T ASK OTHERS TO INVEST IF I'M NOT COMPLETELY INVESTED MYSELF. THAT MEANS NO FALL-BACK PLAN.
OK, SETH. YOU CAN COUNT ON ME TO BE THERE FOR YOU.
YOU CAN COUNT ON ME TO BE THERE FOR YOU, TOO. JUST NOT RIGHT NOW.
WHAT? WHY NOT?
?
WE'VE BEEN DRINKING A LOT OF TEA. I'LL BE RIGHT BACK.
AHHH!

4. WEEK 1

FEBRUARY 2, 1998. SETH LAUNCHES THE COMPANY OUT OF HIS HOUSE.

INSTALLS ACCOUNTING SOFTWARE.

DAY 1

HI! I'D LIKE TO OPEN A P.O. BOX.

UNITED STATES POSTAL SERVICE

BETHESDA, MD 20814

DAY 2

Are you sure you want to delete Solitaire?

CONFIRM   CANCEL

CLICK!

MOST IMPORTANT KEY-STROKE IN THE HISTORY OF HONEST TEA

DAY 3

BUSINESS PLAN

HONEST TEA SEEKS TO PROVIDE BOTTLED TEA THAT TASTES LIKE TEA—A WORLD OF FLAVOR, FRESHLY BREWED, AND BARELY SWEETENED. WE SEEK TO PROVIDE BETTER-TASTING, HEALTHIER TEAS THE WAY NATURE AND THEIR CULTURES OF ORIGIN INTENDED THEM TO BE. WE STRIVE FOR RELATIONSHIPS WITH OUR CUSTOMERS, EMPLOY-EES, SUPPLIERS, AND STAKEHOLDERS THAT ARE AS HEALTHY AND HONEST AS THE TEA WE BREW.

DAY 4

WE LOOKED AT DOZENS OF BOTTLE DESIGNS...

zuckerman honickman

MEETING WITH A GLASS SUPPLIER

AND THIS ONE SEEMS TO FIT OUR BRAND PERFECTLY.

IT'S BEAUTIFUL. YOU DON'T SEE MANY SQUARE BOTTLES. YOU'LL NEED A MOLD—TWO MOLDS, ACTUALLY. THEY RUN $90,000 EACH.

NOW I KNOW WHY YOU DON'T SEE MANY SQUARE BOTTLES.

UH, WHAT KIND OF BOTTLE CAN I GET WITHOUT A MOLD?

Rio Grande
mexican cuisine

YOU'RE LAUNCHING A WHAT???!!

A BOTTLED-TEA COMPANY.

TRY THIS. IT'S CALLED GOLD RUSH, A CINNAMON TEA WITH JUST HALF A TEASPOON OF SUGAR PER SERVING.

SETH HAS LUNCH WITH JOE DOBROW, A FELLOW YALE SOM ALUM WHO WAS WORKING AT WHOLE FOODS.

YOU REALLY LEFT CALVERT? ARE YOU DOING THIS ALONE?

TASTES GREAT!

NOT EXACTLY. DID YOU TAKE ANY CLASSES WITH BARRY NALEBUFF WHEN YOU WERE AT YALE?

HOW COULD I FORGET HIM? HE CALLED ON ME ON THE FIRST DAY. IS YOUR PARTNER ONE OF HIS STUDENTS?

ACTUALLY, BARRY IS MY CO-FOUNDER.

NO WAY! HE ALWAYS HAD THE MOST OFF-THE-WALL IDEAS.

INDEED. DO YOU KNOW THE STORY OF HOW HE ENDED UP BEING A PROFESSOR AT YALE?

1985

HARVARD BUSINESS SCHOOL FACULTY CLUB

BARRY, YOU HAVE IMPRESSIVE ACADEMIC CREDENTIALS: MIT, RHODES SCHOLAR, D.PHIL. FROM OXFORD IN TWO YEARS, AND NOW A HARVARD JUNIOR FELLOW.

BUT WHAT DO YOU KNOW ABOUT BUSINESS? HAVE YOU EVER CONSIDERED WORKING OUTSIDE ACADEMIA?

25

I'VE THOUGHT ABOUT SELLING FORTUNE COOKIES IN CHINA.

I MEANT CONSULTING OR INVESTMENT BANKING.

FORTUNE COOKIES ARE ACTUALLY AN AMERICAN INVENTION, BASED ON A JAPANESE COOKIE POPULARIZED BY AMERICAN CHINESE RESTAURANTS DURING WWII.

WHAT'S THIS?

IT IS A SPECIAL WESTERN COOKIE.

"EVERY WISE MAN STARTED OUT BY ASKING MANY QUESTIONS."

CRACK

WISE SAYINGS FIT THEIR CULTURE. I'D LOVE TO BE KNOWN AS THE GUY WHO BROUGHT THE FORTUNE COOKIE TO CHINA.

next stop...

THESE ARE GOOD-QUALITY ICE BLOCKS.

THIS GUY MAY BE SMART...

BUT HE DOESN'T KNOW THE FIRST THING ABOUT BUSINESS.

HE'S WAY TOO WACKY FOR US.

I KINDA LIKE THE FORTUNE COOKIE IDEA.

CAN YOU HELP US GET AN APPOINTMENT WITH YOUR BUYER?

BLAH BLAH

AND THAT'S WHY BARRY DIDN'T GET A JOB AT HARVARD.

WELL, I'M IN MARKETING, BUT I CAN INTRODUCE YOU TO A FORMER BUYER, AND SHE MIGHT BE ABLE TO HELP.

WE HAD A NAME, A BOTTLE, AND SOME RECIPES. WE STILL NEEDED TO RAISE MONEY, FIND OUR FIRST CUSTOMER, AND DESIGN A LABEL—NOT NECESSARILY IN THAT ORDER.

DAY 8

SLOAN, I ASKED YALE SCHOOL OF ART FACULTY TO RECOMMEND A RECENT GRAD FOR DESIGN HELP, WHICH LED ME TO YOU.

GLAD TO HEAR IT.

THE PRODUCT IS SIMPLE: BOTTLED ICED TEA THAT'S FRESHLY BREWED AND BARELY SWEETENED.

WE WANT THE LABEL TO CONVEY THAT THE PRODUCT IS WHAT IT SAYS IT IS. THAT YOU CAN TRUST US. THAT WE HAVE NOTHING TO HIDE.

IF YOUR NAME IS HONEST TEA, DOES THAT IMPLY OTHERS ARE DISHONEST?

SIP

I LIKE THIS TEA!

CONSUMERS HAVE BEEN FOOLED BEFORE BY COMPANIES SELLING SUGARY DRINKS THAT PRETEND TO BE HEALTHY. WE WANT OUR DESIGN TO BE THE OPPOSITE OF KITSCH—SOMETHING THAT COMMUNICATES AUTHENTIC, NATURAL INGREDIENTS.

FIGHTS CANCER

LIVE LONGER!

IMPROVES MEMORY

BETTER SEX

IF YOU WANT TO EMPHASIZE AUTHENTICITY, HOW ABOUT USING AN OLD MAP OR WOOD FROM A TEA CRATE?

INTERESTING.

WHAT ARE SOME LABELS THAT YOU LIKE?

I LOVE THE MOUTON ROTHSCHILD WINE LABELS. THEY ARE BEAUTIFUL. THEY CONVEY HIGH QUALITY WHILE ALSO SHOWING SOME PERSONALITY.

IS SELLING TEA ANYTHING LIKE SELLING WINE?

TEA TODAY IS A LOT LIKE WINE 20 YEARS AGO. FOLKS USED TO ORDER RED OR WHITE. THEN THEY LEARNED ABOUT MERLOT AND CHARDONNAY.

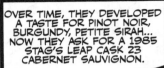

OVER TIME, THEY DEVELOPED A TASTE FOR PINOT NOIR, BURGUNDY, PETITE SIRAH... NOW THEY ASK FOR A 1985 STAG'S LEAP CASK 23 CABERNET SAUVIGNON.

WITH TEA, PEOPLE JUST ORDER BLACK OR GREEN.

THAT'S RIGHT. THEY'VE NEVER HEARD OF ASSAM, OOLONG, DARJEELING, GENMAICHA, OR GUNPOWDER.

GREEN

BLACK

SO YOU'RE NOT JUST TRYING TO APPEAL TO TEA SNOBS.

EXACTLY. WE'RE SELLING GREAT-TASTING TEA AT AN AFFORDABLE PRICE.

LET ME PLAY AROUND WITH SOME ART IMAGES I HAVE HERE.

THIS ANTIQUE SCROLL PAINTING WOULD EMPHASIZE THE CULTURAL AUTHENTICITY.

OR I COULD USE A WILLIAM BLAKE PAINTING TO CONNECT THE TEA TO NATURE.

Honest Tea

THEY'RE BEAUTIFUL, BUT I'D LIKE THE TEA TO PLAY A LARGER ROLE. AND OUR BRAND NAME NEEDS TO BE RECOGNIZABLE AT A DISTANCE.

BEFORE WE GO TOO FAR, LET'S DISCUSS COMPENSATION.

I'D LIKE TO PROPOSE THAT WE PAY YOU IN A WAY THAT ALLOWS YOU TO SHARE IN THE SUCCESS YOU HELP CREATE.

IN ADDITION TO $4,000 UP FRONT, WE'LL PAY 0.2¢ PER BOTTLE ON SALES FROM 2 MILLION TO 20 MILLION BOTTLES. THAT WOULD COME TO ANOTHER $36,000.

HOW LONG DO YOU THINK IT WILL TAKE TO SELL 20 MILLION BOTTLES?

WE'RE HOPING TO HIT THAT MILESTONE BY YEAR FIVE. OF COURSE, WE'LL PAY YOU ALONG THE WAY.

OK. I'M WILLING TO BET ON MY DESIGN AND YOUR TEA. I CAN SHOW YOU SOME DESIGNS NEXT WEEK.

 DAY 15

AND LIKE A WINE BOTTLE, I'VE GOT SEPARATE FRONT AND BACK LABELS. THE GAP IN BETWEEN WILL SHOW MORE OF THE PRODUCT AND THAT YOU HAVE NOTHING TO HIDE.

I'M USING A LARGE "T" AS A KEYHOLE AND PLACING THE ART INSIDE IT. YOU'LL BE ABLE TO RECOGNIZE THE T FROM 20 FT AWAY.

I'VE MADE THE CAP BLACK SO IT WILL STAND OUT AND LOOK LIKE THE FOIL ON TOP OF A WINE BOTTLE.

THAT'S STUNNING. AND I LIKE HOW YOU CONNECTED THE ART TO THE ORIGIN OF EACH TEA.

COULD YOU USE THIS MINIATURE PORTRAIT I BROUGHT BACK FROM INDIA?

SURE.

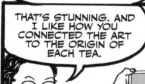

HONEST TEA®
HONESTLY BREWED & BARELY SWEETENED

KASHMIRI CHAI
(SPICED INDIAN BLACK TEA)
16 FLUID OUNCES (1 PINT) 473ML

WITH THE LABELS DONE, FOCUS GROUPS HELPED US CHOOSE FLAVORS.

DAY 19

DO I REALLY HAVE TO DRINK THIS ONE?

YES. THAT'S WHY WE'RE PAYING YOU.

IT TASTES LIKE LAKE WATER. ACTUALLY, LAKE WATER'S BETTER.

THEY'RE ABOUT TO TRY HOJICHA, A JAPANESE TWIG TEA.

I THINK WE NEED TO GO MORE MAINSTREAM.

DAY 21

WE GOT THE OPPORTUNITY WE WERE HOPING FOR! I HAVE AN APPOINTMENT WITH THE WHOLE FOODS* BUYER AT 10:00 AM ON FEBRUARY 27. CAN YOU COME DOWN AND HELP ME MAKE THE SAMPLES?

I'LL BE THERE.

*TECHNICALLY, THE BUYER COVERED FRESH FIELDS STORES FOR FRESH FIELDS/WHOLE FOODS MARKET. THE STORES AND THE COMPANY WOULD BE RENAMED WHOLE FOODS MARKET IN 2000, SO FOR SIMPLICITY, WE'LL USE THAT NAME THROUGHOUT THE BOOK.

DAY 25

← MAPLE SYRUP

ASSAM

← HONEY

MOROCCAN MINT

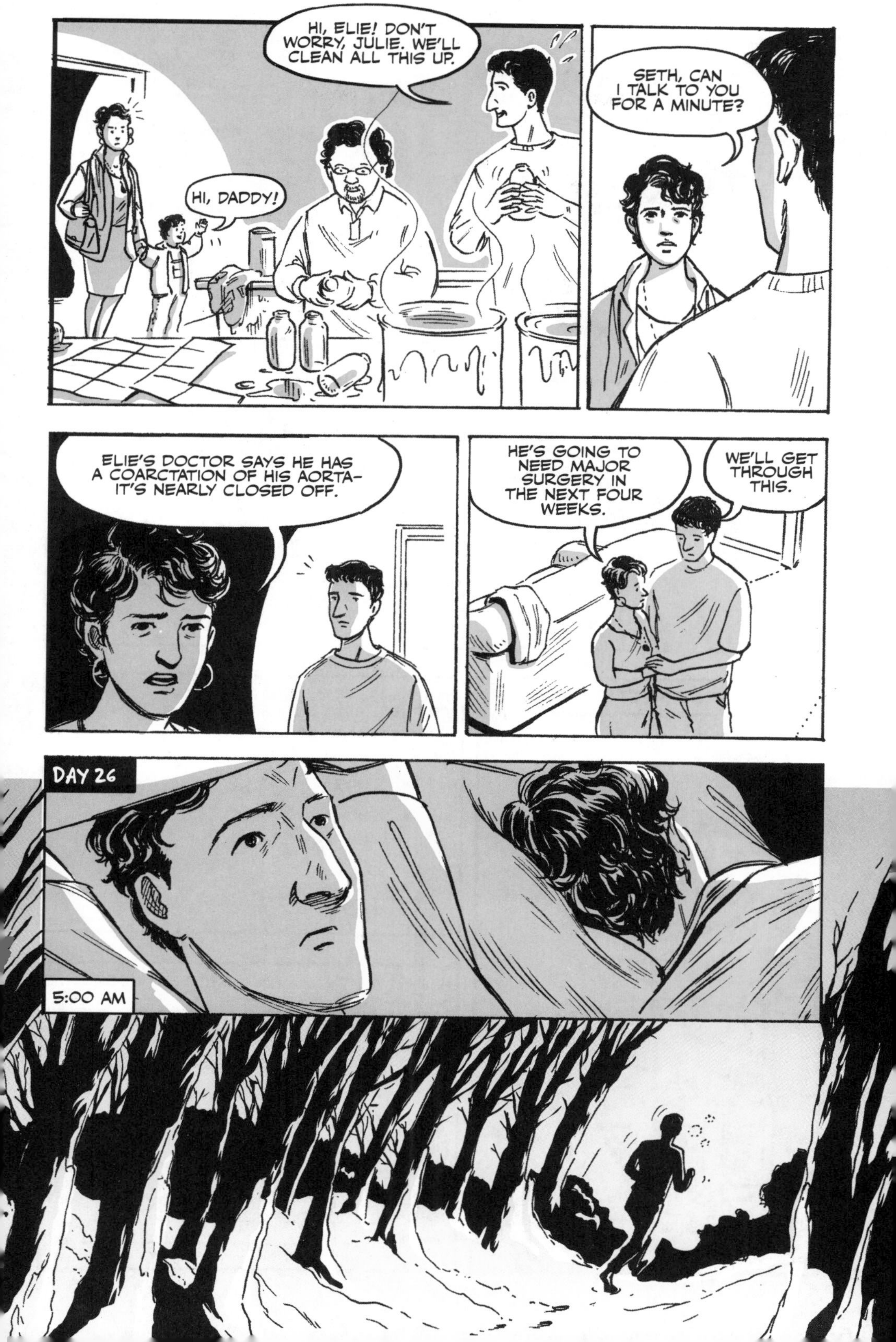
HI, ELIE! DON'T WORRY, JULIE. WE'LL CLEAN ALL THIS UP.
HI, DADDY!
SETH, CAN I TALK TO YOU FOR A MINUTE?
ELIE'S DOCTOR SAYS HE HAS A COARCTATION OF HIS AORTA- IT'S NEARLY CLOSED OFF.
HE'S GOING TO NEED MAJOR SURGERY IN THE NEXT FOUR WEEKS.
WE'LL GET THROUGH THIS.
DAY 26
5:00 AM

LATER THAT MORNING

I'LL CHECK ON THE TEA.

OOPS! THE TEA DIDN'T COOL DOWN IN THE CAR OVERNIGHT. THESE THERMOSES WORKED TOO WELL.

THAT'S NOT THE IDEAL WAY TO SAMPLE ICED TEA.

I HOPE THE BUYER GOES FOR IT.

HE SHOULD. WE DESIGNED THE TEA WITH WHOLE FOODS CUSTOMERS IN MIND.

WHOLE FOODS BUYER'S OFFICE

HONEST TEA IS TEA THAT TASTES LIKE TEA...

THE LABEL ART IS CONNECTED TO THE CULTURE OF EACH TEA.

...LY BREWED & BARELY SWEETENED

TEA·

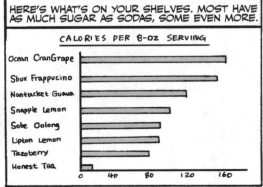

HERE'S WHAT'S ON YOUR SHELVES. MOST HAVE AS MUCH SUGAR AS SODAS, SOME EVEN MORE.

CALORIES PER 8-OZ SERVING

Ocean CranGrape
Sbux Frappucino
Nantucket Guava
Snapple Lemon
Sobe Oolong
Lipton Lemon
Tazoberry
Honest Tea

0   40   80   120   160

I'M ASKING YOU TO BUY MORE THAN JUST SOME TEA. I'M ASKING YOU TO BUY INTO A DIFFERENT APPROACH TO BEVERAGES: A PRODUCT THAT IS WHAT IT SAYS IT IS.

I GET IT. THERE'S NOTHING LIKE THIS ON THE MARKET. BUT IT'LL BE TOUGH GOING AGAINST SNAPPLE AND ARIZONA...

HOW DO YOU PLAN TO MARKET IT?

WE'LL DO SAMPLING EVENTS AT ALL 17 OF YOUR STORES.

I'LL POUR THEM MYSELF!

I'M IMPRESSED! I'LL TAKE 3,000 BOTTLES OF EACH FLAVOR!

WE EXPECT THE FIRST CASES TO BE FREE. ONCE THOSE SELL, WE'LL PAY FOR REORDERS.

FREE?

I REALLY CAN'T AFFORD TO GIVE ANYTHING AWAY FOR FREE. THE WHOLE COMPANY IS ME, THESE THERMOSES, AND SOME REUSED SNAPPLE BOTTLES.

ACTUALLY, THE THERMOSES ARE BARRY'S, SO IT'S JUST ME AND THE BOTTLES.

I CAN'T BELIEVE I'M SAYING THIS!

I GUESS WE'LL MAKE AN EXCEPTION.

LATER

WE GOT OUR FIRST ORDER! 15,000 BOTTLES!

15,000 BOTTLES? THAT'S GREAT!

HOW ARE WE GOING TO MAKE THAT MUCH TEA?!

33

7. GEORGE MOVES IN

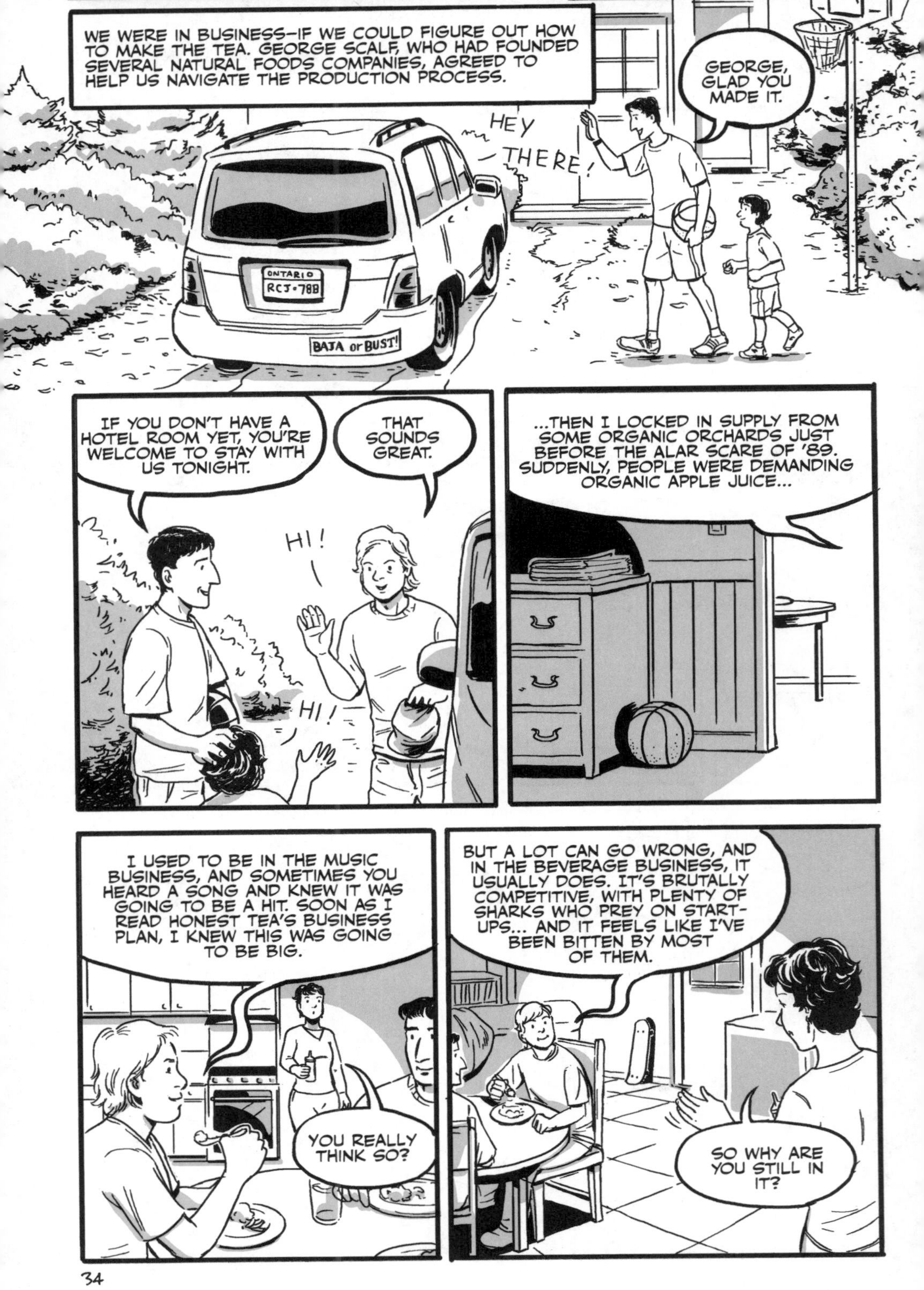

WE WERE IN BUSINESS—IF WE COULD FIGURE OUT HOW TO MAKE THE TEA. GEORGE SCALF, WHO HAD FOUNDED SEVERAL NATURAL FOODS COMPANIES, AGREED TO HELP US NAVIGATE THE PRODUCTION PROCESS.
HEY THERE!
GEORGE, GLAD YOU MADE IT.
ONTARIO
RCJ-788
BAJA or BUST!
IF YOU DON'T HAVE A HOTEL ROOM YET, YOU'RE WELCOME TO STAY WITH US TONIGHT.
THAT SOUNDS GREAT.
HI!
HI!
...THEN I LOCKED IN SUPPLY FROM SOME ORGANIC ORCHARDS JUST BEFORE THE ALAR SCARE OF '89. SUDDENLY, PEOPLE WERE DEMANDING ORGANIC APPLE JUICE...
I USED TO BE IN THE MUSIC BUSINESS, AND SOMETIMES YOU HEARD A SONG AND KNEW IT WAS GOING TO BE A HIT. SOON AS I READ HONEST TEA'S BUSINESS PLAN, I KNEW THIS WAS GOING TO BE BIG.
YOU REALLY THINK SO?
BUT A LOT CAN GO WRONG, AND IN THE BEVERAGE BUSINESS, IT USUALLY DOES. IT'S BRUTALLY COMPETITIVE, WITH PLENTY OF SHARKS WHO PREY ON START-UPS... AND IT FEELS LIKE I'VE BEEN BITTEN BY MOST OF THEM.
SO WHY ARE YOU STILL IN IT?

JUST WHEN I THOUGHT I WAS OUT, SETH PULLED ME BACK IN. I WAS ABOUT TO LEAVE FOR BAJA WHEN HE CALLED. HE GOT ME EXCITED ABOUT STARTING SOMETHING FROM SCRATCH.

IT'S A BIT LIKE BEING BACK IN THE MUSIC BUSINESS. AND SETH COULD BE A ROCK STAR.

IS THAT A GOOD THING?

TWO WEEKS LATER

I LIKE GEORGE, BUT WASN'T HE JUST GOING TO STAY ONE NIGHT?

MM-HMM.

WHY WOULD HE WANT TO STAY HERE IN OUR UNFINISHED BASEMENT WITH THE SPIDER CRICKETS?

AND WHO CAN SLEEP WITH A BABY IN THE HOUSE AND TWO BOYS RUNNING AROUND?

GEORGE IS ON A BIT OF A JOURNEY. I'M NOT SURE EXACTLY WHAT HE'S BEEN THROUGH, BUT HE'S IN A RECOVERY MODE. HE SPENDS HIS FREE TIME AT BARNES & NOBLE READING SELF-HELP BOOKS.

SELF-HELP

I GUESS HE LIKES BEING PART OF A FAMILY, EVEN IF IT IS A LITTLE CHAOTIC.

YES, I THINK WE'RE PART OF HIS RECOVERY.

WELL, THE BOYS LOVE HIM, AND IT SEEMS LIKE HE'S CRITICAL TO YOUR START-UP, SO WE'LL MAKE IT WORK.

HA HA
HA
HA HA
HA HA
HA

35

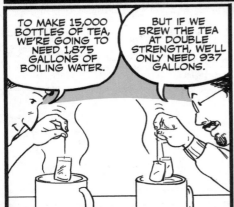

TO MAKE 15,000 BOTTLES OF TEA, WE'RE GOING TO NEED 1,875 GALLONS OF BOILING WATER.

BUT IF WE BREW THE TEA AT DOUBLE STRENGTH, WE'LL ONLY NEED 937 GALLONS.

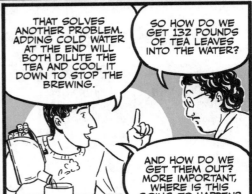

THAT SOLVES ANOTHER PROBLEM. ADDING COLD WATER AT THE END WILL BOTH DILUTE THE TEA AND COOL IT DOWN TO STOP THE BREWING.

SO HOW DO WE GET 132 POUNDS OF TEA LEAVES INTO THE WATER?

AND HOW DO WE GET THEM OUT? MORE IMPORTANT, WHERE IS THIS GOING TO HAPPEN?

SETH AND GEORGE HIT THE ROAD. FIRST STOP: FREDERICK BREWING CO., FREDERICK, MD.

WE'D LIKE TO BOTTLE OUR TEA AT YOUR PLANT.

WHO'S SUPPLYING YOUR CONCENTRATE?

ACTUALLY, WE DON'T USE CONCENTRATE. WE WANT TO BREW THE TEA HERE.

WE KNOW HOW TO STEEP INGREDIENTS AND FILL BOTTLES, BUT WE'RE NOT SET UP TO PASTEURIZE.

A JELLY-PACKING PLANT IN A BARN IN VIRGINIA

WE CAN PUT JELLY IN A JAR, BUT OUR LINE ISN'T SET UP FOR BEVERAGE BOTTLES.

A SODA PLANT IN WILKES-BARRE, PA

BOTTLING IS NO PROBLEM—WE RUN SODA 20 HOURS A DAY. BUT WE HAVE NO WAY OF HEATING WATER TO MAKE TEA.

I THINK JUICE PACKING PLANTS ARE OUR BEST BET. THEY HAVE THE EQUIPMENT TO HEAT WATER FOR BREWING AND PASTEURIZATION.

OUR LINES ARE
ALL FULL.

NO CAPACITY FOR
NEW BRANDS.

OUR MINIMUM
RUN IS 100,000
BOTTLES.

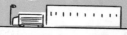

A JUICE PLANT IN
NEW JERSEY

THIS PLACE IS
SCARY! I WOULDN'T
FEEL COMFORTABLE
OPENING A CAN OF
LYSOL IN HERE.

MAYER BROTHERS,
NEAR BUFFALO, NY

I THINK WE HAVE
A SHOT HERE. I'LL
CALL YOU AFTER
THE MEETING.

SETH AND BARRY WANT TO
MAKE TEA BY BREWING
REAL TEA LEAVES INSTEAD
OF USING A CONCENTRATE,
SYRUP, OR POWDER.

HMMM...

SO HOW ARE
YOU GONNA
DO THAT?

WE'VE GOT SOME
IDEAS, LIKE USING
LARGE FILTER
BAGS LIKE THIS.

HMMM...

ALSO, WE WANT TO USE ONLY
ORGANIC SWEETENERS, LIKE
CANE SUGAR, HONEY, AND
MAPLE SYRUP.

WE'VE BEEN HAPPY WITH
HIGH-FRUCTOSE CORN
SYRUP—IT BLENDS IN
EASILY, AND WE GET IT
DELIVERED BY
THE TANK.

BUT I
SUPPOSE WE
CAN WORK WITH
YOU THERE.

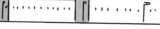

AND BECAUSE THE TEA IS LIGHTLY SWEETENED, WE DON'T WANT TO ADD A LOT OF ACID TO GET THE PH DOWN. WE'LL SHIP IN SPRING WATER THAT HAS A NATURALLY LOW PH.

WATER

WELL, I GUESS THAT WILL WORK, AS LONG AS YOU MAKE THE ARRANGEMENTS.

AS FAR AS LABELS GO, WE WANT TO HAVE SPOT LABELS ON THE FRONT AND BACK.

IS THAT SOMETHING YOU CAN DO?

NOPE, WE ONLY HAVE A WRAPAROUND LABELER.

AND I'M GUESSING YOU WANT TO PACK 25 BOTTLES TO THE CASE INSTEAD OF THE USUAL 24.

WHY WOULD WE WANT TO DO THAT?

'CAUSE WE DON'T DO THAT EITHER.

HA HA HA!

I DON'T KNOW EXACTLY WHY, BUT THEY'RE WILLING TO GIVE US A TRY. WE CAN START NEXT MONTH.

THAT'S AWESOME!

WE WERE ALMOST READY TO DO OUR FIRST PRODUCTION RUN. WE HAD ALL THE TEA DELIVERIES TO BUFFALO LINED UP.

FAR AWAY SPRINGS

BLACK TEA

SUGAR

MAPLE SYRUP

GREEN TEA

WE LOVE YOUR CHAI BLEND AND WANT TO ORDER A LOT OF IT.

6:30 AM

I'M HEADING TO WORK NOW, BUT I COULD MAKE A BATCH WHEN I GET HOME. HOW MUCH DO YOU NEED? TEN POUNDS?

WE'D ORDERED THE ORGANIC CANE SUGAR, HONEY, AND MAPLE SYRUP. BUT WE COULDN'T FIND ANYONE TO SUPPLY THE SPICES FOR OUR KASHMIRI CHAI.

MORE LIKE 200.

UHHH, I DON'T THINK I CAN HELP YOU.

BUT DID YOU TELL HIM HOW MUCH WE WANTED TO ORDER? THAT SHOULD HAVE MOTIVATED HIM TO DO SOME EXTRA WORK.

HE ONLY MAKES CHAI AS A HOBBY. HE GRINDS SPICES ON WEEKENDS IN HIS BACKYARD.

THAT'S WHAT SCARED HIM AWAY.

THEN WE'LL JUST HAVE TO MAKE OUR OWN CHAI RECIPE.

HOW ARE WE GOING TO DO THAT?? ASIDE FROM SCRAMBLED EGGS, I'M NOT MUCH OF A COOK.

WHAT'S SO COMPLICATED? WE KNOW WHAT'S IN EVERY CHAI RECIPE. WE JUST NEED TO FIND THE RIGHT BLEND.

CINNAMON   HMM...
GINGER
CLOVES
PEPPER
ORANGE
PEEL...

I GUESS WE'LL NEED TO FIND A SPICE COMPANY, THEN.

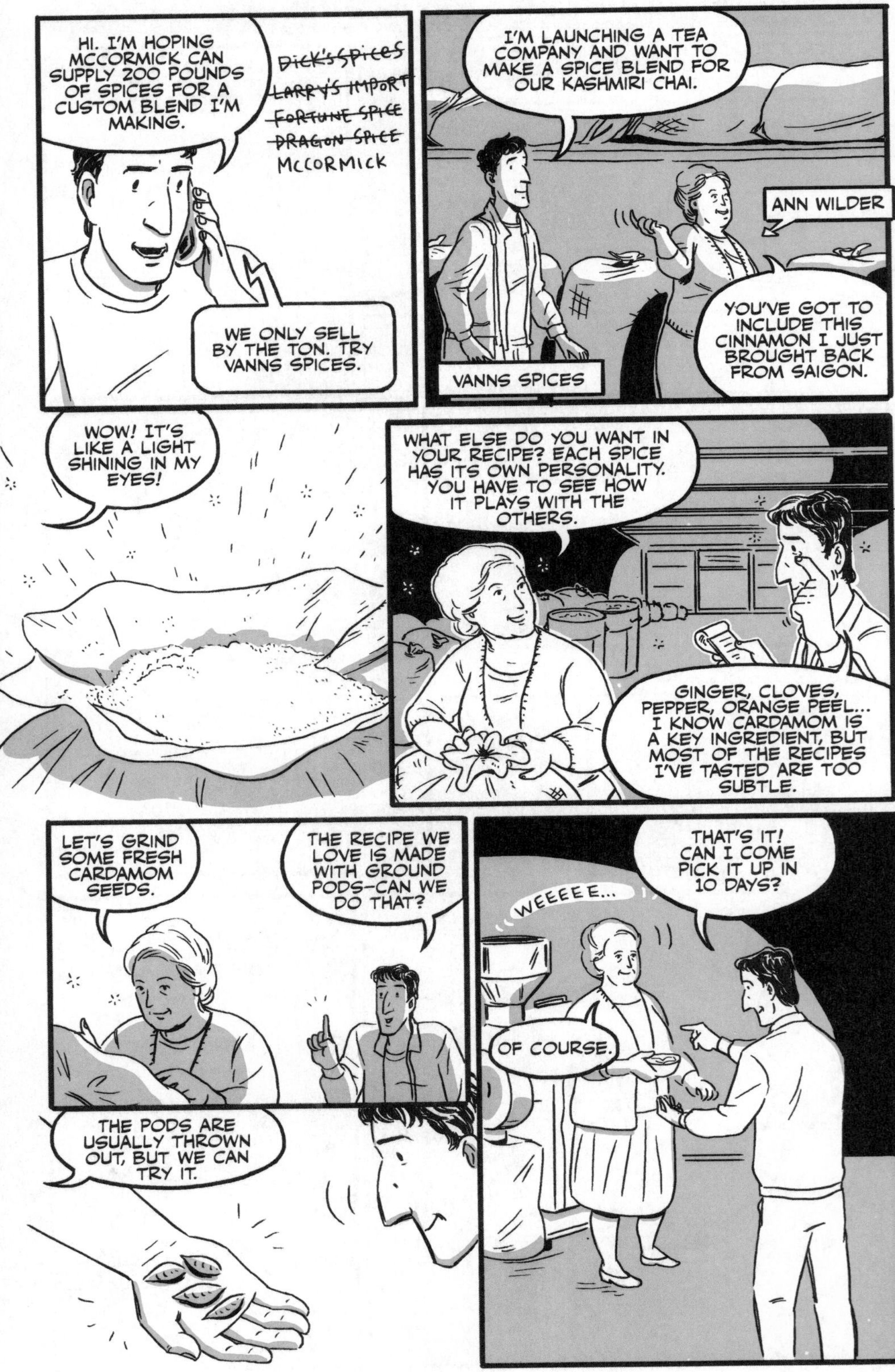
HI. I'M HOPING MCCORMICK CAN SUPPLY 200 POUNDS OF SPICES FOR A CUSTOM BLEND I'M MAKING.
DICK'S SPICES
LARRY'S IMPORT
FORTUNE SPICE
DRAGON SPICE
MCCORMICK
WE ONLY SELL BY THE TON. TRY VANNS SPICES.
I'M LAUNCHING A TEA COMPANY AND WANT TO MAKE A SPICE BLEND FOR OUR KASHMIRI CHAI.
ANN WILDER
VANNS SPICES
YOU'VE GOT TO INCLUDE THIS CINNAMON I JUST BROUGHT BACK FROM SAIGON.
WOW! IT'S LIKE A LIGHT SHINING IN MY EYES!
WHAT ELSE DO YOU WANT IN YOUR RECIPE? EACH SPICE HAS ITS OWN PERSONALITY. YOU HAVE TO SEE HOW IT PLAYS WITH THE OTHERS.
GINGER, CLOVES, PEPPER, ORANGE PEEL... I KNOW CARDAMOM IS A KEY INGREDIENT, BUT MOST OF THE RECIPES I'VE TASTED ARE TOO SUBTLE.
LET'S GRIND SOME FRESH CARDAMOM SEEDS.
THE RECIPE WE LOVE IS MADE WITH GROUND PODS—CAN WE DO THAT?
THE PODS ARE USUALLY THROWN OUT, BUT WE CAN TRY IT.
WEEEEE...
THAT'S IT! CAN I COME PICK IT UP IN 10 DAYS?
OF COURSE.

PROF. NALEBUFF, WHY SETH?

I FIRST MET SETH AS A STUDENT IN MY POLITICAL & ECONOMIC MARKETING CLASS.

1994

LATER, I ADVISED HIM ON A BUSINESS PLAN.

THE IDEA IS TO PUT A TEST STRIP FOR URINARY TRACT INFECTIONS INTO AN ADULT INCONTINENCE DIAPER.

CONGRATULATIONS ON WINNING YALE'S FIRST BUSINESS PLAN COMPETITION. WE'D LIKE TO INVEST.

I'M FLATTERED, BUT I'M NOT SURE I HAVE THE PASSION FOR A DIAPER BUSINESS.

IT WASN'T A QUESTION OF IF SETH WOULD START A BUSINESS, BUT WHEN AND WHAT KIND. HE NEEDED TO FIND SOMETHING THAT HAD A SOCIAL MISSION.

OUR FIRST CASE STUDY IS RAINFOREST CRUNCH, A SOCIAL VENTURE THAT TRIED TO SAVE THE RAIN FOREST BY SELLING CANDY MADE WITH INDIGENOUS NUTS.

WHAT AN AMAZING CONCEPT!

YEAH, BUT THE BUSINESS FAILED.

I MEAN THAT A BUSINESS COULD MAKE CHANGE HAPPEN AND FUND ITS GROWTH THROUGH PROFITS.

SOM CLASSROOM, 1993

LIKE ALL OF YOU, SETH IS PLENTY SMART. BUT HE HAS SOME OTHER VERY SPECIAL QUALITIES. HE'S AN ETERNAL OPTIMIST.

IT MAY NOT BE HALF FULL, BUT IT LOOKS LIKE PLENTY TO ME.

ENTREPRENEURS HAVE TO LIVE WITH CONSTANT REJECTION.

CAN WE SELL YOU SOME GOLF BALLS?

NEHOIDEN GOLF CLUB, WELLESLEY, MA, 1973

NOT TODAY, BOYS.

BUT THESE BALLS ARE FRESH FROM THE WOODS. I'VE EVEN GOT THE POISON IVY TO PROVE IT.

SOME OF THESE BALLS ARE HARDLY USED. WE'RE RUNNING A SPECIAL: BUY 3 BALLS FOR $2, AND GET A FREE CUP OF LEMONADE.

THIS LOOKS LIKE THE BALL I HIT INTO THE WOODS LAST WEEK! DO I STILL HAVE TO PAY FOR IT?

YOU'RE NOT THE ONE WITH THE POISON IVY.

JUST BECAUSE THEY DON'T SAY YES THE FIRST TIME DOESN'T MEAN NO.

THAT PERSISTENCE CONTINUES TO THIS DAY.

SETH'S A RISK TAKER. AND HE'S AN ALL-IN KIND OF GUY.

GOOD LUCK WITH LAW SCHOOL.

GOOD LUCK IN CHINA.

HARVARD UNIVERSITY, JUNE 1987

SETH'S DAY JOB WAS TEACHING ENGLISH.

WHEN MARTIN LUTHER KING JR. GAVE HIS "I HAVE A DREAM" SPEECH, HE WAS TALKING ABOUT HIS HOPES FOR A BETTER WORLD.

FOREIGN AFFAIRS COLLEGE, BEIJING

MUCH LATER THAT NIGHT

04:30

OUR DEADLINE IS IN 30 MINUTES. I NEED TO KNOW WHAT YEAR ZHAO ZIYANG JOINED THE POLITBURO.

1979.

TAP TAP

WASHINGTON POST, CHINA BUREAU

A YEAR LATER

你现在回家吗？

是的，回去做总统工作。之后，我就去俄罗斯教书。

(ARE YOU HEADED HOME NOW?)

(YES, TO WORK ON THE PRESIDENTIAL CAMPAIGN. THEN I'M OFF TO TEACH IN RUSSIA.)

LONGVIEW, TX, 1988

HI, I'M JULIE FARKAS, HERE TO HELP YOU GET OILMEN EXCITED ABOUT THE DEMOCRATIC TICKET.

Dukakis Bentsen

Bentsen Vice President '88

THAT WAS ONE OF THE BEST EVENTS WE'VE HAD THIS MONTH. WELL DONE.

THANK YOU, SENATOR.

NOT BAD FOR A FIRST EVENT. I'M STILL NOT SURE HOW YOU SWEET-TALKED THAT REPUBLICAN INTO LENDING US HIS OIL DERRICK. WE MAKE A GREAT TEAM.

THANKS. MOST PEOPLE HERE THOUGHT WE WERE A COUPLE. I GUESS NEITHER OF US BLENDS IN HERE IN LONGVIEW.

I KNOW WE JUST MET, BUT I'M HEADING OFF TO TEACH ENGLISH IN RUSSIA IN A FEW MONTHS. ANY CHANCE YOU'D COME ALONG?

MOSCOW, 1989

AFTER CHINA AND RUSSIA, SETH RETURNED TO THE U.S. TO RUN A DEMONSTRATION PROGRAM FOR AMERICORPS. HE THEN ENROLLED HERE AT SOM, WHERE HE WAS ONE OF THE FOUNDERS OF NET IMPACT. HIS INTEREST IN BUSINESS AS AN AGENT OF CHANGE LED HIM TO AN INTERNSHIP, AND A JOB UPON GRADUATION, AT CALVERT INVESTMENTS.

SETH, AS MUCH AS YOU CAN DO VIA NOT-FOR-PROFITS, YOU MIGHT CHANGE THE WORLD EVEN MORE THROUGH BUSINESS.

WAYNE SILBY, CALVERT CO-FOUNDER

THROUGH BIOTECHNOLOGY, WE CAN END WORLD HUNGER.

ROBERT SHAPIRO, CEO OF MONSANTO

SETH'S JOB TOOK HIM TO THE BUSINESS FOR SOCIAL RESPONSIBILITY CONFERENCE (1997).

I APPLAUD YOUR BEING HERE TODAY AND YOUR DESIRE TO END WORLD HUNGER. BUT I CHALLENGE MONSANTO TO STOP SELLING RECOMBINANT BOVINE GROWTH HORMONE.

GARY HIRSHBERG, CE-YO OF STONYFIELD FARM

IT'S INHUMANE TO COWS AND UNHEALTHY FOR PEOPLE.

AT STONYFIELD, WE BUY FROM FARMERS WHO DON'T USE RBGH, BUT AT OUR SIZE, WE ONLY AFFECT A FEW THOUSAND COWS AND A FEW HUNDRED THOUSAND PEOPLE.

MONSANTO COULD PUT THEIR TECHNICAL KNOW-HOW INTO DEVELOPING ADVANCED FEED SUPPLEMENTS THAT ENHANCE ANIMAL HEALTH AND BUILD NATURAL RESISTANCE USING ORGANIC METHODS.

YOU'D MAKE HUNDREDS OF MILLIONS IN PROFITS AND IMPROVE BILLIONS OF LIVES.

THAT GUY'S NOT AFRAID TO TELL IT LIKE IT IS. I NEED TO GET CLOSER TO THE ACTION!

FUELED IN PART BY HIS SENSE OF PURPOSE, SETH HAS AMAZING STAMINA. THAT'S KEY IN A START-UP, WHICH IS MORE LIKE A MARATHON THAN A SPRINT.

20 DONUTS

OK, SETH, YOU WIN THE BET.

10 miles

SETH'S PERSONALITY MAKES HIM A GREAT MATCH FOR ME AS A BUSINESS PARTNER; OUR SKILL SETS COMPLEMENT EACH ANOTHER.

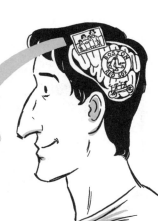

CONCEPTUALIZER	PROTECTOR
logical analytical fact-based	Dutiful Meticulous Supportive
☑ Organized ☑ Practical ☑ Outgoing	Optimistic Enthusiastic Values - driven
COORDINATOR	ENTHUSIAST

PERHAPS MOST IMPORTANT, YOU SPEND A LOT OF TIME WITH A BUSINESS PARTNER, SO YOU SHOULD ENJOY BEING WITH THAT PERSON.

I KNOW IT SOUNDS CORNY, BUT SETH HELPS ME BE A BETTER PERSON.

WHAT WOULD SETH DO?

HMMM

WE FIGURED OUR TARGET CUSTOMER WAS A LABEL READER. SINCE WE COULDN'T AFFORD TO ADVERTISE, THE BACK LABEL WAS THE BEST (AND, FOR NOW, ONLY) PLACE TO EXPLAIN WHAT WE WERE DOING AND HOW WE WERE DIFFERENT. OF COURSE, WE STILL HAD TO WRITE IT—AND QUICKLY—TO MEET THE PRINTING DEADLINE AHEAD OF OUR PRODUCTION RUN.

HONEST TEA

FRONT

BACK

WE NEED TO MAKE IT PERSONAL. HOW ABOUT JUST TELLING OUR STORY?

WE WERE THIRSTY. WE SEARCHED FOR BOTTLED TEA THAT TRULY TASTED LIKE TEA, BUT COULDN'T FIND ANY. SO WE DECIDED TO MAKE OUR OWN. HONEST TEAS ARE SELECT BLACK, GREEN, AND HERBAL TEAS MICROBREWED IN SPRING WATER, FINELY FILTERED, AND NOT TOO SWEET.

GIVEN ALL THE SEDIMENT, I'M NOT SURE ABOUT "FINELY FILTERED." AND WE SHOULD EXPLAIN THAT THE TASTE WON'T HIT THEM OVER THE HEAD. TRY THIS:

WE WERE THIRSTY. WE SEARCHED FOR BOTTLED TEA THAT TRULY TASTED LIKE TEA, BUT COULDN'T FIND ANY. SO WE DECIDED TO MAKE OUR OWN.

HONEST TEAS ARE MICROBREWED IN SPRING WATER AND SWEETENED—JUST BARELY. EACH HAS A SUBTLE, AROMATIC FLAVOR AND ONE-SIXTH OF THE CALORIES OF THOSE SUPER-SWEET, TEA-FLAVORED DRINKS.

THAT'S A BIT NEGATIVE AT THE END.

RE THIRSTY. WE HED FOR BOTTLED RULY TASTED LIKE , BUT COULDN'T FIND ANY. SO WE DECIDED TO MAKE OUR OWN. HONEST TEAS ARE MICROBREWED IN SPRING WATER AND SWEETENED—JUST BARELY. EACH HAS A SUBTLE, AROMATIC FLAVOR AND ONE-SIXTH OF THE CALORIES OF THOSE SUPER-SWEET, TEA-FLAVORED DRINKS.

BUT IT'S TRUE.

OK. BUT LET'S SWITCH...

WE WERE THIRSTY. WE SEARCHED FOR BOTTL TEA THAT TRULY TAST LIKE TEA, BUT COULDN FIND ANY. SO WE DEC TO MAKE OUR OWN. HONEST TEAS ARE MIC BREWED IN SPRING W AND SWEETENED—JUST BARELY. EACH HAS A SUBTLE, AROMATIC FLA AND ONE-SIXTH OF TH CALORIES OF THOSE SUPER-SWEET, TEA-FLAVORED DRINKS.

JUST BARELY SWEETENED

WHAT DO WE DO ABOUT THE SEDIMENT IN THE TEA?

LET'S USE A P.S. TO TURN IT INTO A POSITIVE.

WE WERE THIRSTY. WE SEARCHED FOR BOTTLED TEA THAT TRULY TASTED LIKE TEA BUT COULDN'T FIND ANY. SO WE DECIDED TO MAKE OUR OWN. HONEST TEAS ARE MICROBREWED IN SPRING WATER AND JUST BARELY SWEETENED. EACH HAS A SUBTLE, AROMATIC FLAVOR AND ONE-SIXTH OF THE CALORIES OF THOSE SUPER-SWEET, TEA-FLAVORED DRINKS.

P.S. LIKE FINE WINE, OUR TEA CONTAINS NATURAL SEDIMENT BECAUSE, UNLIKE THE OTHER GUYS, WE BREW OUR TEA NATURALLY AND HONESTLY.

I'D RATHER NOT END ON A DIG AT THE COMPETITION.

OUR OWN. HONEST TEAS ARE BREWED IN SPRING WATER JUST BARELY SWEETENED. HAS A SUBTLE, AROMATIC FLAVOR AND ONE-SIXTH OF THE CALORIES OF THOSE SUPER-SWEET, TEA-FLAVORED DRINKS.

P.S. LIKE FINE WINE, OUR TEA CONTAINS NATURAL SEDIMENT. OR AS OUR KIDS SAY: DON'T MIND THE FLOATIES.

THE P.S. MESSAGES SHOULD BE FUN AND POSITIVE. FOR OUR GREEN TEA WE COULD TRY:

WE DECIDED TO HONEST TEAS ARE IN SPRING WATER SWEETENED. SUBTLE, AROMATIC ONE SIXTH OF THE OF THOSE SUPER-SWEET, TEA-FLAVORED DRINKS.

P.S. LAB TESTS DETERMINED THAT OUR MOROCCAN MINT HAS 20 TIMES MORE EGCG, A KEY ANTIOXIDANT, THAN BROCCOLI.

FOR OUR KASHMIRI CHAI WE COULD SAY:

HONEST TEA
KASHMIRI CHAI

P.S. GREAT COLD, HOT, OR WITH MILK. AND BARRY LIKES IT WITH PIZZA.

WHICH IS TRUE!

SINCE THE MESSAGE IS COMING FROM US, WE SHOULD SIGN IT.

WE CAN SCAN IN OUR ACTUAL SIGNATURES.

HONESTLY YOURS,

Seth + Barry

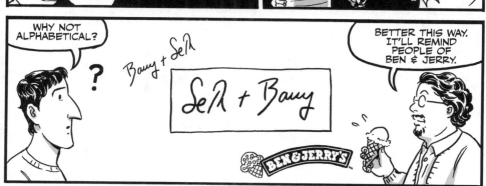

WHY NOT ALPHABETICAL?

? Barry + Seth

Seth + Barry

BETTER THIS WAY. IT'LL REMIND PEOPLE OF BEN & JERRY.

BEN & JERRY'S

WE ALSO NEED A TAGLINE.

HOW ABOUT...

REAL TEA, REAL TASTE, NO SH*T

ARE YOU KIDDING?

NO. NONE OF OUR INGREDIENTS ARE BAD QUALITY, AND WE'RE TELLING THE TRUTH. IT HAS A GREAT DOUBLE MEANING.

I DON'T THINK SO. REMEMBER, OUR TARGET AUDIENCE IS A LITTLE MORE MATURE, IS MORE LIKELY TO PRACTICE YOGA THAN SKATEBOARD, AND LISTENS TO NPR. LET'S GO WITH:

FRESHLY BREWED AND BARELY SWEETENED

A BIT BORING, BUT IT EXPLAINS OUR KEY SELLING POINTS.

SOME WEEKS LATER

THE BACK LABEL MESSAGE IS WORKING, BUT THE TAGLINE, NOT SO MUCH.

THIS IS SWEETENED WITH BARLEY? WHAT DOES THAT TASTE LIKE?

TEA FRESHLY BREWED & BARLEY SWEETENED

HONEST TEA

LET'S TRY "REAL TEA, REAL TASTE, HONEST."

Making a Pictogram

MEGHAN, I COULD USE YOUR HELP ON A TECHNICAL PROBLEM.

KNOCK KNOCK

OK, WHAT'S THE PROBLEM?

WE'RE TRYING TO MAKE A LITTLE PICTOGRAM FOR THE BACK LABEL TO ILLUSTRATE THE CAFFEINE LEVEL.

AND HERE I THOUGHT YOU WERE GOING TO ASK ME SOMETHING ABOUT ECONOMICS.

WELL, IT IS, SORT OF. HAVE A LOOK.

about ¼ the caffeine of coffee

HOW BIG SHOULD THE INNER CUP BE?

THE INNER CUP LOOKS TO BE ABOUT 40% AS BIG IN EACH DIMENSION, SO IT'S REALLY 16% THE SIZE. IT'S TOO SMALL.

I KNOW. IN FACT, IF THE CUP IS THREE-DIMENSIONAL, THEN IT'S ONLY 6% OF THE VOLUME.

3D

$(0.4)^2 = 16\%$

$(0.4)^3 = 6\%$

IS THAT HONEST?

THAT'S WHY I'M ASKING YOU. IF WE DRAW IT TO SCALE, IT JUST LOOKS WRONG.

63%

I AGREE. THE WAY YOU'VE DONE IT SEEMS HONEST TO ME.

about ¼ the caffeine of coffee

EVEN IF IT'S TECHNICALLY WRONG, PEOPLE WILL SEE IT AS 25%, AND THAT'S WHAT MATTERS.

12. GOOD TASTE ISN'T EVERYTHING

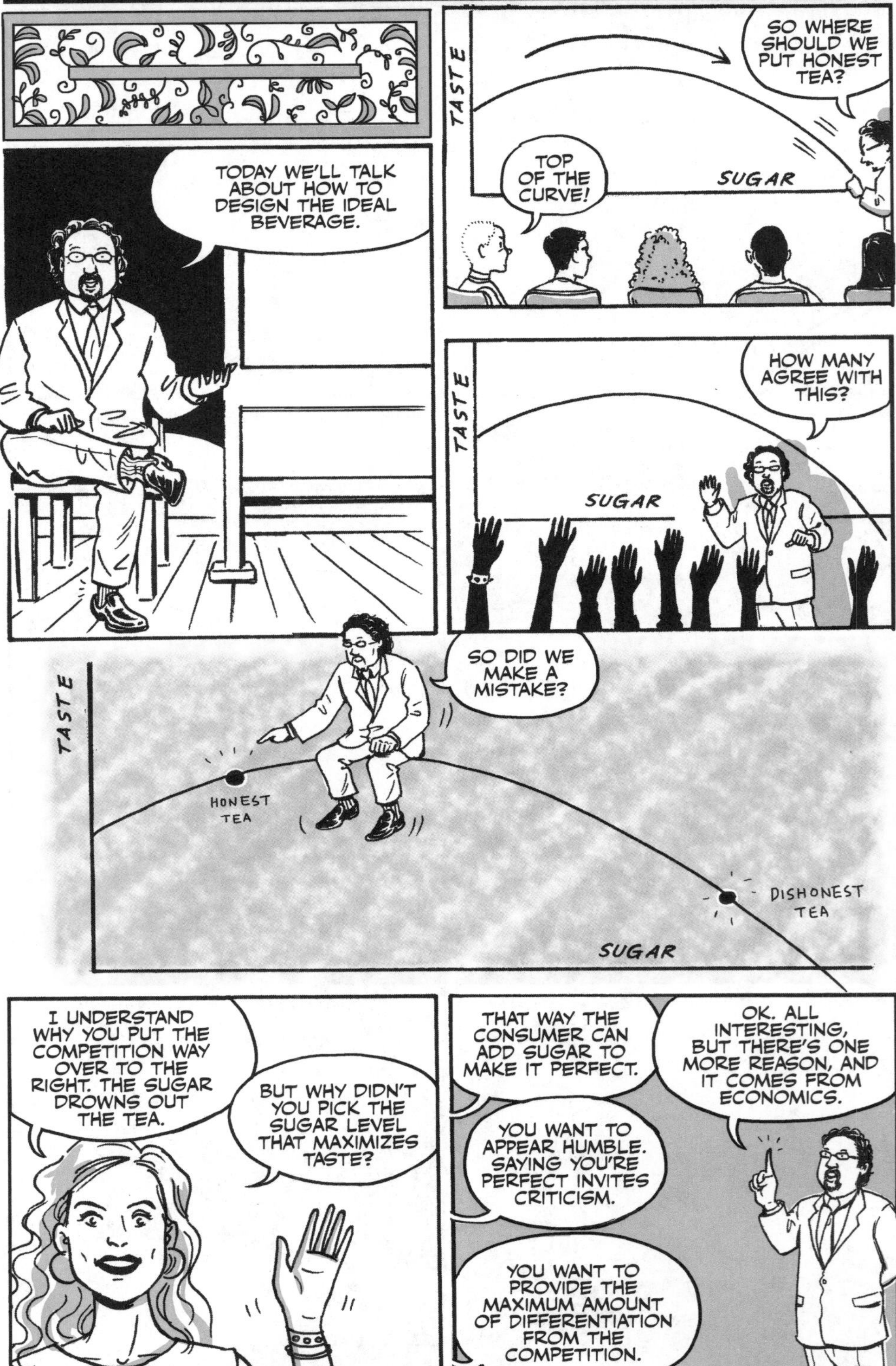
TODAY WE'LL TALK ABOUT HOW TO DESIGN THE IDEAL BEVERAGE.
TASTE
SO WHERE SHOULD WE PUT HONEST TEA?
TOP OF THE CURVE!
SUGAR
TASTE
HOW MANY AGREE WITH THIS?
SUGAR
TASTE
SO DID WE MAKE A MISTAKE?
HONEST TEA
DISHONEST TEA
SUGAR
I UNDERSTAND WHY YOU PUT THE COMPETITION WAY OVER TO THE RIGHT. THE SUGAR DROWNS OUT THE TEA.
BUT WHY DIDN'T YOU PICK THE SUGAR LEVEL THAT MAXIMIZES TASTE?
THAT WAY THE CONSUMER CAN ADD SUGAR TO MAKE IT PERFECT.
YOU WANT TO APPEAR HUMBLE. SAYING YOU'RE PERFECT INVITES CRITICISM.
YOU WANT TO PROVIDE THE MAXIMUM AMOUNT OF DIFFERENTIATION FROM THE COMPETITION.
OK. ALL INTERESTING, BUT THERE'S ONE MORE REASON, AND IT COMES FROM ECONOMICS.

DIFFERENT PEOPLE HAVE DIFFERENT TASTES.

TRUE. BUT EVEN IF WE WERE DESIGNING THIS TEA JUST FOR YOU, WE WOULDN'T GO TO THE PEAK.

WHY NOT?

I'M STILL HERE

BECAUSE IF YOU CUT BACK ON SUGAR, YOU SAVE MONEY.

AND WHAT ELSE IS SAVED?

CALORIES!

CUSTOMERS NOT ONLY CARE ABOUT TASTE, THEY CARE ABOUT COST, AND THEY CARE ABOUT CALORIES.

DIET COKE

HERE'S WHERE ECON 101 COMES IN.

IT IS ALWAYS FLAT AT THE TOP OF A CURVE. THUS, CUTTING BACK ON SUGAR MEANS WE GIVE UP ALMOST NOTHING IN TERMS OF TASTE.

BUT THE CUSTOMER SAVES CALORIES AND WE SAVE MONEY ON INGREDIENTS.

TASTE

SUGAR

USING LESS SUGAR ALSO MEANS WE CAN AFFORD TO USE ORGANIC HONEY, AGAVE, AND MAPLE SYRUP.

MAPLE

HONEY

AGAVE

THE IDEAL BEVERAGE MAXIMIZES THE CUSTOMER'S OVERALL HAPPINESS.

WE'RE THE ONLY BEVERAGE COMPANY WITH A TASTE VERSUS SUGAR CURVE ON OUR BACK LABEL.

IT DOESN'T TAKE AN ECON PH.D. TO BREW TEA—BUT BARRY HAS ONE AND SOMETIMES IT ACTUALLY HELPS. HERE'S HOW. SUGAR, LIKE MOST GOODS HAS A DECLINING MARGINAL UTILITY. ONE TEASPOON TAKES AWAY TEA'S BITTERNESS. ANOTHER ADDS A NICE SWEETNESS. THAT'S WHERE WE STOP. MORE SUGAR ADDS CALORIES BUT NOT MUCH MORE TASTE. BY THE TIME YOU'VE GOT SIX TEASPOONS PER SERVING, IT'S LIQUID CANDY. GREEN DRAGON TEA IS ORGANIC AND JUST A TAD SWEET.
HONESTLY YOURS,

P.S. THE ANTIOXIDANT DRAGON TEA CAN PLAY ROLE IN A HEALTHY DIET MORE, VISIT THE AMERI FOR CANCER RESEARCH AT

DO YOU REALLY EXPECT CONSUMERS TO UNDERSTAND ALL THIS?

WE'D LIKE THE CONSUMER TO THINK:

BOY, THIS TASTES GREAT! I CAN'T BELIEVE IT HAS ONLY 30 CALORIES.

I GET IT! TASTE ISN'T THE ONLY THING THAT'S IMPORTANT. CUTTING BACK ON SUGAR IS HOW YOU MAXIMIZE THE WHOLE PACKAGE.

I THINK THEY'LL JUST ASSUME YOU MADE A TYPO.

PERHAPS. BUT OVER TIME WE'RE BETTING WE HAVE THE RIGHT COMBINATION TO KEEP THEM COMING BACK.

13. A WARRANTED VALUATION

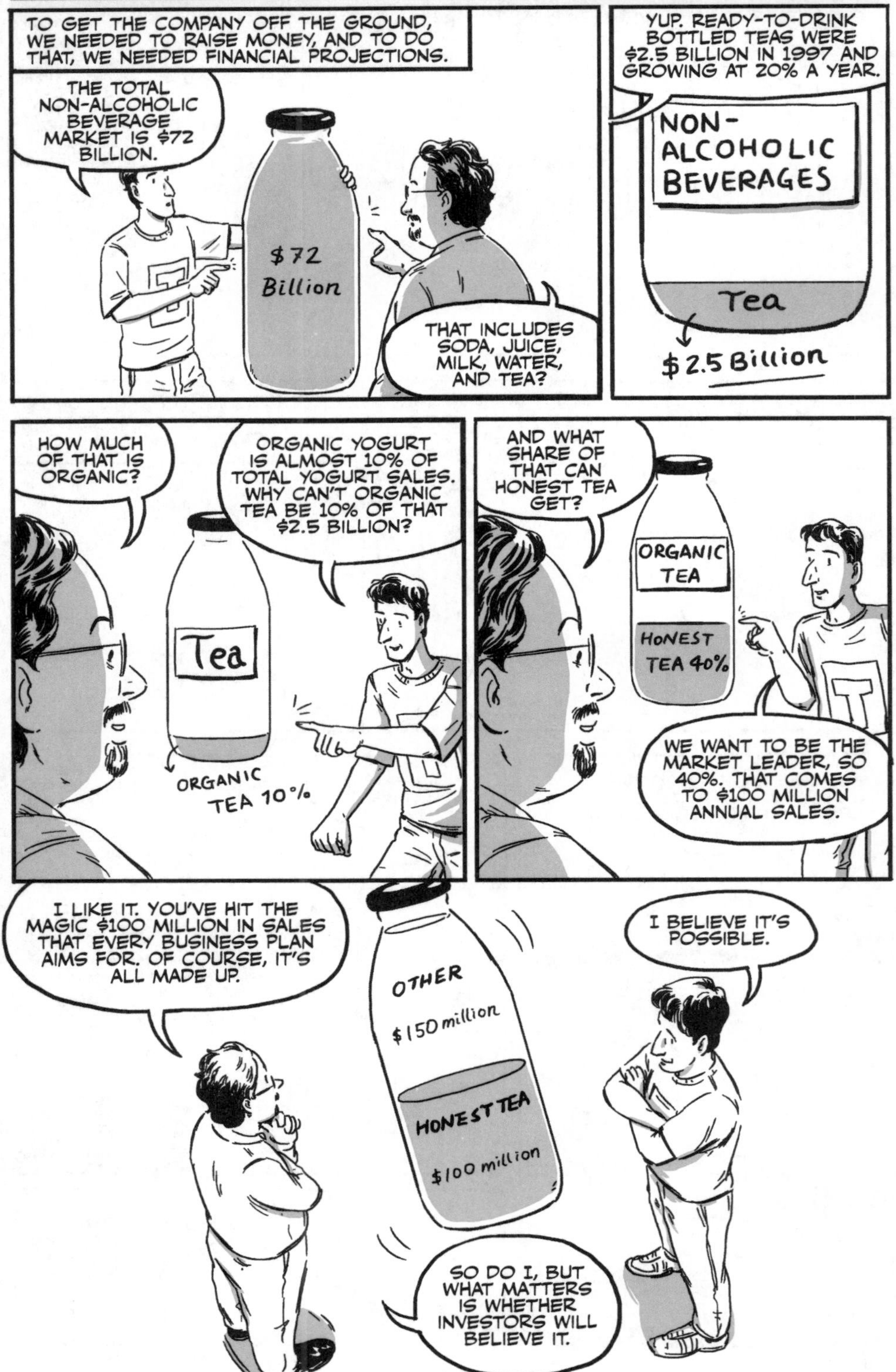

TO GET THE COMPANY OFF THE GROUND, WE NEEDED TO RAISE MONEY, AND TO DO THAT, WE NEEDED FINANCIAL PROJECTIONS.
THE TOTAL NON-ALCOHOLIC BEVERAGE MARKET IS $72 BILLION.
$72 Billion
THAT INCLUDES SODA, JUICE, MILK, WATER, AND TEA?
YUP. READY-TO-DRINK BOTTLED TEAS WERE $2.5 BILLION IN 1997 AND GROWING AT 20% A YEAR.
NON-ALCOHOLIC BEVERAGES
Tea
$2.5 Billion
HOW MUCH OF THAT IS ORGANIC?
ORGANIC YOGURT IS ALMOST 10% OF TOTAL YOGURT SALES. WHY CAN'T ORGANIC TEA BE 10% OF THAT $2.5 BILLION?
Tea
ORGANIC TEA 10%
AND WHAT SHARE OF THAT CAN HONEST TEA GET?
ORGANIC TEA
HONEST TEA 40%
WE WANT TO BE THE MARKET LEADER, SO 40%. THAT COMES TO $100 MILLION ANNUAL SALES.
I LIKE IT. YOU'VE HIT THE MAGIC $100 MILLION IN SALES THAT EVERY BUSINESS PLAN AIMS FOR. OF COURSE, IT'S ALL MADE UP.
OTHER
$150 million
HONEST TEA
$100 million
I BELIEVE IT'S POSSIBLE.
SO DO I, BUT WHAT MATTERS IS WHETHER INVESTORS WILL BELIEVE IT.

IN THE LAST FEW YEARS, OVER 1,000 TEAHOUSES HAVE OPENED IN THE U.S. AND NATURAL FOODS ARE PROJECTED TO GROW FROM $11.5 BILLION TO $50 BILLION BY 2003.

POP
POP
NATURAL FOODS
$11.5
$50
2003

OK, OK. BUT IF ANYONE REALLY BELIEVED WE'D HIT $100 MILLION IN SALES, WE'D RAISE MONEY AT A $100 MILLION VALUATION, NOT THE $5 MILLION VALUATION WE'D BE LUCKY TO GET TODAY.

WELL, EITHER IT'S GOING TO WORK OR IT'S NOT. THE LOW VALUE TODAY REWARDS INVESTORS FOR TAKING A BET ON US.

WITH THAT IN MIND, I WANT TO TRY SOMETHING RADICALLY DIFFERENT.

INSTEAD OF PRETENDING THE COMPANY IS WORTH SOME MADE-UP AMOUNT, OUR LEVEL OF SUCCESS SHOULD DETERMINE WHAT PERCENTAGE OF THE COMPANY THE INVESTORS GET FOR THEIR MONEY.

WHAT DO YOU MEAN?

WE NEED TO RAISE $1 MILLION. NORMALLY, WE'D ASSIGN A VALUE TO THE COMPANY, SAY $5 MILLION.

INVESTORS GET 20% OF THE COMPANY FOR THEIR $1 MILLION, WHILE WE KEEP 80%.

Founders

80%

20%

Investors

MY IDEA IS: LET'S GIVE INVESTORS 100% OF THE COMPANY RIGHT OFF THE BAT. WE'LL START SHARING THE GAINS ONLY AFTER WE'VE DOUBLED THEIR MONEY.

HOW WOULD THAT WORK?

THANKS!

100% INVESTORS

WE'LL SELL A MILLION SHARES AT $1/SHARE. AS FOUNDERS, WE'LL GET A MILLION LONG-TERM OPTIONS—THAT IS, WARRANTS—TO BUY STOCK AT $2, $3, $5, $10, AND $15 A SHARE.

$2

$3

$5

$10

$15

WARRANTS

THAT SOUNDS COMPLICATED. NO ONE WILL UNDERSTAND IT. I'M NOT SURE I UNDERSTAND IT.

YOU'RE PROBABLY RIGHT. BUT THEY'LL UNDERSTAND THE BIG PICTURE: WE ARE PUTTING THE INVESTORS AHEAD OF OURSELVES.

ALL OUR WARRANTS ARE WORTHLESS TODAY. EVEN WHEN WE GROW THE COMPANY TO $2/SHARE, WE STILL WON'T HAVE ANYTHING.

0 value

ONCE WE TRIPLE THEIR INVESTMENT, OUR WARRANTS WILL FINALLY HAVE VALUE. AT $3/SHARE, THE WARRANTS WITH A $2/SHARE EXERCISE PRICE WILL EACH BE WORTH $1.

$3/SHARE	
INVESTORS	1M SHARES = $3M
FOUNDERS	1M WARRANTS AT $2 = $1M ALL OTHER WARRANTS = $0

THE COMPANY WOULD BE WORTH $4 MILLION TOTAL, AND WE'D HAVE A 25% SHARE.

AS THE COMPANY GROWS, SO DOES OUR SHARE. IF WE CAN GROW THE TOTAL VALUE TO $40 MILLION, THAT TRANSLATES TO $12/SHARE. OUR WARRANTS WOULD BE WORTH $28 MILLION, OR 70%.

$12/SHARE	
INVESTORS	1M SHARES = $12M
FOUNDERS	1M WARRANTS AT $2 = $10M 1M WARRANTS AT $3 = $9M 1M WARRANTS AT $5 = $7M 1M WARRANTS AT $10 = $2M 1M WARRANTS AT $15 = $0 $28M

LET ME SEE IF I HAVE THIS STRAIGHT: INSTEAD OF GIVING OURSELVES A BUNCH OF STOCK AT THE BEGINNING, WE HAVE TO EARN OUR SHARE.

AS THE COMPANY GROWS IN VALUE, THE STOCK PRICE GOES UP AND OUR WARRANTS GAIN VALUE. BUT IF WE ONLY DOUBLE THE STOCK PRICE, WE WON'T SEE A DIME.

EXACTLY. TYPICALLY, AS A COMPANY RAISES MORE MONEY, THE FOUNDERS GET DILUTED. BUT IF WE'RE ABLE TO KEEP INCREASING THE VALUATION, OUR STAKE WILL GO UP.

THAT'S NOT NORMALLY HOW PEOPLE RAISE MONEY, BUT DOING THINGS DIFFERENTLY HASN'T STOPPED US BEFORE.

WAIT. WHAT ABOUT LOSING CONTROL? IF WE DON'T HOLD A MAJORITY STAKE, HOW DO WE PROTECT OURSELVES?

GOOD POINT. ON MATTERS OF CONTROL, THE INVESTORS WILL NEED TO AGREE TO VOTE WITH US—AT LEAST FOR THE FIRST 10 YEARS.

NOTE: WE'VE SIMPLIFIED OUR STORY TO MAKE THE MATH A BIT EASIER. WE ACTUALLY SOLD 1.24 MILLION SHARES AT 50¢ AND HAD 800K WARRANTS AT $1, $1.50, $2.50, $5.00, AND $7.50.

I LOVE GEORGE, BUT WE NEED SOME FAMILY TIME DURING ELIE'S OPERATION.

MY FRIEND LAWRENCE IS A QUALITY CONTROL MANAGER AT A LOCAL BOTTLING PLANT.

HE CAN HELP YOU FINALIZE THE FORMULATIONS. I'LL DRIVE DOWN TO THE BOTTLING PLANT FROM TORONTO AND MAKE SURE EVERYTHING'S READY FOR THE FIRST PRODUCTION RUN.

ALRIGHT. I'LL SEE YOU IN BUFFALO IN A FEW WEEKS.

YOU GOING TO BE OK?

WE'LL FIGURE OUT A WAY TO BE OK.

FORTUNATELY, SETH'S FAMILY HAD INSURANCE THROUGH JULIE'S JOB.

6:30 AM

LOOK, DADDY, THERE'S A BEE!

HE'S GOING TO BE OK, BUT HIS AORTA WAS ALMOST COMPLETELY CLOSED OFF. BARELY ANY BLOOD WAS GETTING THROUGH.
AORTIC ARCH
AORTIC Valve
Intensive Care Unit
I WANT TO GO HOME.
I KNOW YOU DO, SWEETIE, AND YOU WILL. WE JUST HAVE TO STAY HERE FOR A FEW DAYS UNTIL YOU GET ALL THE WAY BETTER.
DAY 2
Z Z Z
DAY 3
Z Z Z
DAY 4

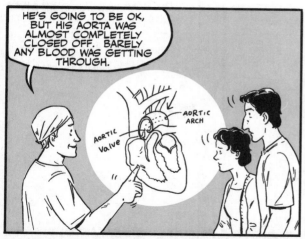

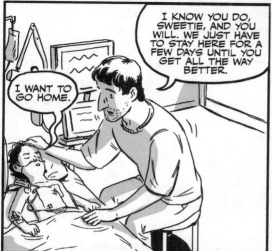

DAY 5

HOW'S YOUR SON?

HE'S RECOVERING, BUT WE'LL ALL FEEL BETTER WHEN WE CAN GO HOME. I APPRECIATE YOU MEETING ME HERE SO LATE.

THIS ACTUALLY WORKS OUT WELL FOR ME—MY SHIFT ENDED AT 11 PM.

I KNOW WE NEED TO ADD ACID TO LOWER THE TEA'S PH SO BACTERIA CAN'T GROW IN THE BOTTLES.

HERE'S WHAT ASSAM TASTES LIKE WITH LEMON JUICE.

NOW I SEE WHY EVERYONE WANTS TO PUT SO MUCH SUGAR IN. AREN'T THERE ANY OTHER ACIDS WE CAN USE THAT HAVE LESS IMPACT ON THE TASTE?

HERE'S WHAT IT TASTES LIKE WHEN YOU JUST USE CITRIC ACID.

BETTER, BUT IT STILL CHANGES THE FLAVOR. IS THERE ANYTHING ELSE WE CAN USE?

WELL, THERE'S MALIC ACID, AN ACID THAT OCCURS NATURALLY IN APPLES. TRY THIS.

MUCH BETTER! LET'S USE THAT IN OUR BLACK TEAS, AND THE CITRIC ACID IN OUR GREEN TEAS.

DAY 6

I THINK WE'RE READY TO GO HOME.

15. FIRST RUN

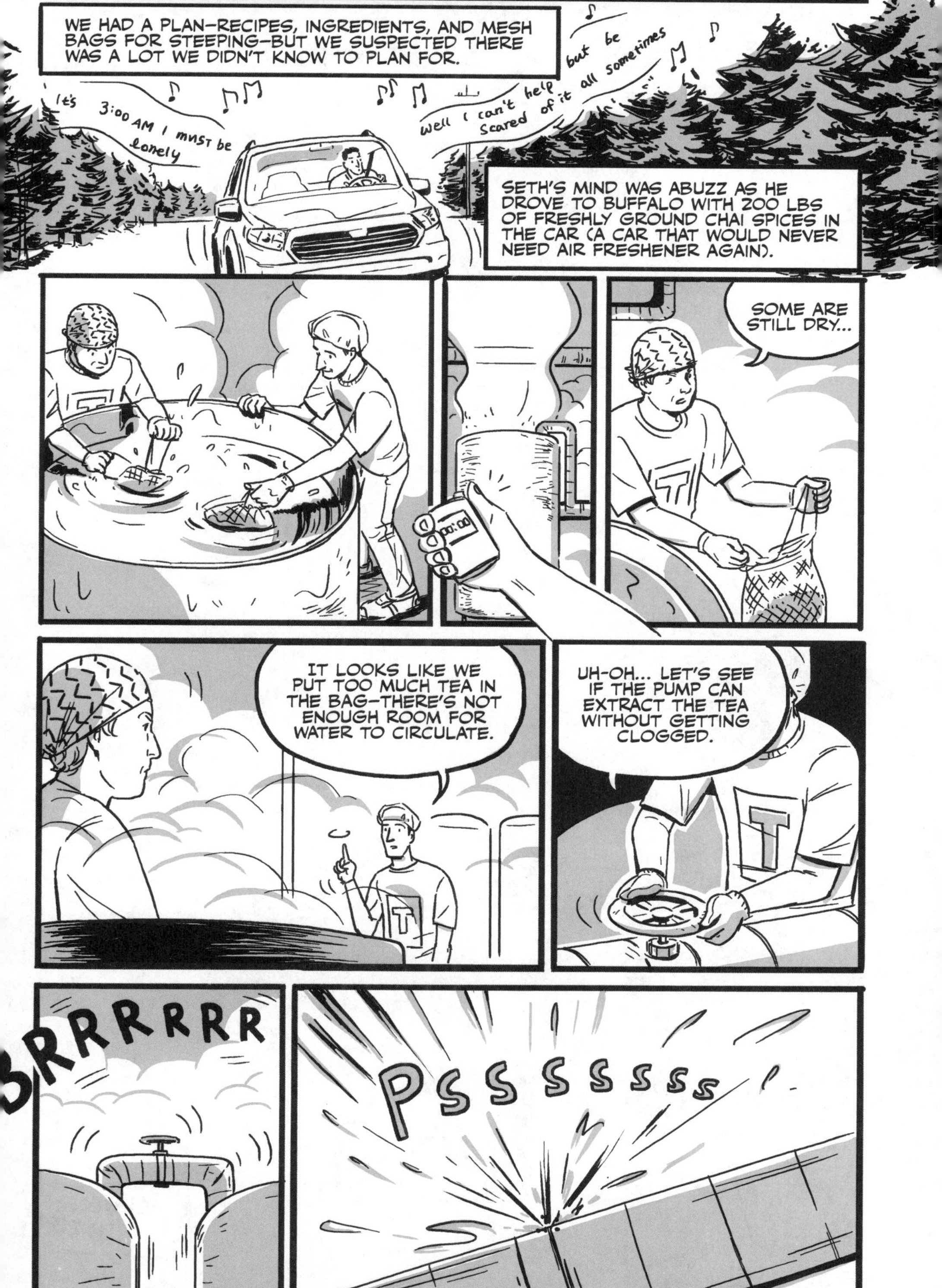

WE HAD A PLAN—RECIPES, INGREDIENTS, AND MESH BAGS FOR STEEPING—BUT WE SUSPECTED THERE WAS A LOT WE DIDN'T KNOW TO PLAN FOR.
It's 3:00 AM I must be lonely
well I can't help but be scared of it all sometimes
SETH'S MIND WAS ABUZZ AS HE DROVE TO BUFFALO WITH 200 LBS OF FRESHLY GROUND CHAI SPICES IN THE CAR (A CAR THAT WOULD NEVER NEED AIR FRESHENER AGAIN).
SOME ARE STILL DRY...
IT LOOKS LIKE WE PUT TOO MUCH TEA IN THE BAG—THERE'S NOT ENOUGH ROOM FOR WATER TO CIRCULATE.
UH-OH... LET'S SEE IF THE PUMP CAN EXTRACT THE TEA WITHOUT GETTING CLOGGED.
BRRRRRRR
PSSSSSSS

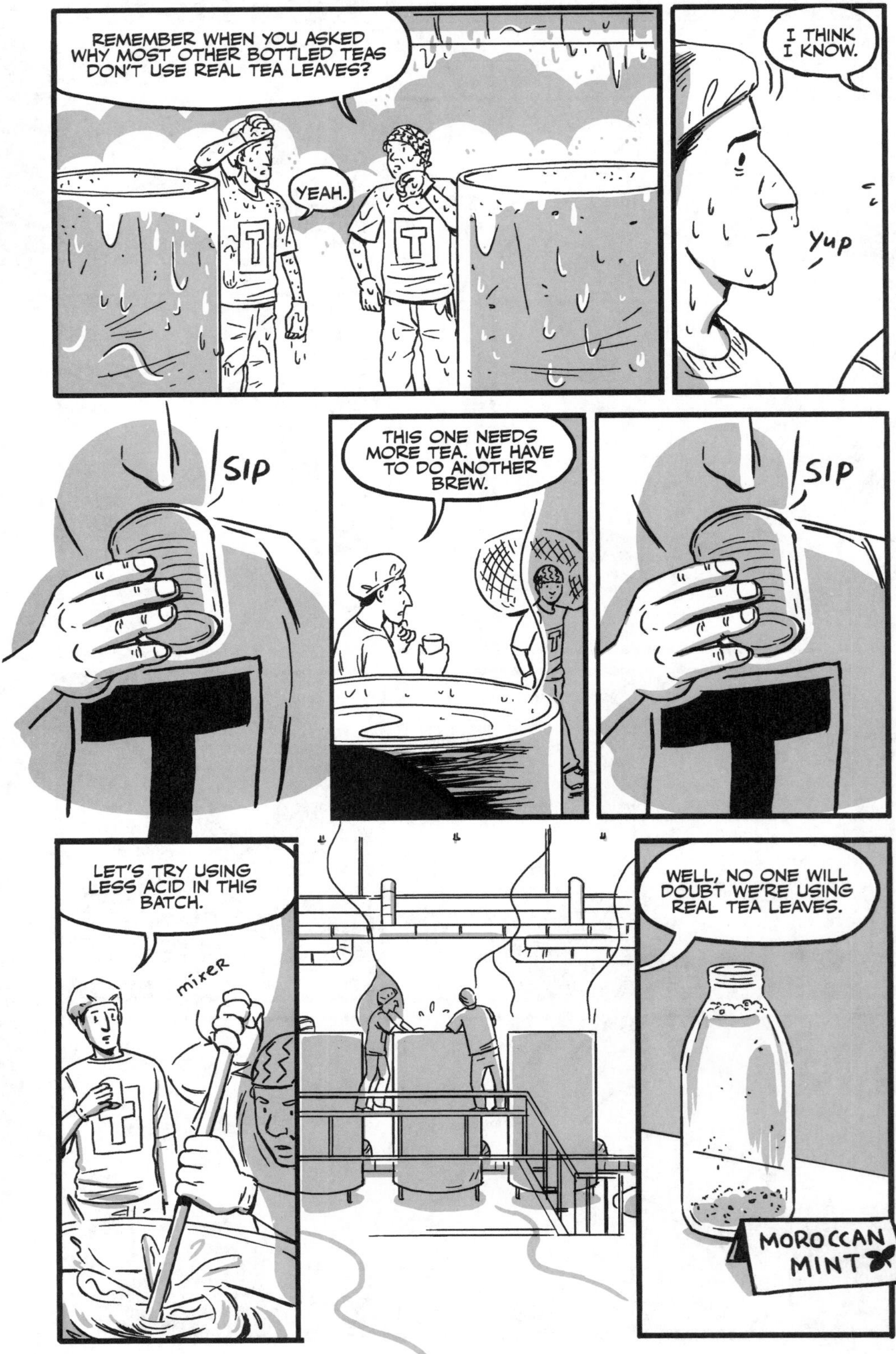
REMEMBER WHEN YOU ASKED WHY MOST OTHER BOTTLED TEAS DON'T USE REAL TEA LEAVES?
YEAH.
I THINK I KNOW.
yup
SIP
THIS ONE NEEDS MORE TEA. WE HAVE TO DO ANOTHER BREW.
SIP
LET'S TRY USING LESS ACID IN THIS BATCH.
mixer
WELL, NO ONE WILL DOUBT WE'RE USING REAL TEA LEAVES.
MOROCCAN MINT

IT NEEDS MORE ACID—THE PH ISN'T LOW ENOUGH.

SIP

BUT LET'S ADD JUST A LITTLE AT A TIME. I DON'T WANT TO THROW OFF THE TASTE.

ACID POWDER

TOO MUCH. NOW IT NEEDS MORE TEA.

I DON'T KNOW HOW EXACTLY, BUT WE RUINED THE TASTE OF THE ASSAM. I DON'T THINK WE SHOULD BOTTLE IT.

moroccan mint

assam

IT'S NOT IDEAL, BUT I'D RATHER DUMP THE ASSAM BATCH THAN BOTTLE SOMETHING THAT DOESN'T TASTE GREAT.

I AGREE.

HOPEFULLY, THE NEXT PRODUCTION RUN WON'T TAKE THREE DAYS.

YEAH, WE WON'T SURVIVE IF IT TAKES US THAT LONG TO PRODUCE 48,000 BOTTLES. AT LEAST NOW WE KNOW WHAT WE NEED TO WORK ON.

I'LL HEAD DOWN TO NEW JERSEY TO SEE HOW THE LABELING IS GOING.

AT THE LABELING PLANT

NORMALLY, WE PUT LABELS ON SHAMPOO BOTTLES, BUT WE'VE BEEN ABLE TO MAKE IT WORK.

WE DON'T HAVE A HEAT TUNNEL TO SHRINK-WRAP THE CASES, SO WE HAD TO IMPROVISE.

WAAA

HAPPY 40th BIRTHDAY

SURPRISE!

I DON'T THINK I'VE EVER BEEN SO COMPLETELY FOOLED.

WE HAVE ONE MORE SURPRISE. THERE'S ANOTHER BIRTHDAY TO CELEBRATE.

SURPRISE!

I CAME STRAIGHT FROM THE LABELING PLANT. THESE ARE THE FIRST BOTTLES WE'VE EVER PRODUCED.

IT'S REAL. AND ALL I HOPED IT WOULD BE.

SETH, THIS IS JEFF MACKLIS, MY COLLEGE ROOMMATE.

THE TEA IS GREAT.

HOW DO I INVEST?

HI, PROFESSOR OSTER.

HI, SETH. THIS IS A CUTE IDEA.

BUT IT'LL NEVER WORK AS A BUSINESS.

LET'S JUST HOPE WE DON'T SELL TOO MANY BOTTLES.

WHAT DO YOU MEAN?

WELL, WE CAN'T MAKE THAT MUCH TEA, AND WHAT WE DO MAKE WE LOSE MONEY ON.

AS LONG AS WE HAVE A PATH TO PROFITABILITY, WE'LL BE FINE.

TEA LEAVES · · · · · · · · · · · · · · · 4¢
SPRING WATER · · · · · · · · · · · · · · 1¢
FRUIT PUREES & BOTANICALS · · · · 3¢
HONEY, SUGAR, AGAVE · · · · · · · · · 4¢
CERTIFICATION
(KOSHER, USDA ORGANIC) · · · · · · · 1¢
TOTAL · · · · · · · · · · · · · · 13¢/BOTTLE

filler

CLINK CLINK CLINK CLINK

Bottle
8.7¢

Capper

Cooling
tunnel

Bottle
Cap
3.4¢

Case
Tray
1.3¢

HONEST TEA

Pallet
0.7¢

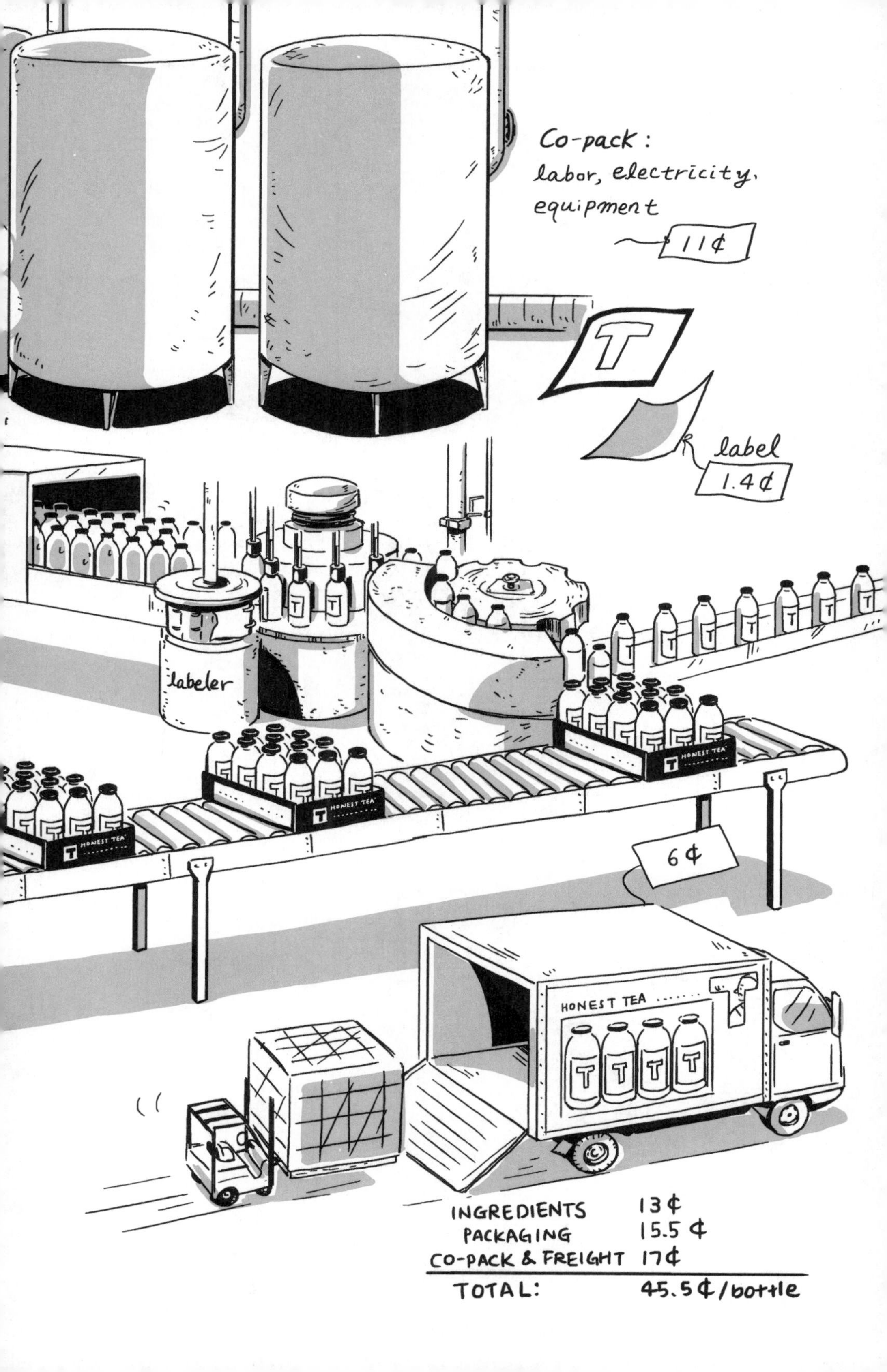

Co-pack:
labor, electricity,
equipment
11¢
label
1.4¢
labeler
HONEST TEA
6¢
HONEST TEA
INGREDIENTS 13¢
PACKAGING 15.5¢
CO-PACK & FREIGHT 17¢
TOTAL: 45.5¢/bottle

HOW MUCH SHOULD WE CHARGE?

TO KEEP THE EVERYDAY PRICE BELOW $1.39, WE CAN'T CHARGE DISTRIBUTORS MORE THAN 70¢.

HONEST TEA

AND WE'LL NEED TO GIVE THEM DISCOUNTS TO SUPPORT PRICE PROMOTIONS.

4 for $5

THAT MEANS OUR NET SALES PRICE PER BOTTLE WILL BE DOWN TO 60¢.

IF WE ONLY CLEAR 14.5¢ A BOTTLE, THEN A MILLION BOTTLES GIVES US $145,000 TO COVER RENT, SALARIES, SAMPLING, LAWYERS, KITCHEN SINK...

WE'LL NEVER MAKE ANY MONEY.

BUT IF WE CHARGE MORE THAN 70¢ A BOTTLE WHOLESALE, WE WON'T GROW BEYOND A NICHE PRODUCT.

HONEST TEA T

AS OUR BUSINESS GROWS, WE CAN BUY MORE IN BULK, AND OUR COSTS WILL COME DOWN TO SOMETHING CLOSER TO 37¢ A BOTTLE.

10% DISCOUNT

20% DISCOUNT

15% DISCOUNT

IF WE PRICE BASED ON OUR CURRENT COSTS, WE'LL NEVER SELL ENOUGH TO BRING OUR COSTS DOWN. THE ONLY SOLUTION IS FIELD-OF-DREAMS PRICING.

PRICE IT LOW, SALES WILL COME, COSTS WILL FALL, AND THE PRICE WILL BE RIGHT AFTER ALL.

WE JUST HAVE TO BE CAREFUL NOT TO GO OUT OF BUSINESS ALONG THE WAY.

TODAY'S QUESTION IS A CLASSIC ECONOMICS PUZZLE. WHY ARE THE BEST FLORIDA ORANGES SOLD IN NEW YORK RATHER THAN FLORIDA? ROGER?

UH... COULD YOU REPEAT THE QUESTION?

MR. SCHOLL, YOU'VE GOT TO STAY ALERT. THIS CLASS IS GOING TO BE IN MY NEXT BOOK.

PEOPLE IN NEW YORK ARE RICHER THAN PEOPLE IN FLORIDA. THEY GET THE BEST ORANGES SINCE THEY'RE WILLING TO PAY MORE.

FLORIDIANS ARE JUST AS WEALTHY AS NEW YORKERS. IN FACT, A LOT OF THEM ARE FROM NEW YORK.

SHOPPERS IN NEW YORK ARE MORE DISCERNING!

PEOPLE IN FLORIDA DON'T THINK ORANGES ARE ANYTHING SPECIAL. NEW YORKERS ARE WILLING TO PAY MORE FOR A GOOD ORANGE.

OK, THOSE ARE ALL FINE MARKETING EXPLANATIONS, BUT I'M LOOKING FOR AN ECONOMICS EXPLANATION. WHY DOES FLORIDA EXPORT ITS BEST ORANGES?

MY FAMILY IS IN THE EXPORT BUSINESS. WE ONLY EXPORT THE HIGHEST QUALITY PRODUCTS—THAT'S WHAT "EXPORT QUALITY" MEANS.

ALL TRUE, BUT WHY IS EXPORT QUALITY THE HIGHEST QUALITY? WHY NOT EXPORT GOOD QUALITY?

GOOD   EXCELLENT

BECAUSE FOREIGN BUYERS ARE MORE DEMANDING.

YOU'RE BACK TO MARKETING. LET'S STICK TO ECONOMICS.

THE EXPLANATION CAN BE FOUND IN WHAT'S CALLED "THE BABYSITTER THEOREM."

HERE WE HAVE TWO COUPLES, THE SAME AGES, EARNING THE SAME AMOUNT.

WHERE TO?

LET'S GO TO THE MOVIES.

THE COUPLE WITH A KID HAS LESS MONEY TO SPEND AND YET GOES OUT TO A BROADWAY SHOW. WHY?

WHAT TIME DOES THE PLAY START?

7:30.

WHEN I USED TO BABYSIT, I CHARGED $40 FOR AN EVENING. THERE'S NO WAY SOMEONE WOULD PAY ME THAT MUCH AND JUST GO TO A MOVIE.

WHEN YOU FACTOR IN THE COST OF THE BABYSITTER, GOING TO SEE A MOVIE COSTS $60 AND JUST ISN'T WORTH IT.

IF YOU'RE GOING TO SPEND $40 TO WALK OUT THE DOOR, YOU MIGHT AS WELL MAKE A NIGHT OF IT.

I GET IT. IT'S THE SAME WITH ORANGES. A GOOD ORANGE IN FLORIDA MIGHT COST A NICKEL, WHILE A GREAT ONE COSTS A DIME. THE COST OF SENDING THE ORANGE UP TO NEW YORK IS LIKE HIRING THE BABYSITTER. IT COSTS, SAY, A DOLLAR.

THERE'S NO POINT SPENDING $1 TO SHIP A 5¢ ORANGE WHEN, FOR AN EXTRA 5¢, YOU CAN SHIP A GREAT ORANGE. THE PRICE DIFFERENCE IN NY WOULD BE TRIVIAL.

NOW WE'RE TALKING ECONOMICS! WHEN THE TRANSPORT COST IS LARGE RELATIVE TO THE PRODUCT COST, IT ONLY MAKES SENSE TO SHIP THE HIGHEST-QUALITY ITEMS.

NEW YORK

CAN ANYONE TELL ME HOW THIS APPLIES TO HONEST TEA?

FOR YOU, THE BOTTLE IS LIKE THE BABYSITTER. THERE'S NO POINT PUTTING CHEAP TEA IN AN EXPENSIVE BOTTLE.

EXACTLY.

TO BUY THIS GLASS BOTTLE, FILL IT WITH AIR,

RUN IT THROUGH THE FILLING LINE, CAP IT, LABEL IT,

PACK IT IN A CASE, AND SHIP IT TO A DISTRIBUTOR AND THEN TO A STORE WOULD COST 32.5¢.

THE COST OF THE TEA IS THE SMALLEST PART OF THE PACKAGE. OTHERS SPEND LESS THAN A PENNY A BOTTLE ON TEA. WE SPEND 4¢ ON BETTER TEA AND ANOTHER 8¢ ON FRUIT PUREES AND ORGANIC SWEETENERS.

NO SURPRISE, BUT CONSUMERS CAN REALLY TELL THE DIFFERENCE. PREMIUM WHOLE-LEAF TEA TASTES A LOT BETTER THAN DUST AND FANNINGS.

WHILE WE SPEND FOUR TIMES AS MUCH ON TEA, IT'S STILL A TINY FRACTION OF THE OVERALL COST.

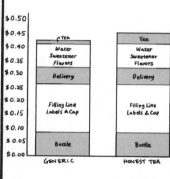

SO THEN WHY DON'T OTHER COMPANIES USE HIGHER-QUALITY INGREDIENTS?

THEY SAY THEY DO. YOU KNOW, "MADE FROM THE BEST STUFF ON EARTH."

WELL, WE DON'T USE ANY "STUFF." OUR ORGANIC SWEETENERS COST THREE TIMES AS MUCH AS HIGH-FRUCTOSE CORN SYRUP, BUT SINCE WE ONLY USE A THIRD AS MUCH, IT BALANCES OUT. WHY OTHERS DON'T SPEND MORE ON BETTER TEA, THAT'S STILL A PUZZLE.

WE MADE THE DELIVERY TO WHOLE FOODS AND LANDED ORDERS FROM SOME OF THE MOST PRESTIGIOUS RETAILERS IN NEW YORK.

BUT HOW WOULD WE GET OUR TEAS TO ALL THOSE STORES?

THE CHALLENGE IS WHEN THEY REORDER. I CAN'T BE DRIVING UP TO NYC EVERY WEEK.

BUT THESE SHOWCASE ACCOUNTS IN NEW YORK HELP OPEN DOORS.

TRUE. THAT'S WHY WE'VE GOT OUR TWO MBA INTERNS OUT MAKING DELIVERIES.

JULIE MAKES STOPS ON THE WAY TO HER JOB AT THE HOMELESS SHELTER.

YOU'RE COVERING NEW HAVEN.

AND WE'VE EVEN GOT MY DAD MAKING DELIVERIES IN CAMBRIDGE.

THIS ISN'T SUSTAINABLE OR SCALABLE. OUR PROBLEM ISN'T LANDING NEW ACCOUNTS; IT'S DISTRIBUTING TO THE STORES WE'VE ALREADY SIGNED.

WHAT ABOUT USING SOBE, SNAPPLE, OR NANTUCKET NECTARS DISTRIBUTORS?

I GOT A MEETING WITH ONE OF THE MOST POWERFUL BEVERAGE DISTRIBUTORS ON THE EAST COAST. LET'S SEE WHAT HAPPENS.

HONICKMAN GROUP
Canada Dry Potomac Corp.
Canada Dry Delaware Valley
Canada Dry Bottling of Philadelphia
Canada Dry New York

HAROLD HONICKMAN

YOU CAN SEE HOW HONEST TEA IS DIFFERENT FROM ALL THE OTHER TEAS ON THE MARKET.

T

WHAT THEY CALL TEA

NOT SWEET ENOUGH, AND IT TASTES GRASSY. BESIDES, IT'S TOO EXPENSIVE. CONSUMERS WON'T PAY THAT MUCH.

BUT IT'S BEEN SELLING WELL IN THE ACCOUNTS WE'RE IN.

YEAH, BUT NOT AS WELL AS THAT BOTTLE ON THE RIGHT.

IN ANY CASE, OUR CONTRACT WITH SNAPPLE PROHIBITS US FROM CARRYING OTHER TEAS.

HOW'D IT GO?

I GUESS IT COULD HAVE GONE BETTER.

HE SAID NO?

HE DIDN'T SAY YES... YET. IN THE MEANTIME, A COLLEGE FRIEND IS GOING TO HELP ME DO A SALES RUN IN BOSTON.

U-HAUL

71

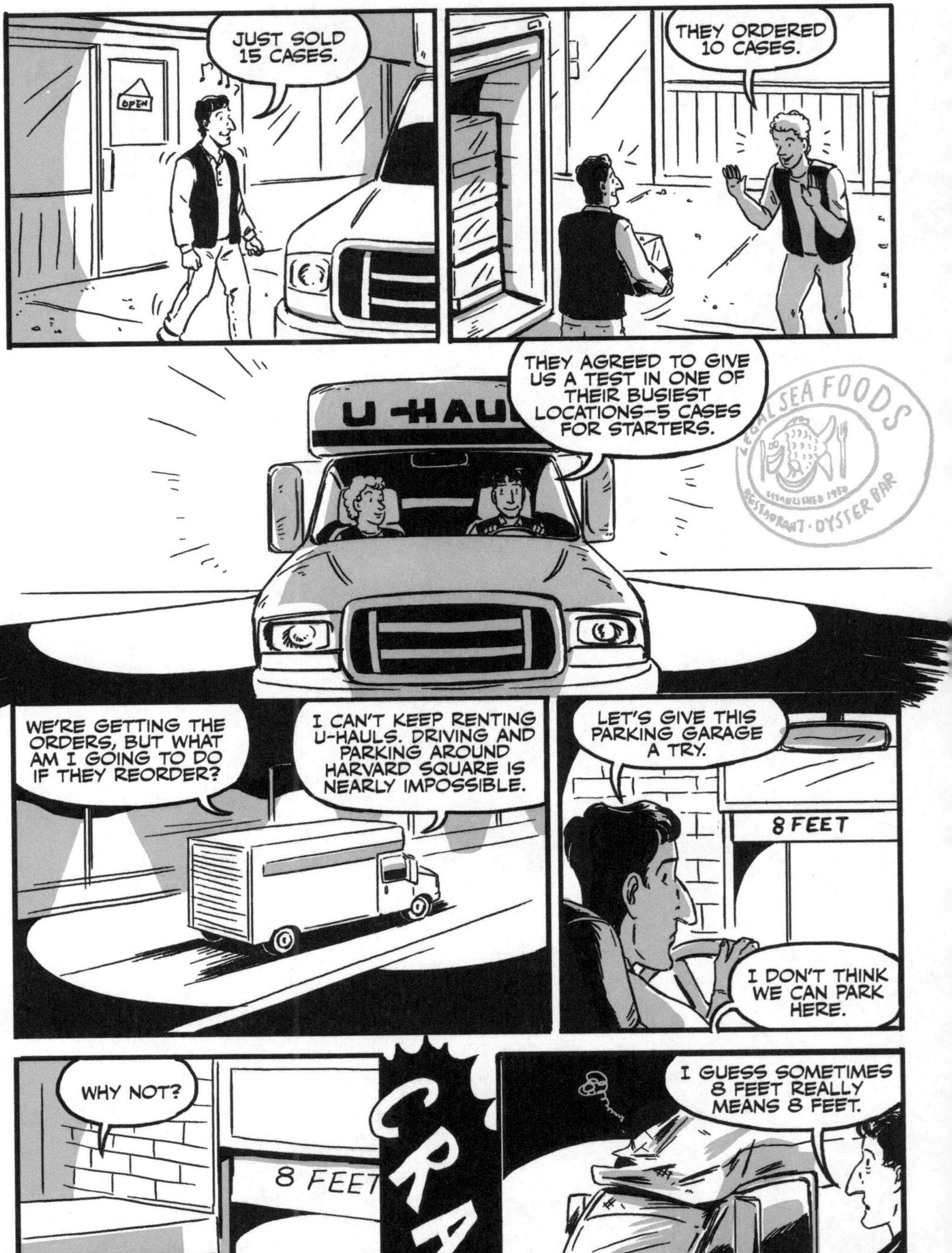
JUST SOLD 15 CASES.
OPEN
THEY ORDERED 10 CASES.
U-HAU
THEY AGREED TO GIVE US A TEST IN ONE OF THEIR BUSIEST LOCATIONS—5 CASES FOR STARTERS.
LEGAL SEA FOODS
ESTABLISHED 1950
RESTAURANT · OYSTER BAR
WE'RE GETTING THE ORDERS, BUT WHAT AM I GOING TO DO IF THEY REORDER?
I CAN'T KEEP RENTING U-HAULS. DRIVING AND PARKING AROUND HARVARD SQUARE IS NEARLY IMPOSSIBLE.
LET'S GIVE THIS PARKING GARAGE A TRY.
8 FEET
I DON'T THINK WE CAN PARK HERE.
WHY NOT?
8 FEET
THIS IS A 10-FOOT TRUCK.
CRACK
I GUESS SOMETIMES 8 FEET REALLY MEANS 8 FEET.

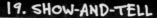

N.A.S.F.T.
Welcomes You to the
Fancy Food Show

800

THE JAVITS CENTER,
NYC, JUNE 1998

SO MANY COMPANIES TRYING TO DO THE SAME THING! HOW MANY SALSAS DOES THE WORLD NEED?

400

MUNCH MUNCH

IT SHOWS JUST HOW COMPETITIVE THIS INDUSTRY IS.

THERE MUST BE A HUNDRED BOOTHS SELLING BISCOTTI.

I KNOW. I'VE TRIED HALF OF THEM. I DON'T THINK I COULD EAT ONE EVER AGAIN.

OH, LOOK, RUSKS! GOTTA TRY THAT.

THERE'S GOURMECO. THEY DISTRIBUTE HIGH-END CHEESES AND OLIVE OILS.

Gourmeco
imports

HI THERE. I'M BARRY.

AND I'M SETH, TEA-EO OF HONEST TEA.

GO

OH, THAT'S... CREATIVE. I'M JUST MELANIE.

WOULD YOU LIKE TO TRY SOME OF OUR TEAS? THEY'LL PAIR WELL WITH YOUR MERRY-GOAT-ROUND CHEESES.

WHY DON'T I COME BY YOUR BOOTH LATER? WE'RE REALLY HERE TO SELL PRODUCTS, NOT BUY THEM.

ACTUALLY... WE DON'T HAVE A BOOTH. WE JUST STARTED UP AND THIS IS OUR FIRST SHOW.

HONEST T

WOW, THIS ISN'T AT ALL WHAT I EXPECTED. IT'S NOT TOO SWEET AND TASTES JUST LIKE HOMEMADE.

WE'LL TAKE THAT AS A COMPLIMENT.

WE THINK IT'S EVEN BETTER THAN HOMEMADE. WE BREW FRESH TEA LEAVES IN SPRING WATER FOR JUST THE RIGHT AMOUNT OF TIME AT JUST THE RIGHT TEMPERATURE.

SEVERAL RETAILERS HERE SUGGESTED THAT YOU WOULD BE A GREAT DISTRIBUTOR FOR US.

I LIKE YOUR PRODUCT, BUT OUR PRESIDENT MAKES THOSE DECISIONS. CAN YOU GET SAMPLES TO OUR OFFICE IN VIRGINIA?

NO PROBLEM. WE'RE JUST IN BETHESDA.

A FEW WEEKS LATER

GOOD NEWS! WE WANT TO CARRY HONEST TEA. AND I'VE GOT A MEETING NEXT WEEK WITH THE BUYER AT GIANT FOOD. CAN YOU JOIN ME?

OF COURSE!

HI, I'M MELANIE FROM GOURMECO. WE HAVE A 3:00 APPOINTMENT TO SEE THE SPECIALTY BUYER.

2:45 PM

I'M EXCITED FOR OUR FIRST SALES CALL TOGETHER. IT'S GREAT THAT THE BUYER GETS TO MEET THE CEO.

TEA-EO.

GOTCHA, TEA-EO.

IT'S NOT UNUSUAL FOR MEETINGS TO START LATE. DON'T WORRY.

3:15 PM

I'LL ASK THE RECEPTIONIST FOR AN UPDATE. THE BUYER REALLY IS A GREAT GUY.

3:45 PM

SOMETHING'S COME UP. I'M SORRY I CAN'T MEET WITH YOU. LEAVE ME SOME SAMPLES AND LITERATURE.

4:35 PM

I'M SO SORRY TO HAVE WASTED YOUR TIME.

NOT AT ALL. WE GOT TO KNOW EACH OTHER BETTER. WE MET THE BUYER, ALBEIT BRIEFLY. AND HE DIDN'T SAY NO.

NEXT DAY

THE BUYER AGREED TO PUT HONEST TEA ON THE SHELF! I THINK HE FELT BAD ABOUT STANDING US UP.

20. EXCLUSIVE CONTRACTS

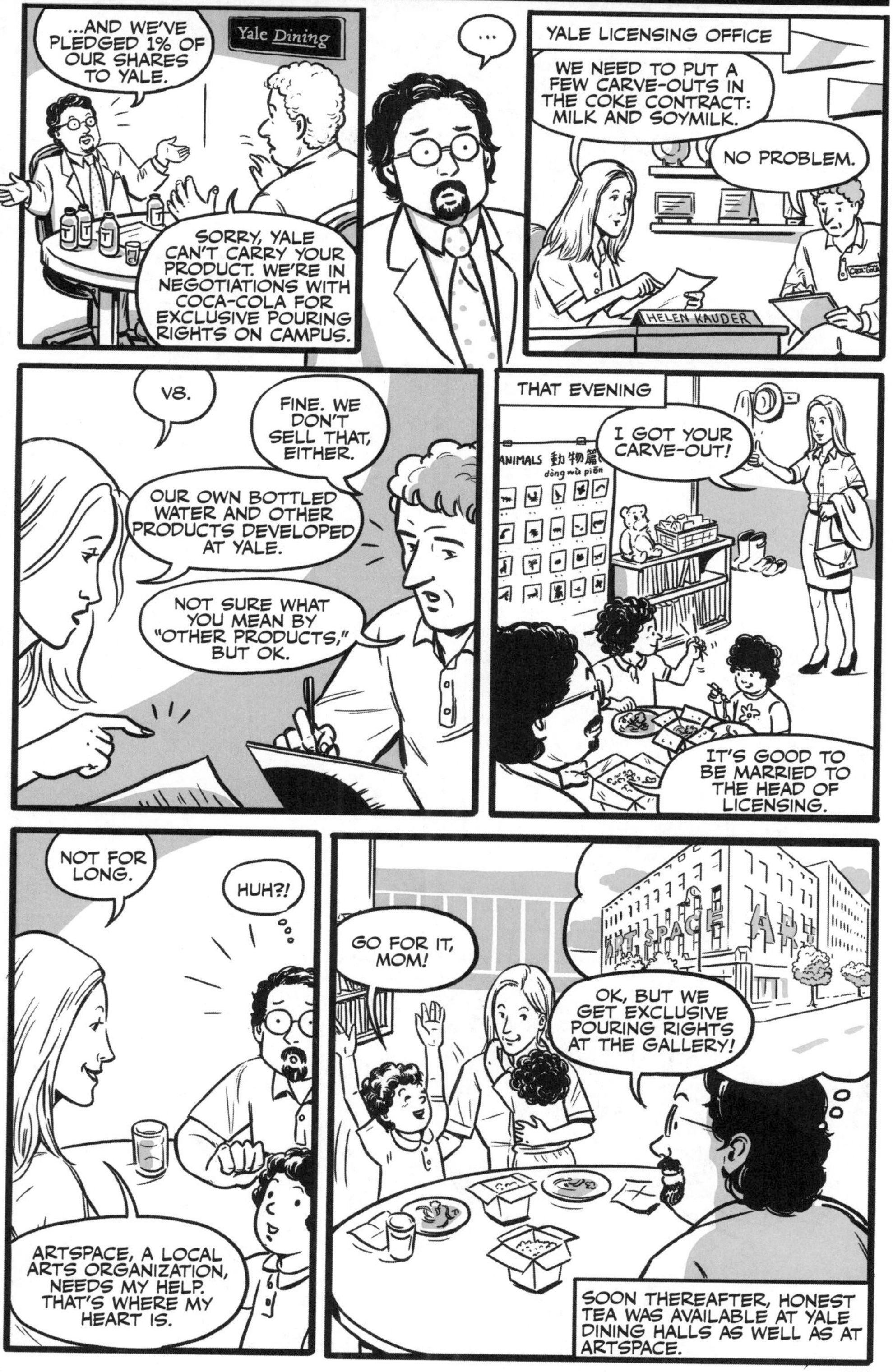
...AND WE'VE PLEDGED 1% OF OUR SHARES TO YALE.
Yale Dining
SORRY, YALE CAN'T CARRY YOUR PRODUCT. WE'RE IN NEGOTIATIONS WITH COCA-COLA FOR EXCLUSIVE POURING RIGHTS ON CAMPUS.
...
YALE LICENSING OFFICE
WE NEED TO PUT A FEW CARVE-OUTS IN THE COKE CONTRACT: MILK AND SOYMILK.
NO PROBLEM.
HELEN KAUDER
V8.
FINE. WE DON'T SELL THAT, EITHER.
OUR OWN BOTTLED WATER AND OTHER PRODUCTS DEVELOPED AT YALE.
NOT SURE WHAT YOU MEAN BY "OTHER PRODUCTS," BUT OK.
THAT EVENING
I GOT YOUR CARVE-OUT!
IT'S GOOD TO BE MARRIED TO THE HEAD OF LICENSING.
NOT FOR LONG.
HUH?!
ARTSPACE, A LOCAL ARTS ORGANIZATION, NEEDS MY HELP. THAT'S WHERE MY HEART IS.
GO FOR IT, MOM!
OK, BUT WE GET EXCLUSIVE POURING RIGHTS AT THE GALLERY!
SOON THEREAFTER, HONEST TEA WAS AVAILABLE AT YALE DINING HALLS AS WELL AS AT ARTSPACE.

21. EARLY MARKETING EFFORTS

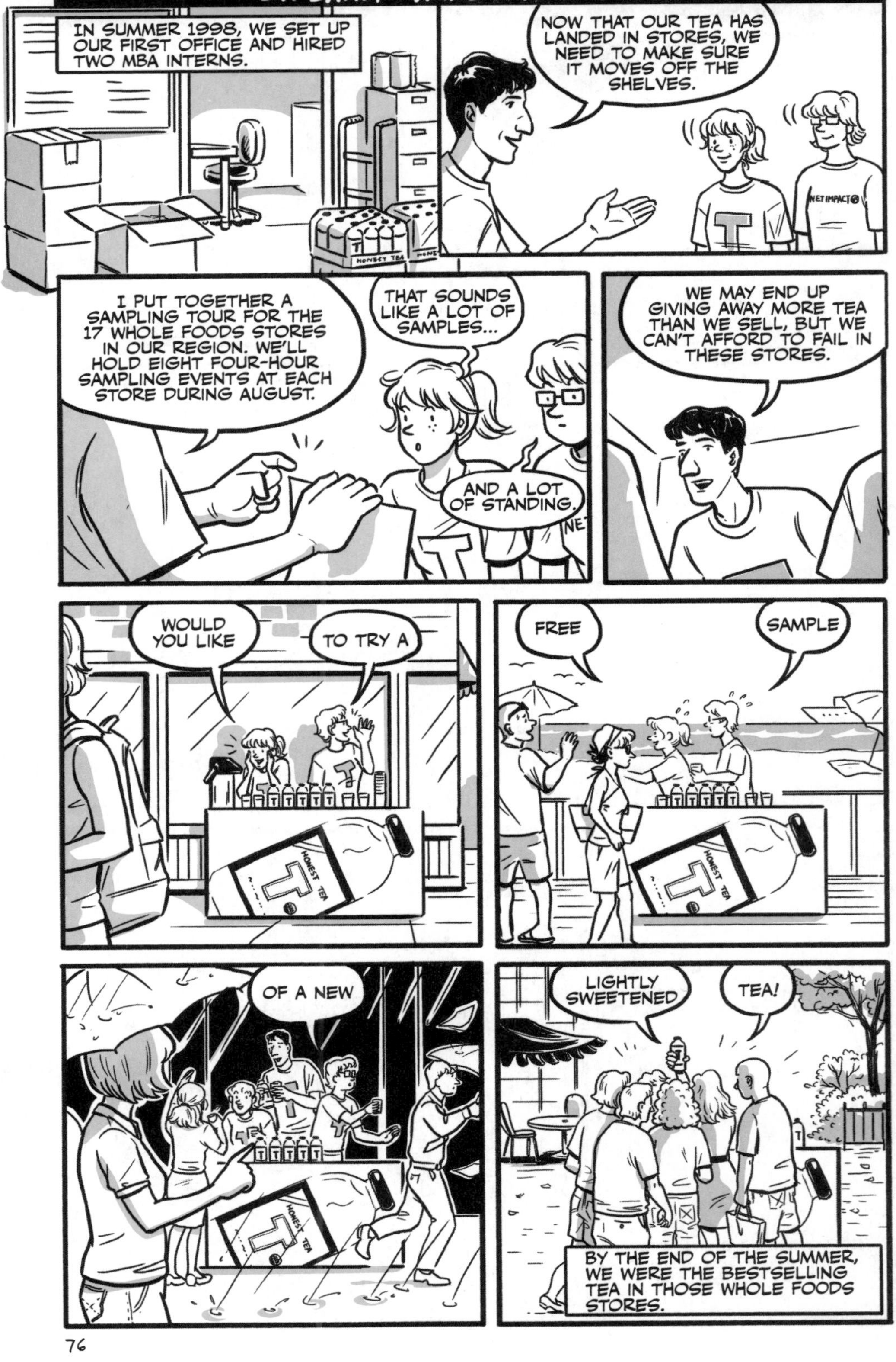
IN SUMMER 1998, WE SET UP OUR FIRST OFFICE AND HIRED TWO MBA INTERNS.
HONEST TEA
NOW THAT OUR TEA HAS LANDED IN STORES, WE NEED TO MAKE SURE IT MOVES OFF THE SHELVES.
NET IMPACT
I PUT TOGETHER A SAMPLING TOUR FOR THE 17 WHOLE FOODS STORES IN OUR REGION. WE'LL HOLD EIGHT FOUR-HOUR SAMPLING EVENTS AT EACH STORE DURING AUGUST.
THAT SOUNDS LIKE A LOT OF SAMPLES...
AND A LOT OF STANDING.
WE MAY END UP GIVING AWAY MORE TEA THAN WE SELL, BUT WE CAN'T AFFORD TO FAIL IN THESE STORES.
WOULD YOU LIKE
TO TRY A
HONEST TEA
FREE
SAMPLE
HONEST TEA
OF A NEW
HONEST TEA
LIGHTLY SWEETENED
TEA!
BY THE END OF THE SUMMER, WE WERE THE BESTSELLING TEA IN THOSE WHOLE FOODS STORES.

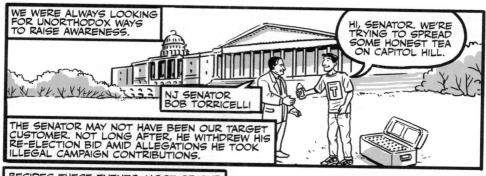

WE WERE ALWAYS LOOKING FOR UNORTHODOX WAYS TO RAISE AWARENESS.

NJ SENATOR BOB TORRICELLI

HI, SENATOR. WE'RE TRYING TO SPREAD SOME HONEST TEA ON CAPITOL HILL.

THE SENATOR MAY NOT HAVE BEEN OUR TARGET CUSTOMER. NOT LONG AFTER, HE WITHDREW HIS RE-ELECTION BID AMID ALLEGATIONS HE TOOK ILLEGAL CAMPAIGN CONTRIBUTIONS.

BESIDES THESE EVENTS, MOST OF OUR MARKETING WAS WORD-OF-MOUTH. OUR INVESTORS HELPED SPREAD THE WORD, OFTEN CREATING NEW FORUMS FOR BEVERAGE REVIEWS.

SEPTEMBER 1999

Andrew Tobias
Money and Other Subjects

Have I mentioned Honest Tea? I loved the name and the packaging when a Yale School of Management professor first showed it to me—a little side business for him and a young marketing whiz—though, truthfully, I hated the tea. But this was because he had me sample it out of his briefcase in a hallway at room temperature (and on New Year's Eve, no less). It turns out that Honest Tea is better served cold over ice or hot in a cup, surprise, surprise, and that I have become a small investor… A couple of months ago I got the Pioneer Market to order a case of each variety for me. So last night I'm back in the store and the display of Honest Tea is wider than before and filled with bottles. Do you hear what I'm saying? Someone besides me has been buying the product! They like it! I may not die broke after all!

HAPPY NEW YEAR 1999

TRY THIS ONE!

LIKEWISE, OUR SMALL BUT GROWING CUSTOMER BASE ACTED AS A DE FACTO SALES AND MARKETING TEAM.

YOU'RE OUT OF MOROCCAN MINT. IF YOU WON'T CARRY IT, I'LL TAKE MY BUSINESS ELSEWHERE.

CUSTOMER SERVICE

NOT SETH OR BARRY'S MOM

EVEN BETTER, SOME OF OUR FANS WERE BUYERS, WHO COULD PUT PRESSURE ON THEIR STORE MANAGERS.

LETTER FROM A CORPORATE BUYER TO THE MANAGERS AT HER 60 NATURAL FOODS STORES.

WILD OATS

MARK MY WORDS: HONEST TEA WILL BE A SUCCESS. THE ONLY BOTTLED TEA THAT IS NOT LOADED WITH SUGARS AND TASTES GREAT. THIS IS WHAT PEOPLE (LIKE ME) HAVE BEEN SEEKING FOR YEARS. …I MEAN IT NOW—BRING THESE IN!

77

22. MISSION DRIVEN

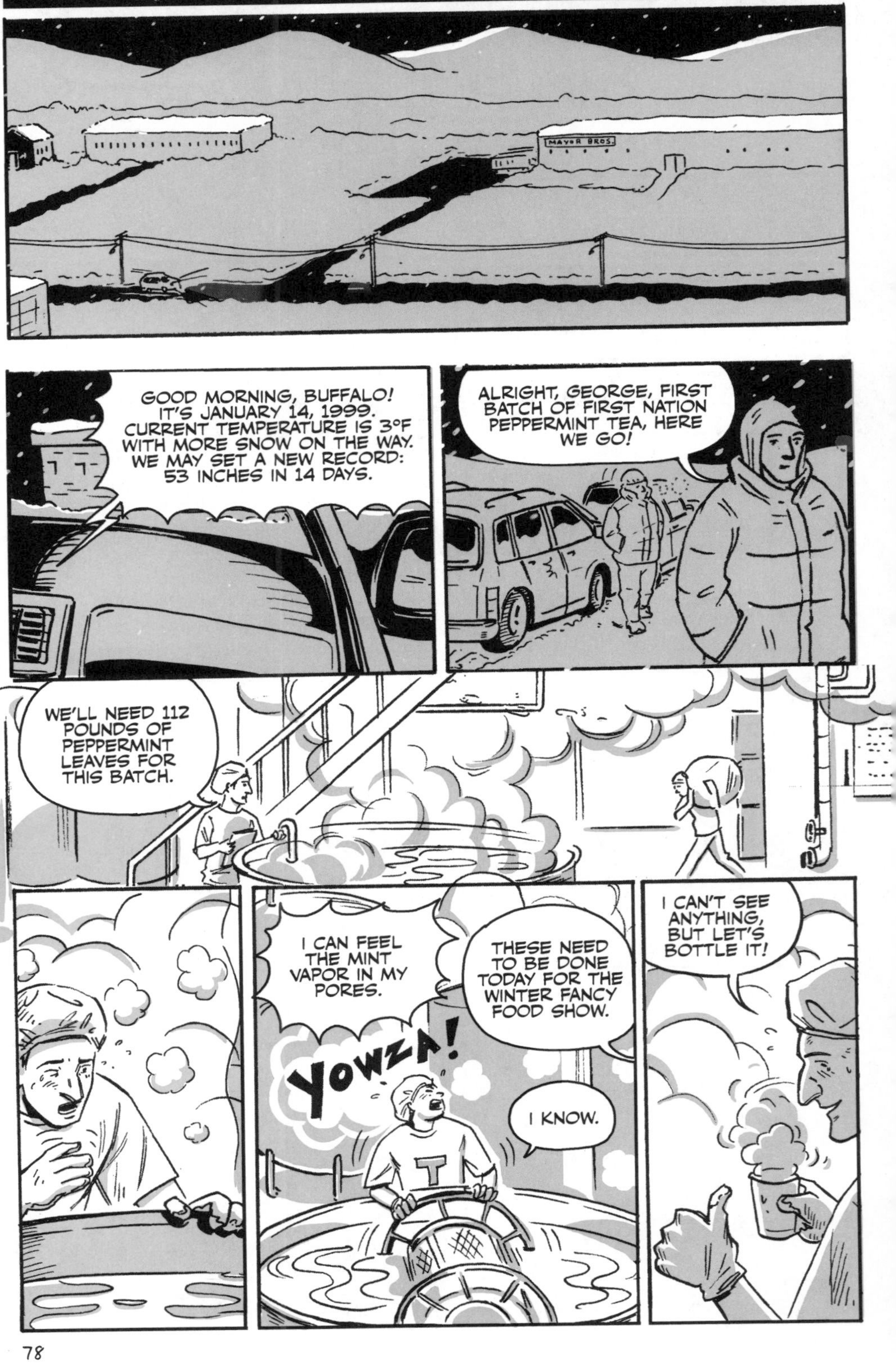
MAYOR BROS.
GOOD MORNING, BUFFALO! IT'S JANUARY 14, 1999. CURRENT TEMPERATURE IS 3°F WITH MORE SNOW ON THE WAY. WE MAY SET A NEW RECORD: 53 INCHES IN 14 DAYS.
ALRIGHT, GEORGE, FIRST BATCH OF FIRST NATION PEPPERMINT TEA, HERE WE GO!
WE'LL NEED 112 POUNDS OF PEPPERMINT LEAVES FOR THIS BATCH.
I CAN FEEL THE MINT VAPOR IN MY PORES.
THESE NEED TO BE DONE TODAY FOR THE WINTER FANCY FOOD SHOW.
YOWZA!
I KNOW.
T
I CAN'T SEE ANYTHING, BUT LET'S BOTTLE IT!

SNAP

UH-OH!

I NEED TO GET HOME AND THEN CATCH A FLIGHT TO MONTANA TO MEET OUR CROW PARTNERS.

GOOD LUCK DRIVING IN THE BLIZZARD.

I'LL JUST HAVE TO BOTTLE THE TEAS MYSELF.

SOUTH OF PITTSBURGH

THIS IS GOING TO TAKE FOREVER.

I CAN MAKE UP SOME TIME IN THE TUNNEL.

I STILL HAVEN'T FOUND

WHAT I'M LOOKING FOR ~

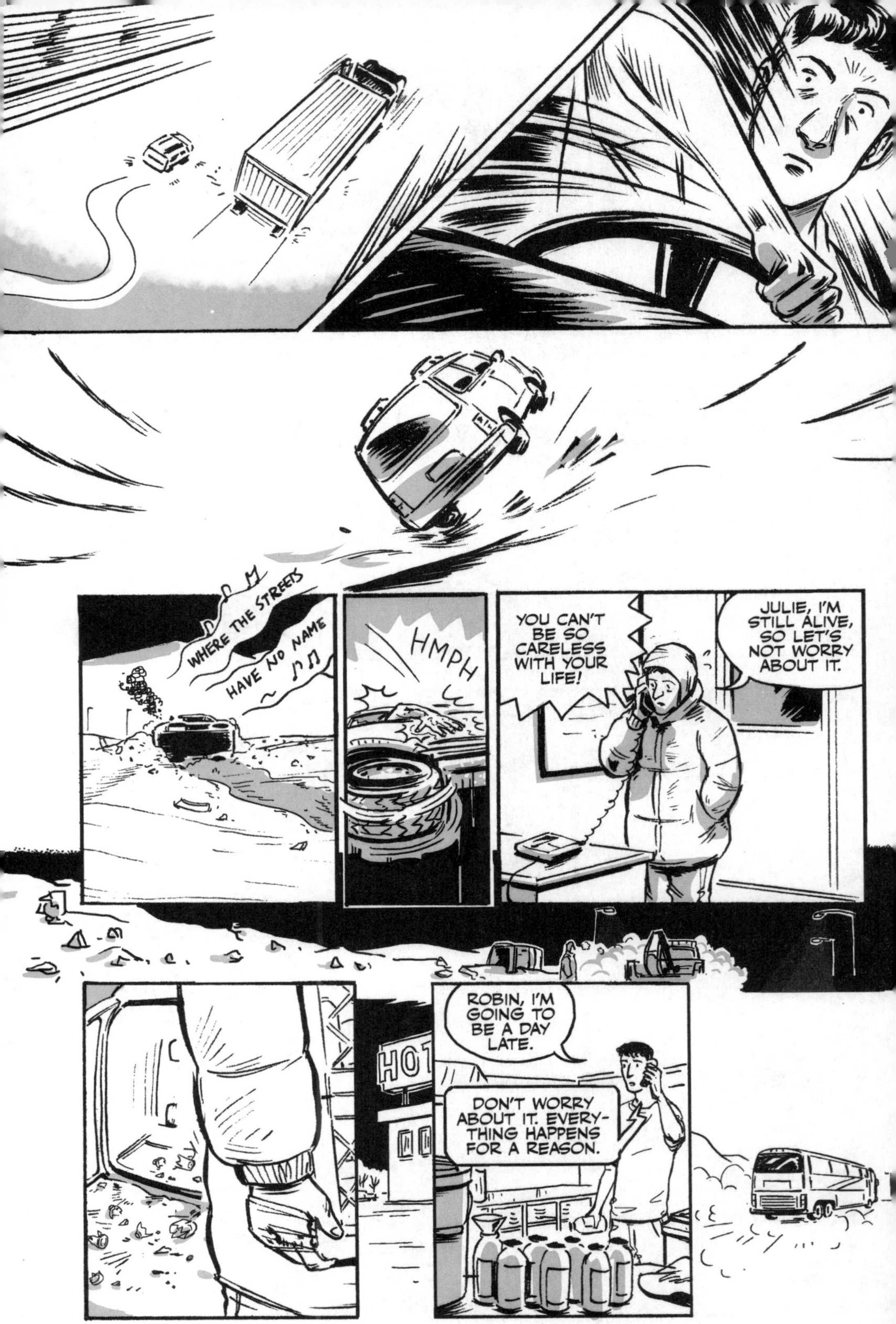
♪ WHERE THE STREETS HAVE NO NAME ♪♪
HMPH
YOU CAN'T BE SO CARELESS WITH YOUR LIFE!
JULIE, I'M STILL ALIVE, SO LET'S NOT WORRY ABOUT IT.
HOT
ROBIN, I'M GOING TO BE A DAY LATE.
DON'T WORRY ABOUT IT. EVERYTHING HAPPENS FOR A REASON.

BACK IN BETHESDA, AFTER A LONG BUS RIDE

ALRIGHTY, THIS TEA IS FINALLY READY TO SHIP TO THE FANCY FOOD SHOW.

2:00 AM

MONTANA

HI! I'M SETH.

THERESA SENDS PART HOME

HI!

ROBIN VALLIE

WHEN YOU FIRST CALLED TO BUY PEPPERMINT FROM US, I WAS SUSPICIOUS.

NATIVE AMERICAN HISTORY IS FILLED WITH PEOPLE WHO WANT TO MAKE MONEY OFF OUR CULTURE.

THAT'S WHY I WANTED TO COME HERE AND MEET YOU IN PERSON.

WE'RE HONORED TO PARTNER WITH THE CROW NATION ON A TEA THAT'S NATIVE TO THE U.S.

THIS PEPPERMINT TEA IS QUITE AUTHENTIC.

THE IN-CARE NETWORK HOME OF THE PRETTY SHIELD FOUNDATION

OUR ROYALTIES FROM THE TEA'S SALES WILL HELP US CARE FOR NATIVE AMERICAN FOSTER CHILDREN.

CROW BUSINESS-PEOPLE ARE WAITING TO TALK TO US ABOUT CULTIVATING PEPPERMINT ON THE RESERVATION.

SHALL WE GO?

81

ACCORDING TO OUR LEGEND, THERE WAS A TIME WHEN PEOPLE MISTREATED THE EARTH AND THE ANIMALS.

THEY TOOK MORE THAN THEY NEEDED FOR SURVIVAL AND TREATED THE EARTH BADLY.

THE ANIMALS DECIDED TO PUNISH HUMANS. THEY PUT A CURSE ON THEM.

THE CURSE WORKED. SO MANY HUMANS DIED THAT THEY NEARED THE BRINK OF EXTINCTION.

THE HUMANS REALIZED THEIR ERRORS AND PRAYED TO THE CREATOR. AS THEY PRAYED, THE PLANT SPIRITS HEARD THEIR CRIES.

THE PLANTS AGREED TO HELP THE HUMANS SO THE EARTH WOULDN'T FALL INTO IMBALANCE.

THEY DECIDED EACH WOULD ACT AS A CURE FOR A SPECIFIC AILMENT.

EACH PLANT ALSO GAVE HUMANS A SONG UNIQUE TO THAT PLANT.

WITHOUT THE SONG, THE PLANT POWER WOULDN'T WORK, SO HUMANS LEARNED TO BE RESPECTFUL OF THE PLANTS.

THIS IS WHY WE CROWS SING WHEN PICKING HERBS AND NEVER TAKE THE WHOLE PLANT.

WE REPLANT SEEDS TO ENSURE PLENTIFUL PLANTS IN THE FUTURE.

OUR PURPOSE IS TO PROTECT ALL LIVING THINGS, SO ALL CAN LIVE IN BALANCE.

I WANT HONEST TEA TO EMBODY THIS MIND-SET.

82

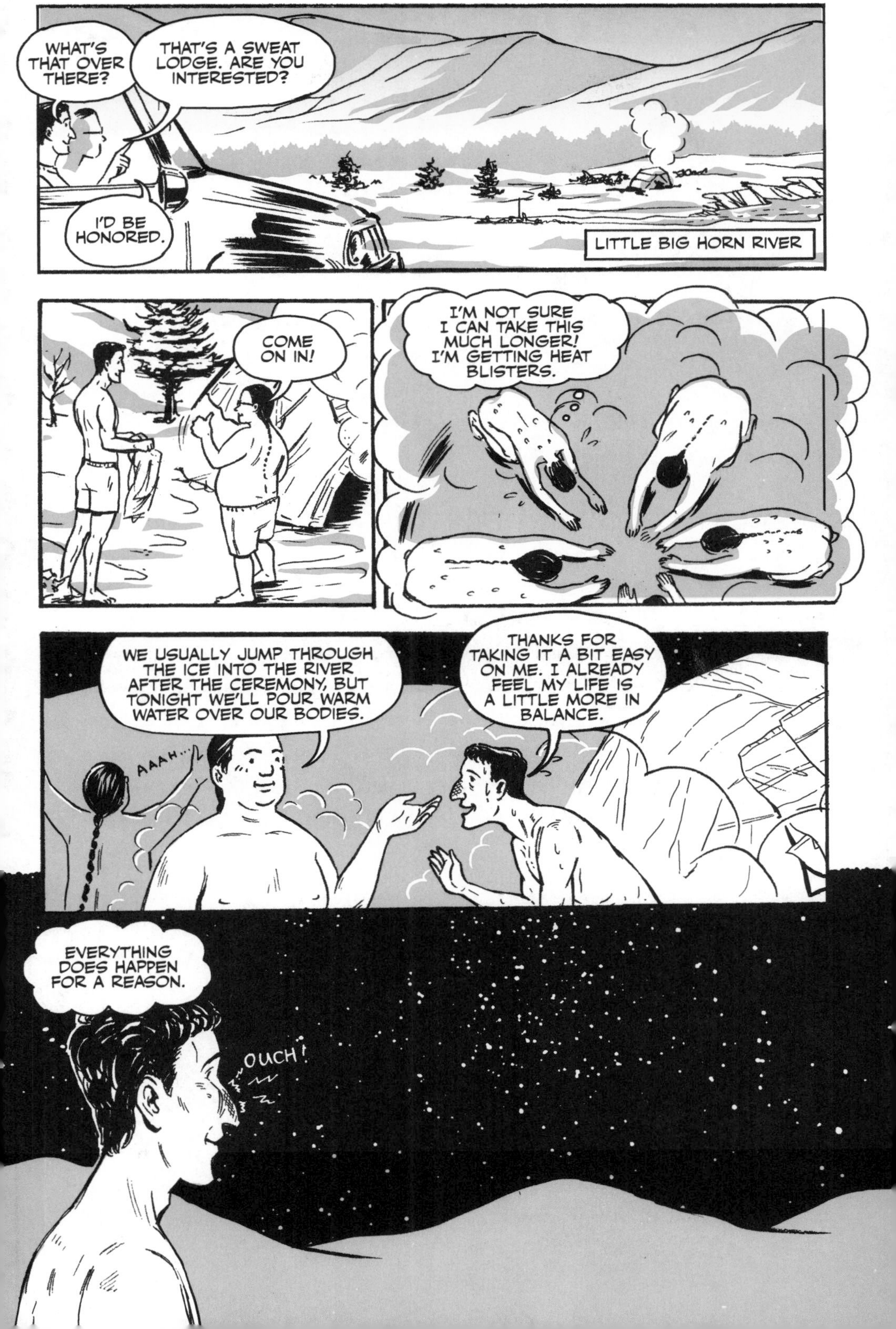
WHAT'S THAT OVER THERE?
THAT'S A SWEAT LODGE. ARE YOU INTERESTED?
I'D BE HONORED.
LITTLE BIG HORN RIVER
COME ON IN!
I'M NOT SURE I CAN TAKE THIS MUCH LONGER! I'M GETTING HEAT BLISTERS.
WE USUALLY JUMP THROUGH THE ICE INTO THE RIVER AFTER THE CEREMONY, BUT TONIGHT WE'LL POUR WARM WATER OVER OUR BODIES.
AAAH...
THANKS FOR TAKING IT A BIT EASY ON ME. I ALREADY FEEL MY LIFE IS A LITTLE MORE IN BALANCE.
EVERYTHING DOES HAPPEN FOR A REASON.
OUCH!

Creating a successful company depends on your ability to answer the following questions:

1. Why will it succeed at first?

2. Why will it continue to succeed once others copy it?

I'll try to explain the importance of these questions and how we answered them at Honest Tea.

WHY WILL IT SUCCEED AT FIRST?

No product has any natural right to exist. In the beverage industry, some 300 new brands are introduced each year. With several varieties in each brand, that translates to more than 1,000 new products. However, the shelf space for beverages isn't expanding—at least, nowhere near that rapidly. To get a place in the market, you have to displace someone already there. Thus, you must be able to answer the basic questions: Why is your product different from all other products? What problem does it solve? How does it make people's lives better?

With Honest Tea, the answer was clear: we found a hole in the market. We couldn't find anything we wanted to drink and figured we weren't alone. So we created a beverage that was just barely sweetened. Since we weren't hiding the flavor behind tons of sugar, we spent more money on better ingredients. Customers didn't have to be tea aficionados to taste the difference.

Just because you find a hole doesn't mean you should step into it. Entrepreneurs are natural optimists. That's an essential ingredient to perseverance, but it can lead to a false sense of invincibility.

Before taking the leap, do a reality check. Odds are you aren't the first person to have this idea. If it's such a great idea, why haven't others done it before? In other words, why will you succeed where others have failed? Unless you have a convincing answer to this question, proceed with extreme caution.

One answer might be a special set of circumstances. In our case, the timing was right. The healthy food movement was starting to take off, and there wasn't a tasty beverage option in the category. Many successful beverages, like Snapple and Clearly Canadian, had been launched under the good-for-you umbrella. They were seen as healthier alternatives to soda because they didn't add carbonation or caramel coloring, but they often contained just as much sugar. We believed Honest Tea would be the first beverage to truly deliver on the good-for-you promise.

Having a great product or service is only a start. You'll need to get the word out. With a new product, traditional advertising isn't cost-effective. Airtime costs the same amount whether your product is in 1 store or 1,000. If you lack store presence, most of the people hearing your ad won't be able to find the product, and the ad is wasted. Thus, you'll most likely rely on some type of word-of-mouth.

Say you've got a great new wart remover. Even if you get people to try it and even if they love it, they probably aren't going to tell their friends about it. In contrast, people walk around with a bottle of Honest Tea and become our billboards. They share our product when friends come over. New products can become "discovery" brands. Consumers take pride in discovering Honest Tea for themselves, and even more pride in introducing it to others.

You might think that finding an opportunity and getting through liftoff is the toughest challenge. Alas, no. Once you've gained some traction, your success will be noticed by others. And they will copy you. Unless you have a patent—and even then, it's hard to stop others from doing pretty much what you are doing.

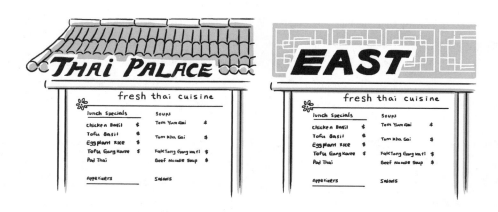

This leads to the second key question—the most important question to ask yourself:

WHY WILL YOU CONTINUE TO SUCCEED EVEN WHEN OTHERS WITH MORE MONEY AND EXPERIENCE ENTER YOUR MARKET?

This is what stopped us from entering the beverage business with a mixture of orange juice and club soda. We thought it would be a great drink—a healthy, all-natural soda with half the calories and half the cost of OJ. But if it worked, we'd just be doing test marketing for Minute Maid and Tropicana. Their costs are so much lower and their distribution so much better, we wouldn't stand a chance. The problem with most great business ideas is they are a great idea for someone else, not you.

So, why was Honest Tea different? What would keep industry incumbents from copying us or, at least, make them hesitate before doing so?

Our position as the anti-Snapple created cognitive dissonance for those selling sugar-laden beverages. It is hard to market supersweet and lightly sweetened drinks at the same time. Their existing customers liked sweet drinks and weren't asking for a less-sweet option. Indeed, they wouldn't like something just a tad sweet. And those looking for something barely sweetened wouldn't be happy with the majority of their product lines. Trying to satisfy both groups at the same time is a recipe for confusion.

It also helped that our production process was artisanal and hard to scale. The industry wasn't set up to make tea by brewing tea leaves. It doesn't fit their high-speed, efficient production model.

Likewise, industry gospel says each bottle should taste the same, whenever and wherever you buy it. Our product was happily inconsistent. Just like wine, each of our "vintages" tasted a bit different. We thought each tasted great, which was more important than uniformity.

We also got some breathing room because natural foods retailers differentiate themselves by carrying products that aren't typically found in mainstream grocery stores. This gave us some protected space in which to build our brand.

These are some of the answers for Honest Tea. Your job is to figure out the answers for your start-up idea.

I'd like to add a few lessons from my perspective.

1. Build something you believe in right from the start.
2. Think ahead about what you want to accomplish.
3. It doesn't matter how good it is for you if it doesn't taste good.
4. Don't delegate at the beginning.

BUILD SOMETHING YOU BELIEVE IN RIGHT FROM THE START.

As a start-up, you'll likely have worse costs, worse distribution—pretty much worse everything. You have to be much better on some important dimension—better enough that consumers will overlook your weaknesses (such as being really hard to find or having an inch of tea sediment). The more you stand for something, the more you matter in their lives, and the more they'll ask for your brand and perhaps even harass a store manager when they can't find it.

Customers want to have a relationship with your brand, but you have to earn their trust. It's rarely credible when a brand (or a person, for that matter) develops a new personality or a new set of values. It's essential that your brand has a clear identity from the outset.

I'll never forget one of the first conversations I had with Jeff Swartz, CEO of Timberland.

THINK ABOUT HOW IMPORTANT IT IS FOR PEOPLE TO TRUST OUR BRAND.

LOOK! PEOPLE PUT OUR PRODUCT ON THEIR BODY AS PART OF THEIR IDENTITY. CAN ANY RELATIONSHIP BE MORE INTIMATE THAN THAT?

ACTUALLY...

THINK AHEAD ABOUT WHAT YOU WANT TO ACCOMPLISH.

If your game plan is to launch your product, market it for a year or two, and get bought out by a large company like Coke or P&G, then you're unlikely to succeed at any level. That's not how you build an enterprise that can stand on its own or that others will want to acquire. You need to build something for the long run and make decisions based on owning the brand forever. We always envisioned that Honest Tea could be more than just another bottled tea—it could be a national brand embodying a different way of doing business.

IT DOESN'T MATTER HOW GOOD IT IS FOR YOU IF IT DOESN'T TASTE GOOD.

If an eco-friendly toilet paper gives people splinters, they won't care how green it is. With tea, there can't be a trade-off between delicious and healthy. It can't taste like lake water. It has to be delicious.

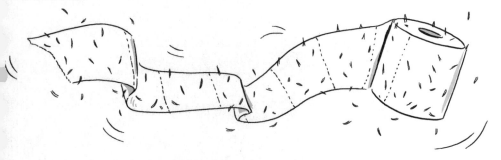

DON'T DELEGATE AT THE BEGINNING.

The best way to get a handle on the business is to learn every aspect. Don't worry, you're not supposed to know what to do, but don't be afraid to try doing it all. If things go well, you'll be able to hire people to take over the tasks where you don't add value. I taught myself how to use accounting software, but certainly not better than a professional. I learned how to buy and brew tea, but we eventually hired food scientists who could do it better. I made sales and deliveries, but dented up trucks along the way. I served more samples of Honest Tea than anyone in our company, but happily I now share the load with our dozens of great brand ambassadors who cover the country. Because I've done all this, I can have a conversation with any employee, supplier, or customer about what they do, ask challenging questions, and not get snowballed.

One downside of not delegating is there's more work to do, but sleep isn't that important the first year. There's enough energy from the thrill and fear of creating something new to keep you going. I was fine operating on five to six hours of sleep a night. Whenever I had an extra 30 to 60 free minutes, I was better off going for a run, which also helped me work through my worries and develop creative ideas.

But I still needed balance. I made sure I was home for dinner whenever I was in town, and I coached my son's baseball team. That sometimes created absurd demands on my schedule, but it ensured I had consistent time with him.

One more personal observation: find a way to manage your stress.

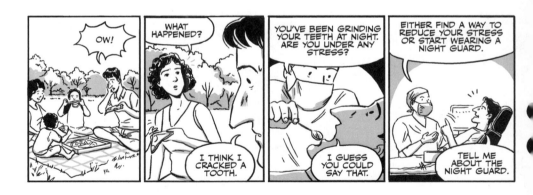

II. GROWING PAINS: 1999–2004

IN OUR FIRST YEAR, WE SOLD $250,000 OF TEA—NOT BAD FOR BEING IN STORES FOR ONLY SIX MONTHS. FOR YEAR TWO, WE WERE ON TRACK TO BREAK $1 MILLION IN SALES. WE WERE ALSO ON TRACK TO LOSE OVER $300,000. WE NEEDED TO RAISE MORE MONEY. AND THIS TIME, WE NEEDED TO PROPOSE A STOCK PRICE.

WHAT DO YOU THINK THE COMPANY IS WORTH?

THERE'S NO RIGHT VALUE. ULTIMATELY, IT'S WHATEVER INVESTORS ARE WILLING TO PAY. I THINK WE CAN SUPPORT A VALUE OF $5 MILLION—THAT'S FIVE TIMES OUR PROJECTED REVENUE FOR THIS YEAR.

WE HAVE 1.24 MILLION SHARES OUTSTANDING. ADD IN THE VALUE OF OUR WARRANTS, AND THAT TRANSLATES TO $2.50/SHARE.

1.24 MILLION SHARES @ $2.50	= $3.1 M
800K WARRANTS WITH $1 STRIKE PRICE	= $1.2 M
800K WARRANTS WITH $1.50 STRIKE PRICE	= $0.8 M
ALL OTHER WARRANTS ARE OUT OF THE MONEY*	
TOTAL	= $5.1 M

*THIS UNDERSTATES THE VALUE OF THE COMPANY, AS THE WARRANTS WERE WORTH MORE THAN THEIR CURRENT EXERCISE VALUE.

RIGHT NOW, WE HAVE A TIGHT-KNIT GROUP OF FOUNDING INVESTORS.

PARENTS

ATTORNEY

SISTER

PARENTS

friend

friend

friend

IT'S A LITTLE EARLY TO ASK THEM TO RE-INVEST. LET'S TRY TO RAISE MONEY FROM PEOPLE BESIDES FRIENDS AND FAMILY.

HONEST TEA HEADQUARTERS

WE LIKE WHAT YOU'RE DOING—HONEST TEA IS A DRUG-DELIVERY DEVICE. YOU MAKE IT EASIER FOR PEOPLE TO GET THEIR DAILY DOSE OF CAFFEINE.

HMMM... I NEVER THOUGHT ABOUT IT LIKE THAT BEFORE.

YOU SHOULD KNOW THAT WE'RE NOT PASSIVE INVESTORS. IF WE WRITE A CHECK, WE'LL WANT TO BE ON THE BOARD. WE'VE GOT BIG IDEAS TO IMPROVE WHAT YOU'RE DOING.

OH, REALLY?

FIRST OF ALL, YOU'VE GOT THIS ALL-NATURAL, HEALTHY TEA, SO YOUR MAILING ADDRESS SHOULDN'T BE IN BETHESDA, MD. YOU COULD SET UP A P.O. BOX IN VERMONT, BUT KEEP YOUR OFFICE HERE.

VERMONT

WHAT'S WRONG WITH BETHESDA? VERMONT ISN'T THE ONLY PLACE FOR ECO-FRIENDLY COMPANIES. BESIDES, THAT DOESN'T SEEM HONEST.

ALSO, WITH THE DOT.COM EXPLOSION GOING ON, INVESTMENT DOLLARS ARE CLAMORING FOR ANYTHING WEB-RELATED.

DOT.com

TELL ME ABOUT IT. MY BUSINESS SCHOOL CLASSMATES RAISE MILLIONS FOR TECH START-UPS NO ONE UNDERSTANDS, WHILE WE TRY TO RAISE FUNDS IN $25,000 UNITS FOR A BUSINESS ANYONE CAN UNDERSTAND.

HAVE YOU CONSIDERED CHANGING YOUR NAME TO HONESTTEA.COM?

I DON'T SEE HOW CALLING US A DOT.COM MAKES US A MORE ATTRACTIVE BUSINESS. THE ECONOMICS OF SHIPPING LIQUID THROUGH THE MAIL AREN'T GOOD, NOT TO MENTION THE ENVIRONMENTAL IMPACT.

WHAT ABOUT ENERGY DRINKS? YOU COULD EXTEND YOUR LINE AND CALL IT HONEST ENERGY.

LOOK, I APPRECIATE YOU ALL COMING HERE, BUT IT FEELS LIKE YOU'RE MORE INTERESTED IN INVESTING IN SOMETHING WE AREN'T, RATHER THAN WHAT WE ARE.

I'M GOING TO BE SEEING THIS GUY FOR 10 MORE YEARS. HOW WILL I FACE HIM IF I LOSE HIS MONEY?

HEY, SETH! WE FOUND YOUR TEA AT WHOLE FOODS AND REALLY LIKE IT. ANY WAY WE COULD INVEST SOME OF OUR KIDS' COLLEGE MONEY IN IT?

THANKS, DOUG. I'LL DEFINITELY KEEP YOU IN MIND.

Some lementary

DID YOU TRY THAT DOCTOR WHO'S CLOSE TO A WEALTHY NEW ENGLAND FAMILY? IT MIGHT BE WORTH MEETING WITH HIM.

I'VE TALKED TO HIM A LOT ON THE PHONE, BUT SO FAR HE HASN'T CONNECTED ME WITH THE FAMILY.

WHY DON'T YOU COME UP TO BOSTON ON FEBRUARY 12 AND WE'LL MAKE A DEAL.

THAT'S MY SON'S BIRTHDAY, SO I'LL NEED TO GET HOME BY DINNERTIME. BUT IF WE CAN MEET AT 2:00, THAT SHOULD BE OK.

ARE YOUR FRIENDS COMING?

HI!

NO, THEY COULDN'T MAKE IT. BUT IF YOU CAN MAKE IT WORTH MY WHILE, I'LL GET THEM INVOLVED.

WE'VE BEEN TALKING FOR MONTHS. IF YOU HAVE SOMEONE WHO WANTS TO MEET ME AND IS READY TO WRITE A CHECK, LET ME KNOW. IF NOT, I'VE GOT A PLANE TO CATCH.

COFFEE

BALTIMORE-WASHINGTON FL1441 4:25PM DEPA...
BALTIMORE-WASHINGTON FL729 7:35 PM DELAYED

11:00 I'M SO SORRY

THIS ISN'T GOING SO WELL. I'M SPENDING MORE TIME TRYING TO SELL SHARES THAN SELLING TEA.

I WAS FINE ASKING MY FAMILY BECAUSE THEY'LL STILL INVITE ME TO THANKSGIVING EVEN IF I LOSE ALL THEIR MONEY. ASKING FRIENDS AND NEIGHBORS TO INVEST FEELS A LOT RISKIER.

THAT'S THE NATURE OF THE BEAST. MY COLLEGE ROOMMATE, HIS OLD GIRLFRIEND, HIS BEST FRIEND, AND HIS BEST FRIEND'S BUSINESS PARTNER ARE ALL INVESTORS. SO IS THE SURGEON WHO REPLACED MY DAD'S HIP.

I'VE BROUGHT IN A CO-AUTHOR AND THREE PEOPLE I'VE WORKED WITH AS A CONSULTANT. WE'VE GOT NELL MINOW, A LEADING EXPERT ON CORPORATE GOVERNANCE, AND ANDY TOBIAS, WHO LITERALLY WROTE THE BOOK ON INVESTING.

IF THIS BOMBS, I'LL HAVE TO MOVE TO AUSTRALIA. BUT IF IT SUCCEEDS, YOU'RE GOING TO FEEL TERRIBLE IF YOU LEAVE PEOPLE OUT.

THE NEXT MORNING

DOUG, IF YOU REALLY ARE INTERESTED IN INVESTING, WE MAY HAVE AN OPPORTUNITY.

A FEW DAYS LATER

The Washington Post

HI, I EMAILED LAST WEEK ABOUT WHERE TO BUY MORE HONEST TEA, AND I READ THAT YOU'RE RAISING MONEY. MY FAMILY INVESTS IN REAL ESTATE, BUT WE'D LIKE TO EXPLORE AN INVESTMENT IN HONEST TEA AS A WAY TO DIVERSIFY OUR PORTFOLIO.

BY THE TIME THE ROUND CLOSED, OUR NETWORK OF INVESTORS HAD GROWN CONSIDERABLY.

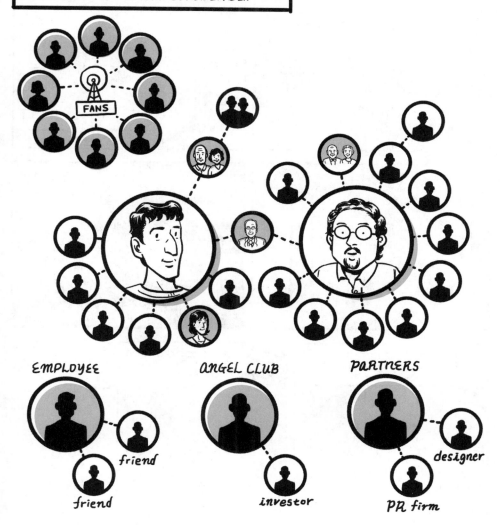

FANS

EMPLOYEE

friend

friend

ANGEL CLUB

investor

PARTNERS

designer

PR firm

WE WERE DOING FINE WITH THE NATURAL FOODS DISTRIBUTORS.

ORGANIC

all about health

GREEN STUFF

BUT WE DIDN'T HAVE A WAY TO REACH ALL THE STORES THEY DIDN'T COVER.

maison de ~

Deli

9 to 5

WE TRIED JUST ABOUT EVERY BEVERAGE DISTRIBUTOR IN EVERY MAJOR CITY.

IT'S NOT SWEET ENOUGH.

IT'S TOO EXPENSIVE.

IT TASTES LIKE GRASS.

THE LABEL ISN'T FLASHY ENOUGH.

AND THE FEW WHO RETURNED OUR CALLS WEREN'T INTERESTED IN WHAT WE WERE OFFERING.

WE HAVE A CONTRACT WITH SNAPPLE THAT PROHIBITS US FROM CARRYING OTHER TEA BRANDS.

WE'RE LOOKING FOR AN ENERGY DRINK. DO YOU MAKE THAT?

HMM. WE'RE GOING TO NEED TO FIND OTHER WAYS TO GET ON THE SHELVES.

GOURMECO, THANKS TO MELANIE, WAS DELIVERING OUR TEA, ALONG WITH THEIR CHEESES, TO GOURMET SHOPS.

CHEESE

HONEST TEA

SINCE YOU DON'T WORK WITH OUR CHEESE DISTRIBUTOR, IS THERE ANOTHER WAY WE CAN GET OUR DRINKS TO YOU?

HERE'S OUR CORNED BEEF DISTRIBUTOR'S CARD—GIVE THEM A CALL.

NOPE, WE DON'T WORK WITH EITHER OF YOUR DISTRIBUTORS.

WELL, WHO ELSE BRINGS THINGS TO YOUR STORES?

HOW ABOUT OUR CHARCOAL DISTRIBUTOR?

WHY NOT?

WE FOUND UNCONVENTIONAL SOLUTIONS IN OTHER CITIES.

CHIPS

A BAGEL DISTRIBUTOR IN BOSTON, A CHIPS AND SNACKS DISTRIBUTOR IN HARTFORD, A GOURMET FOODS DISTRIBUTOR IN CHICAGO...

AND BACK IN NEW HAVEN

HI, BARRY. IS MY RENT DUE?

42½

NO, NOT AT ALL. IF YOU'D LIKE TO MAKE A LITTLE MONEY, I COULD USE HELP DELIVERING TEA TO STORES AROUND TOWN.

DEALING WITH THESE SMALL DISTRIBUTORS HAD ITS COSTS.

YOUR BRAND IS REALLY STARTING TO GROW IN NEW YORK.

BOYLAN

THAT'S GREAT TO HEAR. SO... WHEN ARE YOU GOING TO SEND US A CHECK? YOUR BILL IS 60 DAYS OVERDUE.

HEY, I KNOW WE HAVEN'T PAID YOU YET, BUT WE'RE BUILDING YOUR BRAND IN NEW YORK CITY—A CRITICAL MARKET.

I DON'T WANT TO SOUND UNGRATEFUL, BUT IT'S HARD FOR ME TO BE EXCITED ABOUT THE GROWTH IF YOU CAN'T PAY US.

MEANWHILE, IN CHICAGO

WE'RE SEEING ENCOURAGING THINGS WITH HONEST TEA, BUT THE REST OF OUR BUSINESS IS JUST TOO CHALLENGING. WE'RE CLOSING UP SHOP.

YOU MEAN YOU WON'T BE ABLE TO DISTRIBUTE FOR US ANYMORE?

I'M AFRAID NOT.

THAT'S TERRIBLE. I HATE TO ASK THIS, BUT WHAT ABOUT THE MONEY YOU OWE US?

I'M AFRAID NO

JUST WHEN WE WERE STARTING TO GET THE HANG OF THINGS, THE HEAD OF MAYER BROS. CALLED US IN SEPTEMBER 1998 WITH A SURPRISE: IT WAS APPLE SEASON! FOR THE NEXT FEW MONTHS, THEIR LINES WERE FULLY BOOKED BOTTLING APPLE JUICE AND CIDER.

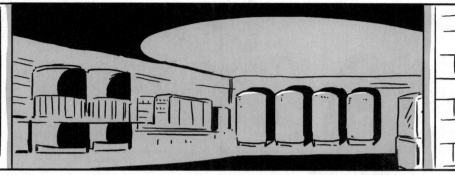

WE WEREN'T YET SELLING ENOUGH TEA IN THE AUTUMN MONTHS TO RUN OUT OF INVENTORY, BUT WE REALIZED NOT HAVING PRODUCT COULD QUICKLY PUT US OUT OF BUSINESS. IF WE EXPECTED TO GROW, WE NEEDED TO FIND A NEW PLANT, AND SOON.

THREE RIVERS BOTTLING, NEW KENSINGTON, PA

THIS PLACE IS HUGE: 85,000 SQ FT. THE LINE RUNS AT 400 BOTTLES/MINUTE.

AND IT'S MUCH CLOSER TO BETHESDA AND TO OUR SPRING WATER SOURCE.

WE COULD PRODUCE 4 MILLION CASES A YEAR—THAT'S $30 MILLION IN SALES!

THIS IS DICK, THE GENERAL MANAGER.

WE'RE STUCK IN A DISPUTE WITH OUR BIGGEST CUSTOMER, WHO REPRESENTS 95% OF OUR BUSINESS. THEY STOPPED PAYING US, SO WE RAN OUT OF CASH AND THE BANK TOOK OVER THE PLANT.

IT'S GOING UP FOR AUCTION, AND I BET YOU COULD BUY IT FOR $500,000.

BUT WE DON'T WANT TO OWN A PLANT.

THIS IS A GREAT DEAL. THE EQUIPMENT ALONE IS WORTH $2 MILLION.

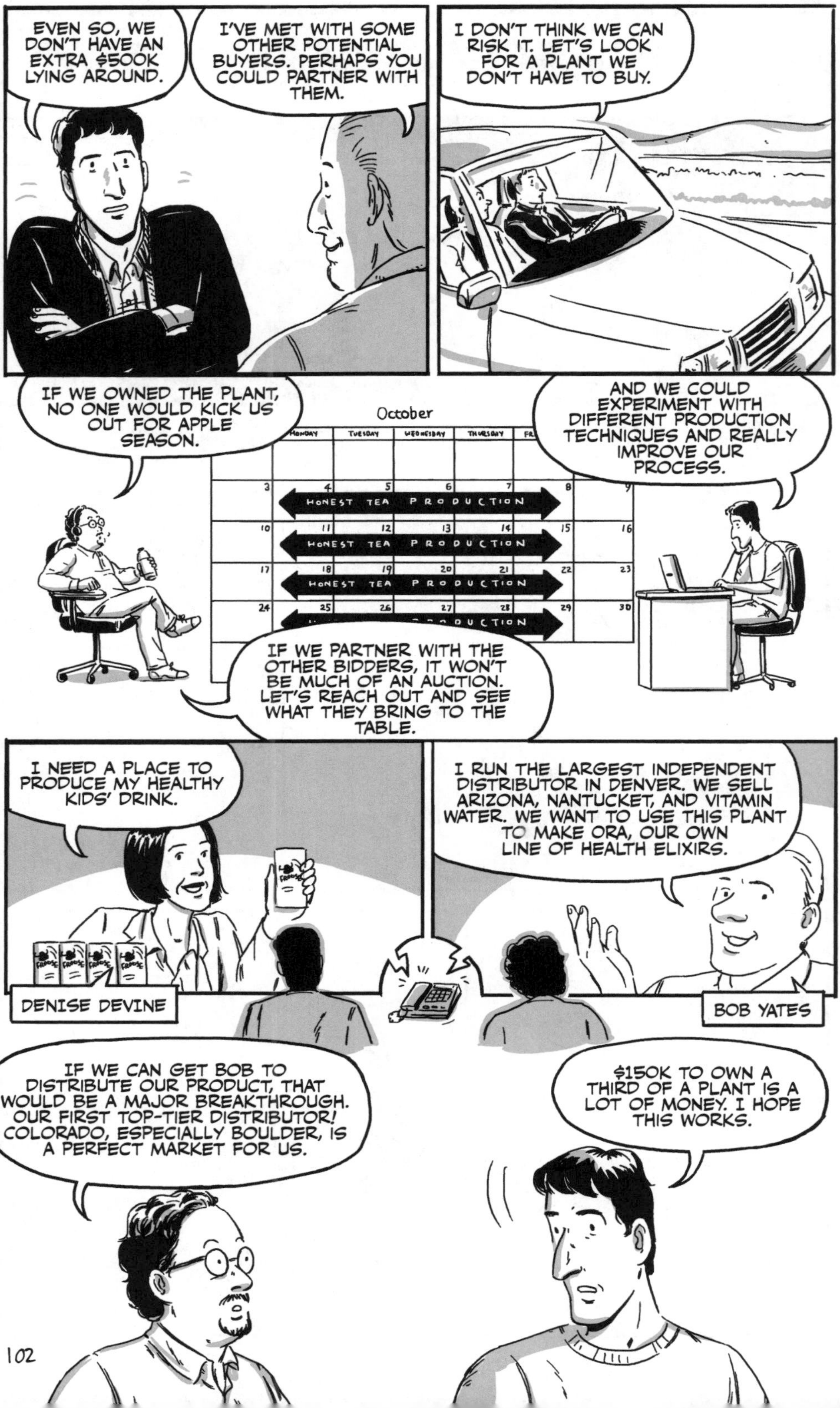
EVEN SO, WE DON'T HAVE AN EXTRA $500K LYING AROUND.
I'VE MET WITH SOME OTHER POTENTIAL BUYERS. PERHAPS YOU COULD PARTNER WITH THEM.
I DON'T THINK WE CAN RISK IT. LET'S LOOK FOR A PLANT WE DON'T HAVE TO BUY.
IF WE OWNED THE PLANT, NO ONE WOULD KICK US OUT FOR APPLE SEASON.
AND WE COULD EXPERIMENT WITH DIFFERENT PRODUCTION TECHNIQUES AND REALLY IMPROVE OUR PROCESS.
October
MONDAY TUESDAY WEDNESDAY THURSDAY
HONEST TEA PRODUCTION
HONEST TEA PRODUCTION
HONEST TEA PRODUCTION
IF WE PARTNER WITH THE OTHER BIDDERS, IT WON'T BE MUCH OF AN AUCTION. LET'S REACH OUT AND SEE WHAT THEY BRING TO THE TABLE.
I NEED A PLACE TO PRODUCE MY HEALTHY KIDS' DRINK.
DENISE DEVINE
I RUN THE LARGEST INDEPENDENT DISTRIBUTOR IN DENVER. WE SELL ARIZONA, NANTUCKET, AND VITAMIN WATER. WE WANT TO USE THIS PLANT TO MAKE ORA, OUR OWN LINE OF HEALTH ELIXIRS.
BOB YATES
IF WE CAN GET BOB TO DISTRIBUTE OUR PRODUCT, THAT WOULD BE A MAJOR BREAKTHROUGH. OUR FIRST TOP-TIER DISTRIBUTOR! COLORADO, ESPECIALLY BOULDER, IS A PERFECT MARKET FOR US.
$150K TO OWN A THIRD OF A PLANT IS A LOT OF MONEY. I HOPE THIS WORKS.

SEVERAL MONTHS LATER

THIS IS THE BEST TEA WE'VE EVER MADE. THE NEW BREWING SYSTEM IS FANTASTIC!

GEORGE, THIS PLANT IS CRITICAL TO OUR BUSINESS. WOULD YOU CONSIDER MOVING TO PITTSBURGH?

THE SURFING HERE IS LOUSY, BUT I'LL GIVE IT A TRY.

CLING

CLING

CLING

CLING

A FEW MONTHS LATER

WE'RE HAVING SOME CHALLENGES HERE. THE BOILER IS DOWN. HOPEFULLY WE'LL HAVE IT UP AND RUNNING IN A FEW DAYS.

A FEW WEEKS LATER

NO PRODUCTION TODAY. IT'S THE FIRST DAY OF BUCK SEASON.

WHAT DOES THAT MEAN?

EVERYONE'S OUT HUNTING.

HONEST TEA ONLY NEEDED 30 PRODUCTION DAYS A YEAR. IF THE PLANT WAS GOING TO SUCCEED, WE HAD TO FIND MORE CLIENTS. EVERY DAY THE PLANT SAT IDLE COST US $5,000.

DO WE HAVE ANY OTHER CUSTOMERS WE CAN RUN?

MCCOYS WANTS US TO MAKE MORE TEA FOR THEM. THEY'RE EVEN THREATENING TO SUE IF WE DON'T, BUT THEY HAVEN'T PAID US FOR THE LAST RUN.

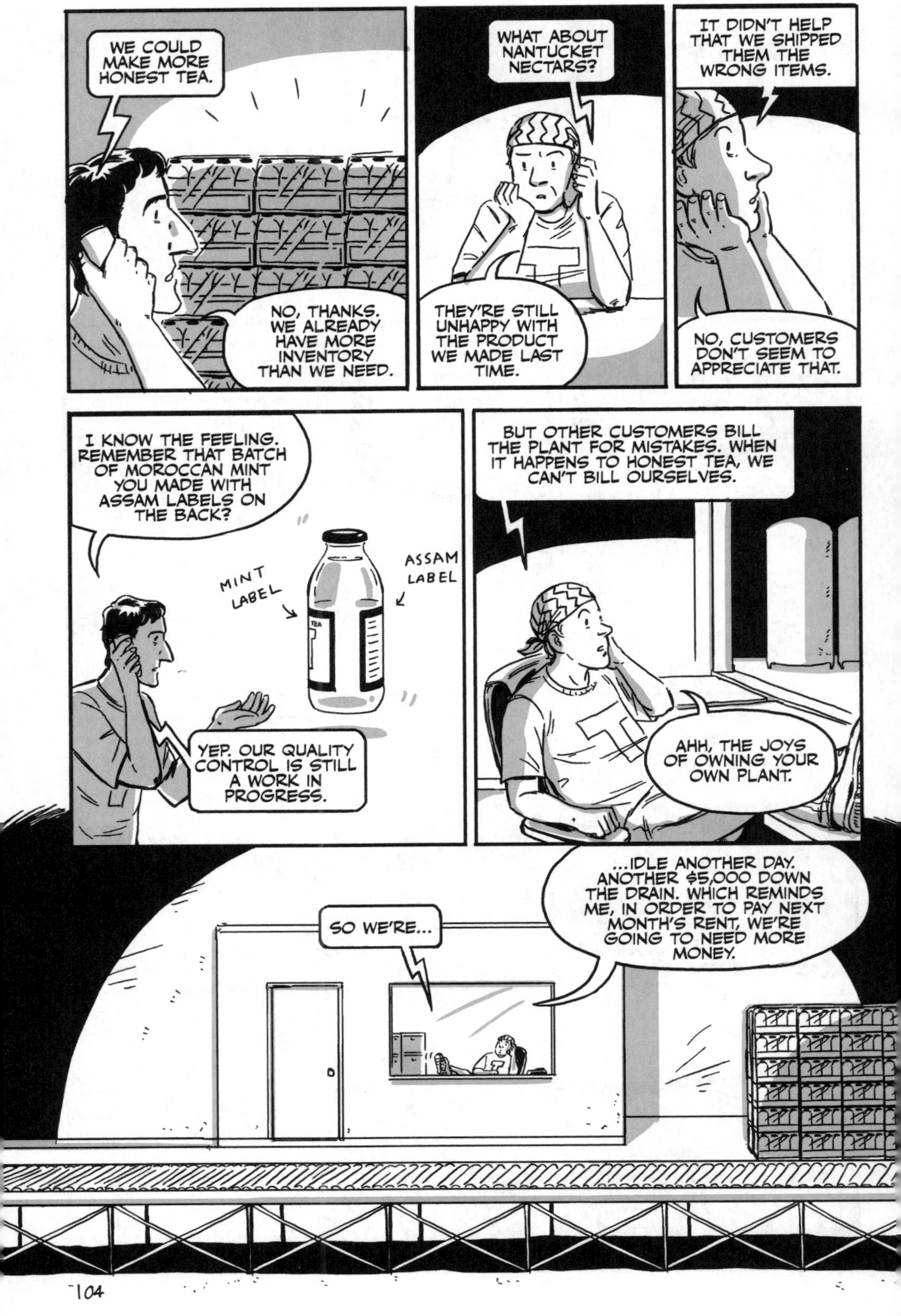
WE COULD MAKE MORE HONEST TEA.
NO, THANKS. WE ALREADY HAVE MORE INVENTORY THAN WE NEED.
WHAT ABOUT NANTUCKET NECTARS?
THEY'RE STILL UNHAPPY WITH THE PRODUCT WE MADE LAST TIME.
IT DIDN'T HELP THAT WE SHIPPED THEM THE WRONG ITEMS.
NO, CUSTOMERS DON'T SEEM TO APPRECIATE THAT.
I KNOW THE FEELING. REMEMBER THAT BATCH OF MOROCCAN MINT YOU MADE WITH ASSAM LABELS ON THE BACK?
MINT LABEL
ASSAM LABEL
YEP. OUR QUALITY CONTROL IS STILL A WORK IN PROGRESS.
BUT OTHER CUSTOMERS BILL THE PLANT FOR MISTAKES. WHEN IT HAPPENS TO HONEST TEA, WE CAN'T BILL OURSELVES.
AHH, THE JOYS OF OWNING YOUR OWN PLANT.
SO WE'RE...
...IDLE ANOTHER DAY. ANOTHER $5,000 DOWN THE DRAIN. WHICH REMINDS ME, IN ORDER TO PAY NEXT MONTH'S RENT, WE'RE GOING TO NEED MORE MONEY.

BY 2000, WE WERE BEGINNING TO FEEL LIKE A REAL COMPANY. IT WAS TIME TO START THINKING BEYOND DAY-TO-DAY SURVIVAL TO BUILDING SOMETHING MORE PERMANENT.

THERE ARE TIMES WHEN I'D LOVE TO GET ADVICE FROM PEOPLE WHO'VE DONE THIS BEFORE.

LET'S TRY TO CREATE THE BOARD OF DIRECTORS OF OUR DREAMS. WHAT KIND OF PEOPLE WOULD WE IDEALLY WANT TO GET ADVICE FROM?

FOR STARTERS, WE NEEDED SOMEONE WHO KNEW NATURAL FOODS. WE REACHED OUT TO MARK ORDAN, THE CO-FOUNDER AND FORMER CEO OF FRESH FIELDS SUPERMARKETS.

THE BIG QUESTION YOU HAVE TO ASK YOURSELF IS WHAT DO YOU REALLY WANT.

WE'RE EXPANDING RAPIDLY. LET'S GO PUBLIC AND TAKE ON WHOLE FOODS.

1996

NO, MARK. THE BOARD HAS DECIDED TO ACCEPT WHOLE FOODS' OFFER TO BUY FRESH FIELDS.

BUT WE'RE JUST GETTING STARTED...

WE'D RATHER LOCK IN THE GAINS. YOU'LL EXIT WITH A NICE PAYDAY AND BE ABLE TO DO WHATEVER YOU WANT TO DO.

I WAS DOING WHAT I WANTED TO DO. BE CAREFUL WHAT YOU WISH FOR.

WE ALSO LOOKED FOR SOMEONE WHO HAD BEEN AROUND THE BEVERAGE BUSINESS.

ROBIN PREVER, CEO OF SARATOGA WATER, IS INTERESTED IN DISTRIBUTING OUR TEA. LET'S GIVE HER A CALL.

YOU WANT CEOS ADVISING YOU. THEY'VE BEEN THROUGH THE SAME PRESSURE AND CHALLENGES YOU'LL EXPERIENCE.

AND WATCH OUT FOR VENTURE CAPITALISTS. THEY'LL TELL YOU ALL SORTS OF WONDERFUL THINGS THEY'LL DO FOR YOU, AND THEN GET YOU HOOKED ON CASH TO GAIN MORE CONTROL.

WE WANTED A BOARD MEMBER WHO COULD HELP US BUILD A BRAND THAT WOULD STAY TRUE TO ITS MISSION.

WE HEARD THAT JEFF SWARTZ, THE CEO OF TIMBERLAND, DRANK HONEST TEA ALL THE TIME.

YOU NEED TO BUILD HONEST TEA LIKE YOU'RE GOING TO OWN IT FOREVER. NEVER MAKE A SHORT-TERM DECISION THAT LIMITS YOUR FUTURE OPTIONS.

YOU HAVE TO BE FANATIC ABOUT YOUR BRAND. EVERYTHING YOU DO, FROM YOUR PACKAGING TO YOUR ON-HOLD MUSIC, HAS TO REFLECT YOUR MISSION.

IF CUSTOMERS DON'T TRUST YOU, IF YOU DON'T STAND FOR SOMETHING, FORGET IT.

WE'RE DOING ONLY $2 MILLION IN SALES, BUT WE'VE GOT A BOARD A $100 MILLION COMPANY WOULD BE LUCKY TO HAVE.

STORES STARTED ASKING US TO BRING OUT A LINE OF TEA BAGS. WHY NOT? HERE WAS AN OPPORTUNITY TO INCREASE SALES AND BUILD OUR BRAND. BUT HOW WOULD WE MAKE AN HONEST TEA BAG—SOMETHING DIFFERENT, BETTER, AND MORE HONEST THAN WHAT WAS OUT THERE?

IT'S OBVIOUS WE SHOULD USE WHOLE-LEAF TEA INSTEAD OF THE USUAL GROUND-UP LEAVES AND TEA DUST.

THE SAME INGREDIENTS WE USE TO BREW OUR BOTTLED TEA?

EXACTLY.

BUT SOME OF OUR TEAS CONTAIN LARGE BERRIES, AND TEA LEAVES EXPAND ENORMOUSLY WHEN STEEPED. HOW WILL THEY FIT IN A TEA BAG?

JUST MAKE THE BAG BIG.

OK, BUT WHY HASN'T ANYONE ELSE DONE THIS?

THERE IS A JAPANESE COMPANY THAT SELLS WHOLE-LEAF TEA IN A BEAUTIFUL SILK PURSE. BUT THEY RETAIL FOR $1 EACH.

WE NEED TO HIT A MUCH LOWER PRICE POINT. IT SHOULD BE POSSIBLE. EVEN WITH GREAT TEA, THE LEAVES IN EACH TEA BAG ONLY COST 2¢.

GIVEN THE EXPENSE OF THE FILTER PAPER, OVERWRAP, CARTON, AND DISTRIBUTION, THAT'S STILL A SMALL FRACTION OF THE TOTAL COST.

2¢

"JUST MAKE THE BAG BIG," OR SO WE THOUGHT. IN 2000, WE LAUNCHED THE PRODUCT USING AN EXTRA-LARGE TEA BAG MADE ENTIRELY OF PAPER. NO STRING, NO STAPLE, NO CARDBOARD TAG. SOME CUSTOMERS THOUGHT IT LOOKED LIKE AN IUD. OTHERS SAW A FRENCH HORN. FUNNY-LOOKING OR NOT, THE TASTE WAS GREAT. IT WAS AFFORDABLE, TOO—ONLY 25¢ PER BAG. SINCE THERE WERE NO STAPLES OR STRINGS, IT WAS MICROWAVABLE AND BIODEGRADABLE.

VERSION 1.0

HONEST TEA
Premium whole-leaf Tea Bags

OTHER BRANDS

AND ITS TAIL HUNG NICELY OVER THE CUP.

WE TURNED TO OUR ORIGINAL DESIGNER, SLOAN WILSON, TO DESIGN THE BOX.

HONEST TEA

T

TO HIGHLIGHT THE INGREDIENTS, WE PUT AN X-RAY (ACTUALLY A SCAN) OF OUR TEA BAG ON THE SIDE OF THE BOX AND A FULL-COLOR PHOTO OF THE TEA LEAVES ON THE TOP.

HONEST TEA

JIANGXI GREEN

ORGANIC GREEN TEA LEAVES IN 15 TEA BAGS

SIDE

TOP

FOR PORTABILITY, WE NEEDED TO PUT THE TEA BAG IN A WRAPPER. SINCE WE WANTED TO SHOW OFF THE BAG AND ITS CONTENTS, A CLEAR OVERWRAP WAS AN EASY CHOICE.

$#@$!!!

THE ONLY PROBLEM WAS THAT PEOPLE COULDN'T GET THE WRAPPER OPEN WITHOUT SCISSORS.

WE SACRIFICED TRANSPARENCY FOR CONVENIENCE AND REPLACED THE PLASTIC WRAPPER WITH A PAPER ONE. BUT THIS LED TO A NEW PROBLEM: THE TEA BAGS SOMETIMES GOT CAUGHT IN THE SEAM AND CUSTOMERS RIPPED THEM BY MISTAKE.

OOPS!

VERSION 2.0

UNDAUNTED, WE MADE THE PAPER OVERWRAP LARGER. PROBLEM SOLVED— EXCEPT THE LARGER WRAPPERS DIDN'T QUITE FIT IN THE BOXES WE HAD PRINTED.

IT WON'T FIT!

VERSION 2.1

WE GAVE UP ON THE WRAPPERS AND JUST PUT OUR TEA BAGS INTO CANISTERS. BUT THE REDUCED PACKAGING MADE IT HARD TO TAKE THEM ON THE GO.

HONEST TEA

VERSION 3.0

THE CANISTERS WERE NICE-LOOKING BUT REQUIRED MORE MATERIAL THAN THE BOXES, SO WE ENCOURAGED OUR CUSTOMERS TO COME UP WITH CREATIVE WAYS TO REUSE THEM.

THE COMPANY MAKING OUR TEA BAGS HAD BEEN HARD TO WORK WITH. THEY WERE REGULARLY OUT OF STOCK AND HAD A NEW EXCUSE EACH WEEK, INCLUDING THAT THEIR ROOF COLLAPSED—WHICH MIGHT HAVE BEEN TRUE. WE HAD HAD ENOUGH. WE SWITCHED TO MORE CONVENTIONAL TEA BAGS AND BOXES.

VERSION 4.0

THE TEA BAGS STILL HAD PREMIUM TEA INSIDE AND NO STAPLES OUTSIDE, BUT THEY WEREN'T DISTINCTIVE ANYMORE.

HONEST TEA

WE PUT A PERFORATION ON THE BOTTOM OF THE CARTON TO MAKE DISPENSING THE TEA BAGS EASIER, BUT THAT MADE THE BOXES TOO WEAK FOR STACKING ON STORE SHELVES.

BY THEN, WE'D BEEN THROUGH FOUR DIFFERENT DESIGNS AND HAD WORN OUT OUR WELCOME WITH RETAILERS. WE HAD A GOOD PRODUCT BUT NO GOOD SOLUTION FOR HOW TO PACKAGE IT.

TO MAKE MATTERS WORSE, SOME RIVALS HAD FIGURED OUT A DIFFERENT WAY TO OFFER WHOLE-LEAF TEA BAGS.

THEIR NYLON PYRAMID DESIGN WASN'T BIODEGRADABLE—SO IT WOULDN'T HAVE WORKED FOR US—BUT IT CERTAINLY WAS NEW AND DIFFERENT. AND THEIR CLEAR OVERWRAP HAD NOTCHES THAT MADE IT EASY TO OPEN.

WE'VE INVESTED OVER $1 MILLION IN THIS PRODUCT LINE, BUT SIX YEARS LATER SALES ARE ONLY $350,000.

IT REMINDS ME OF A RUSSIAN STORY MY DAD TELLS ABOUT A DOCTOR AND HIS PATIENT.

I HAVE TERRIBLE STOMACH PAIN.

YOU SHOULD TRY FASTING FOR THREE DAYS.

I STILL HAVE TERRIBLE STOMACH PAIN.

YOU SHOULD SPEND A WEEK WITHOUT SLEEP.

I STILL HAVE TERRIBLE STOMACH PAIN.

YOU SHOULD TRY EATING NOTHING BUT LEMONS FOR A WEEK.

WHAT A PITY. I HAD SO MANY MORE CURES I WANTED TO TRY.

IT'S A GOOD THING THIS WASN'T THE FIRST PRODUCT WE LAUNCHED, BECAUSE WE WOULD HAVE GONE OUT OF BUSINESS.

I STILL THINK, IF THE COMPANY HAD DEPENDED ON IT, WE MIGHT HAVE MADE IT WORK.

BARRY, YOU'RE NOT GOING TO BELIEVE THE SALES CALL I HAD TODAY...

SETH, I LIKE YOUR PRODUCT, BUT I'M AFRAID IT DOESN'T WORK FOR ME. I NEED TO MAKE $5 A CASE. THE PROFIT JUST ISN'T THERE.

I DON'T GET IT. WE SHOULD BE HIS MOST PROFITABLE BRAND.

HOW MUCH DO YOU MAKE WITH SNAPPLE?

$5.20 A CASE. I ONLY MAKE $4 WITH YOU.

WAIT A SECOND. A CASE OF SNAPPLE HAS 24 BOTTLES. WE ONLY HAVE 12.

snapple   HONEST TEA

ON AN EQUAL BOTTLE BASIS, YOU'LL MAKE MUCH MORE SELLING HONEST TEA.

YEAH, BUT I NEED TO BE MAKING $5 A CASE.

$8.00

$5.20

Snapple

SETH, CAN I FLUNK THIS GUY?

HE'S THINKING ABOUT PROFITS PER CASE WHEN A CASE DOESN'T MEAN ANYTHING. HE SHOULD BE THINKING ABOUT PROFITS PER BOTTLE.

I KNOW, I KNOW.

22¢   Snapple   HONEST TEA T   33¢

IF WE WERE TO TAPE TWO OF OUR CASES TOGETHER, WOULD THAT WORK FOR YOU?

YUP.

CAN WE DO THAT?

I THOUGHT ABOUT IT, AND I'M AFRAID WE CAN'T.

THEN WE ARE GOING TO LOSE OUR CHANCE WITH THIS DISTRIBUTOR.

MAYBE THAT'S A GOOD THING.

WHAT IF WE PUT OUR TEAS IN 24-PACKS?

ACTUALLY, THAT WOULD COST US MORE MONEY.

HOW'S THAT?

HONEST TEA   FREE

WHEN WE GET A NEW ACCOUNT, MOST STORES ASK FOR A FREE FILL, MEANING THEIR FIRST CASE IS FREE.

WITH OUR 12-PACK, WE ONLY HAVE TO GIVE THEM 12 BOTTLES. IF WE HAD 24-PACKS, IT WOULD COST US TWICE AS MUCH.

YOU'RE KIDDING ME.

NO, I'M NOT. AND I DON'T THINK YOU TAUGHT ME THAT IN BUSINESS SCHOOL.

WE STARTED TO BUILD A SALES TEAM. MELANIE CAME TO US FROM GOURMECO TO LEAD OUR NATURAL FOODS SALES. WE HIRED AN INDUSTRY VETERAN, WHOM WE'LL CALL BOB, TO MANAGE OUR FOODSERVICE ACCOUNTS AND BEVERAGE DISTRIBUTORS. HE GOT OFF TO A FINE START, BUT AFTER A YEAR, THINGS CHANGED.

WELL, THAT WAS THE WORST CREW DRIVE I'VE EVER SEEN.

ATLANTIC DISTRIBUTION

WHAT DO YOU MEAN?

BOB PROMISED HE'D BRING A TEAM TO RIDE ALONG WITH MY SALES REPS, BUT NO ONE SHOWED UP, NOT EVEN HIM.

TEAM??

5 Justin
4 Bob
3 Melanie
1 me
2 George

NUMBER OF HONEST TEA EMPLOYEES: 5

LOOK, SETH, I LIKE YOU. BUT IF YOU GUYS DON'T LIVE UP TO YOUR COMMITMENTS, IT'S GOING TO BE A SHORT RUN.

I'LL BE THERE TOMORROW.

A FEW WEEKS LATER

WE'RE DOING GREAT IN NATURAL FOODS BUT STRUGGLING WITH BEVERAGE DISTRIBUTORS AND FOODSERVICE.

WHAT DOES BOB HAVE TO SAY?

I DON'T KNOW. HE WAS SUPPOSED TO BE HERE THIS MORNING, BUT SOMETHING CAME UP. HE SEEMS DISTRACTED.

BOB CAN'T MAKE HIS APPOINTMENT WITH THE COFFEE DISTRIBUTOR. CAN YOU COVER?

I'LL MAKE IT WORK.

A FEW MONTHS LATER

THE FAIRMONT GRILL CALLED. THEY SAY YOU CANCELED ON THEM A SECOND TIME. IS THAT TRUE?

OH, THEY'LL BE FINE. I'LL GO DOWN THERE TODAY.

BOB, WE NEED TO TALK ABOUT YOUR PERFORMANCE. IT'S BEEN A LITTLE... ERRATIC.

I FEEL LIKE I'M DOING MORE DAMAGE CONTROL THAN SALES CALLS.

DON'T WORRY. I'VE GOT A BUNCH OF IRONS IN THE FIRE.

A FEW MONTHS AFTER THAT

HE'S A LIAR.

THE DISTRIBUTOR UP IN HARTFORD ISN'T PAYING BECAUSE HE CLAIMS YOU TOLD HIM HE DIDN'T HAVE TO PAY UNTIL HE ORDERED MORE TEA.

BUT HE'S NOT THE FIRST CUSTOMER TO SAY THAT. LOOK, I LIKE YOU AS A PERSON, BUT WE CAN'T AFFORD TO KEEP YOU IF SALES DON'T PICK UP.

I WAS HOPING TO AVOID TELLING YOU THIS.

MY WIFE IS DIVORCING ME AND TAKING THE KIDS.

OH, NO.

SHE'S BEEN HAVING AN AFFAIR.

OH, NO!

WITH A FAMILY FRIEND.

WHAT??!!

AND SHE'S PREGNANT, TOO.

I'M SO SORRY. IS THERE ANY WAY I CAN HELP?

I JUST NEED YOU TO BE PATIENT UNTIL I CAN WORK THINGS OUT.

I'LL TRY.

AND TIME RAN OUT.

BOB IS STILL STRUGGLING. BUT HOW CAN WE FIRE HIM WHEN HE'S GOING THROUGH SUCH A TERRIBLE LIFE CRISIS?

THE QUESTION IS: HOW CAN WE AFFORD TO HAVE HALF OUR SALES TEAM NOT SELLING?

OK. IF WE LET HIM GO, WE NEED TO GIVE HIM SEVERANCE PAY.

WHAT DID YOU HAVE IN MIND?

HOW ABOUT FOUR MONTHS?

THAT'S TOO MUCH. YOU GAVE HIM A WRITTEN WARNING IN JUNE AFTER HAVING TOLD HIM THE SAME THING IN THE WINTER.

THINGS DID IMPROVE... UNTIL HE STARTED MISSING APPOINTMENTS AGAIN.

IF YOU WANT TO PAY HIM TWO MONTHS' SEVERANCE OUT OF YOUR OWN POCKET, YOU CAN DO IT.

WE CAN'T EXPECT HONEST TEA SHAREHOLDERS TO PAY, ESPECIALLY WHEN OUR SALES ARE GOING TO FALL WELL BELOW OUR BUSINESS PLAN OF $3.4 MILLION.

IT'S STILL 72% GROWTH.

BUT WE CLAIMED WE WOULD GROW 200%.

I'M SO SORRY. SOMETIMES GREAT PEOPLE AND GREAT COMPANIES JUST DON'T WORK OUT.

THAT WAS BRUTAL. I HOPE I NEVER HAVE TO FIRE ANYONE EVER AGAIN. THIS WEEKEND AWAY COULDN'T HAVE COME AT A BETTER TIME.

THIS IS BOB'S BROTHER. HE HAD A HEART ATTACK THIS AFTERNOON AND IS IN THE HOSPITAL.

BEEP

OH MY GOD.

EPILOGUE: THANKFULLY, BOB WAS ABLE TO START OVER. AFTER HIS WIFE REMARRIED AND MOVED TO A NEW CITY, BOB MOVED TO STAY CLOSE TO HIS CHILDREN. HE HAS GONE ON TO A SUCCESSFUL CAREER IN GOURMET FOODSERVICE.

WE NEEDED TO HIRE SOMEONE WHO COULD GET US REAL BEVERAGE DISTRIBUTORS, AND WHO KNEW HOW TO DEAL WITH THEM.

I STARTED IN THE BEVERAGE BUSINESS AT 16, LOADING TRUCKS ALL SUMMER.

LATER, I DROVE A ROUTE IN NEW JERSEY THAT I BUILT UP TO 240,000 CASES A YEAR.

DAN CAVANAUGH

IN JUST ONE ROUTE? THAT'S MORE THAN ALL THE CASES WE SOLD LAST YEAR.

CAN I SEE YOUR RESUME?

I'VE NEVER HAD A RESUME, BUT LET ME SHOW YOU MY PHOTO ALBUM.

WHEN CAN YOU START?

INTERBEV IS THE BIG BEVERAGE INDUSTRY CONFERENCE, AND IT ONLY TAKES PLACE EVERY OTHER YEAR. DECEMBER 2000 WAS OUR FIRST SHOW.

HONEST TEA

NEW ORLEANS CONVENTION CENTER

THE BIGGEST INDEPENDENT BEVERAGE DISTRIBUTION COMPANY IN NEW YORK CITY IS BIG GEYSER, RUN BY IRVING HERSHKOWITZ, OR "H," AS EVERYONE CALLED HIM.

WHAT YOU GOT HERE?

HE WAS WALKING AROUND WITH HIS BADGE REVERSED SO PEOPLE WOULDN'T KNOW WHO HE WAS. THAT INCLUDED US.

IT'S A LINE OF LIGHTLY SWEETENED TEAS MADE WITH ORGANIC INGREDIENTS.

NOT BAD.

TRY BLACK FOREST BERRY. ITS INGREDIENTS ARE SO DELICIOUS, MY CO-FOUNDER BARRY HERE LIKES TO EAT THEM.

OOH, THIS ONE'S GOOD.

I'D LIKE TO COMPLIMENT YOUR WIFE ON HER FINE TASTE.

THAT'S NOT MY WIFE.

UHH, I MEAN YOUR FRIEND.

YOU GOT SOMETHING HERE. IT'S A LITTLE EARLY—PEOPLE AREN'T READY YET—BUT YOU DEFINITELY GOT SOMETHING.

CAN I ASK WHAT KIND OF BUSINESS YOU HAVE?

HE RUNS A DISTRIBUTOR IN NEW YORK.

OH MY GOD, THIS IS "H"!

WHAT DO WE NEED TO DO TO GET YOU TO CARRY OUR TEA?

IF YOU WANT TO BUILD A BRAND IN NEW YORK, YOU NEED TO DO IT ONE BOTTLE AT A TIME. YOU CAN'T JUST COME IN THERE AND PUT IT IN A BUNCH OF CHAINS.

YOU NEED PEOPLE ON THE GROUND TO GO STORE BY STORE AND MAKE IT HAPPEN.

NYC

IN MEMORIAM

IRVING "H" HERSHKOWITZ

1940-2011

THANKS FOR BELIEVING IN US.

SLOWLY, WE STARTED TO SEE PROGRESS. DAN HELPED US SIGN BEVERAGE DISTRIBUTORS IN UPSTATE NEW YORK, VERMONT, SACRAMENTO...

BUT THERE WERE STILL PLENTY OF HICCUPS ALONG THE WAY.

DAN NEEDED TO CLEAN UP WHAT WE HAD.

WHAT'S THE DEAL WITH BRUCE IN CONNECTICUT?

HE LAST ORDERED A FEW MONTHS AGO, BUT HE HASN'T PAID US, AND NOW HE'S NOT RETURNING MY CALLS.

HI. I SEE YOU'RE CARRYING HONEST TEA. CAN I ASK WHERE YOU GOT IT?

OH, THIS GUY BRUCE SOLD IT TO ME—HE'S RUNNING A PROMOTION: BUY THREE CASES, GET ONE FREE.

Convenient St

LOOK, I APPRECIATE YOU DISTRIBUTING OUR PRODUCT, BUT YOU NEED TO PAY US.

UH, I DON'T HAVE MY CHECKBOOK WITH ME. I LEFT IT AT THE OFFICE.

THAT'S NO PROBLEM. I DROVE UP IN MY CAR, SO I'VE GOT ALL DAY.

I GOT HIM TO PAY HALF THE BILL. THAT'S AS GOOD AS WE'RE GONNA GET.

WE NEED TO STOP WORKING WITH GUYS JUST STARTING UP.

NEW YORK

MASSACHUSETTS

CONNECTICUT

NEW HAVEN

DAN, IT'S EMBARRASSING THAT WE STILL DON'T HAVE DISTRIBUTION IN NEW HAVEN. I FOUND A NUMBER ON THE INTERNET FOR A DISTRIBUTOR IN THE AREA. CAN YOU GIVE THEM A CALL?

NEW HAVEN

HI, MY NAME IS DAN CAVANAUGH FROM HONEST TEA. I'D LIKE TO STOP BY TO LEARN MORE ABOUT YOUR BUSINESS.

SURE, HOW ABOUT NEXT WEDNESDAY?

MARYLAND

BETHESDA

THAT'D BE GREAT. I'D LIKE TO GET A SENSE OF WHETHER WE COULD WORK TOGETHER.

WELL, WE'RE VERY PROUD OF HOW WE DO THINGS HERE.

THAT'S NICE TO HEAR. HOW LONG HAVE YOU BEEN IN BUSINESS?

WE'RE IN OUR FIFTH YEAR.

AND WHAT'S YOUR TERRITORY?

WE SERVE FAIRFIELD COUNTY AND THE SURROUNDING AREA.

NEW HAVEN

THAT'S PERFECT. WE'RE GETTING A LOT OF REQUESTS FROM PEOPLE THERE.

ARE YOU AN EMPLOYER?

YEAH, I GUESS YOU COULD SAY THAT. CAN I ASK WHAT OTHER PRODUCTS YOU DISTRIBUTE?

PROSPECT HILL

EDGEWOOD

NEW HAVEN

WEST HAVEN

PRODUCTS?

YES, I MEAN, WHICH OTHER BRANDS? YOU KNOW, LIKE RED BULL OR ARIZONA.

I THINK YOU MIGHT BE MISTAKEN.

THIS IS SMALL WONDERS, RIGHT?

DAY CA

YES, BUT...

120

MORE IMPORTANT THAN NEW HAVEN, WE NEEDED A BEVERAGE DISTRIBUTOR IN OUR HOME MARKET, BALTIMORE-WASHINGTON. THE BEST OPTION WAS CANADA DRY POTOMAC, WHO DISTRIBUTED 7UP, SNAPPLE, VITAMIN WATER, AND SOBE.

WHAT'S OUR PLAN?

BEING PERSISTENT.

HI, DARLENA. IS PHIL IN?

NO, BUT HE'LL BE BACK IN A FEW HOURS.

MIND IF I WORK IN THE LOBBY?

OH!

I KEEP SEEING YOUR DRINKS AROUND. HOW ARE YOU GETTING IT TO THE STORES?

WE'VE GOT A PATCHWORK OF CHEESE, CORNED BEEF, AND CHARCOAL DISTRIBUTORS. IMAGINE WHAT WE COULD DO IF WE HAD A REAL BEVERAGE PARTNER.

WELL, DARLENA'S A FAN. I'M OPEN TO GIVING IT A TRY, BUT YOU'LL HAVE TO CONVINCE MY BOSS, DICK WOLFE. HE'S A SODA GUY AND ISN'T A BELIEVER.

I'VE TRIED CALLING DICK A BUNCH OF TIMES, BUT HE'S NOT RETURNING MY CALLS.

GOOD LUCK!

KEEP TRYING.

HELLO, DICK! I...

YOU AGAIN? LOOK, PHIL TELLS ME YOU'RE DOING WELL, BUT WE'VE GOT A SNAPPLE CONTRACT THAT PROHIBITS US FROM CARRYING OTHER BOTTLED TEAS.

...

TWO YEARS LATER

GUESS WHAT? DICK RETIRED LAST MONTH, AND I'M IN CHARGE NOW.

WE'LL GIVE YOU A TRY.

BUT DON'T GET TOO EXCITED. WE'LL ONLY CARRY FOUR VARIETIES IN ONE WAREHOUSE, AND WE'LL REQUIRE A PERPETUAL CONTRACT.

THAT'S AWESOME!

...I THINK.

WE WANTED OUR BOTTLES TO STAND OUT ON THE SHELF. SINCE WE COULDN'T AFFORD MOLDS FOR A SQUARE BOTTLE, WE CHOSE THE UNIQUE LOOK OF FRONT AND BACK SPOT LABELS INSTEAD OF THE USUAL WRAPAROUND LABELS.

$180,000

WE LOVED THE SPOT LABELS—THEY EVOKED THE LOOK OF A WINE BOTTLE, WHICH HELPED CONVEY THE PREMIUM QUALITY OF OUR TEA.

UNLIKE OTHER BOTTLED TEAS, WHOSE LABELS COVER UP THE LIQUID, OUR LABELS MADE IT CLEAR WE HAD NOTHING TO HIDE—INCLUDING BITS OF TEA LEAVES FLOATING AROUND. BUT THE SPOT LABELS HAD THEIR OWN COSTS.

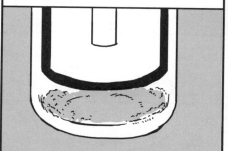

AT FIRST, WE HAD TO SEND OUR BOTTLES TO CINNAMINSON, NJ, TO HAVE THE SPOT LABELS APPLIED.

WE'VE IMPROVED HOW WE BREW AND BOTTLE OUR TEA, BUT WHATEVER MONEY WE'RE SAVING IS GETTING LOST ON THE EXTRA FREIGHT AND LABOR TO SHIP IT TO NEW JERSEY, OPEN THE CASES, LABEL THE BOTTLES, RE-SEAL THE CASES, AND RE-SHIP THEM.

AND, OF COURSE, IT DOESN'T HELP THAT THEY KEEP MAKING BOTTLES WITH A FRONT LABEL FROM ONE TEA AND A BACK LABEL FROM ANOTHER.

WHEN WE BOUGHT THE THREE RIVERS PLANT, WE DECIDED TO BRING THE LABELING ON-SITE. SINCE WE COULDN'T AFFORD $250,000 FOR A NEW LABELER, WE BOUGHT A USED ONE FOR $52,000.

WE'VE GOT THE PRODUCTION LINE AT THREE RIVERS WORKING AT 200 BOTTLES PER MINUTE.

WOW, THAT SOUNDS FAST.

YUP. THERE'S JUST ONE PROBLEM. THE SPOT LABELER CAN ONLY RUN AT 120 BOTTLES PER MINUTE.

SO OUR LABELER IS HOLDING UP THE REST OF THE LINE?

YEAH, AND THAT'S WHEN IT'S IN A GOOD MOOD. WHEN IT'S CRANKY, WE LOSE ALMOST AS MANY LABELS AS WE PUT ON. AND WHEN IT BREAKS DOWN, LIKE IT DID LAST WEEK, WE'RE STUCK.

SETH, SOMETHING'S GOTTA GIVE. I KNOW YOU'RE PART OWNERS OF THE PLANT, BUT WE'RE GOING TO HAVE TO CHARGE YOU MORE.

ALL THIS EXTRA DOWNTIME FROM THE LABELER IS COSTING THE PLANT $500 AN HOUR.

MEANWHILE, WE NEEDED TO PRODUCE ON THE WEST COAST TO SAVE SHIPPING COSTS. WE MANAGED TO FIND A BOTTLING PLANT IN CALIFORNIA THAT HAD A SPOT LABELER, BUT ITS LINE SPEED WAS EVEN SLOWER.

WELL, WE GOT HER UP TO 60 BOTTLES PER MINUTE LAST WEEK... BUT SHE KEEPS BREAKING DOWN.

SOMETIMES I THINK WE MIGHT HAVE SAVED MONEY IF WE HAD INVESTED $180,000 IN THOSE SQUARE BOTTLE MOLDS INSTEAD OF THE SPOT LABELS.

$180,000

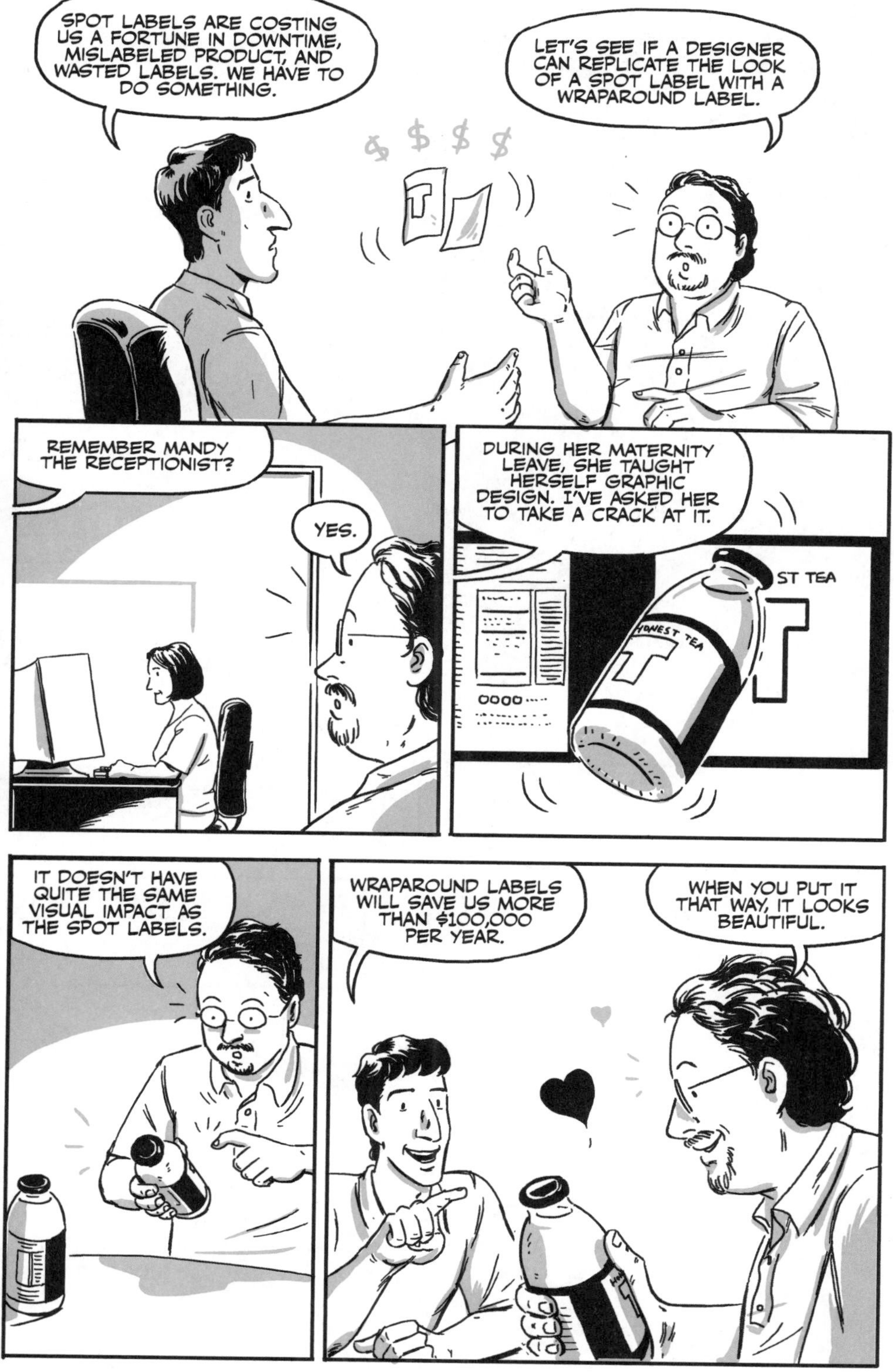
SPOT LABELS ARE COSTING US A FORTUNE IN DOWNTIME, MISLABELED PRODUCT, AND WASTED LABELS. WE HAVE TO DO SOMETHING.
LET'S SEE IF A DESIGNER CAN REPLICATE THE LOOK OF A SPOT LABEL WITH A WRAPAROUND LABEL.
REMEMBER MANDY THE RECEPTIONIST?
YES.
DURING HER MATERNITY LEAVE, SHE TAUGHT HERSELF GRAPHIC DESIGN. I'VE ASKED HER TO TAKE A CRACK AT IT.
ST TEA
HONEST TEA
IT DOESN'T HAVE QUITE THE SAME VISUAL IMPACT AS THE SPOT LABELS.
WRAPAROUND LABELS WILL SAVE US MORE THAN $100,000 PER YEAR.
WHEN YOU PUT IT THAT WAY, IT LOOKS BEAUTIFUL.

OUR ADVERTISING BUDGET WAS ROUGHLY $0, SO OUR NAME ONLY APPEARED IN PRINT WHEN IT WAS FOR FREE. FORTUNATELY, A PROFESSOR AND HIS STUDENT STARTING A COMPANY TOGETHER MADE FOR A GOOD NEWS STORY. THE *NEW YORK TIMES* RAN A LONG PIECE ON THE FRONT PAGE OF THEIR BUSINESS SECTION, AS DID THE *WASHINGTON POST.*

Business Day
The New York Times

MANAGEMENT; TEA BY TWO

BY CONSTANCE L. HAYS
AUGUST 2, 2000

It hardly seems the stuff consumer thrills are made of: a weak, watery tea, brewed the old-fashioned way, with hardly any sugar and even less caffeine. Marketing? There is almost none. Edgy television ads and celebrity endorsements? Zero.

…As luck, or insight, would have it, when Honest Tea started landing on store shelves, consumers were showing a distinct preference for bottled water and other beverages perceived to be more healthful.

Tea by Two

THE TEA ITSELF WAS AN EVEN BETTER MEDIA DRAW, GARNERING COVERAGE IN *PREVENTION, MEN'S HEALTH, FOOD & WINE,* AND THE FRENCH VERSION OF *ELLE*—THOUGH THAT LAST ONE DIDN'T REALLY HELP SALES.

Men'sHealth

WHICH BOTTLED GREEN TEA PACKS THE MOST NUTRITIONAL PUNCH? HONEST TEA'S ORGANIC HONEY GREEN TEA. IT'S THE KING OF CATECHINS, WITH ONLY A SMIDGEN OF SUGAR.

FOOD&WINE

THE NATION'S LEADING PRODUCT-TESTING MAGAZINE—A COMPANY THAT OBJECTS IF YOU QUOTE IT BY NAME—WROTE: "HONEST TEA TOPPED OUR RATINGS AND ALSO HAD THE FEWEST CALORIES OF ANY NON-DIET TEA."

OUR TEA ALSO LANDED SOME TV APPEARANCES.

CBS EARLY SHOW

AFTER TESTING 20 DIFFERENT BOTTLED ICED TEAS, THESE ARE THE THREE WINNERS. THIS IS CALLED LORI'S LEMON FROM HONEST TEA... IT'S DELICIOUS. IT'S GOT A SLIGHTLY HERBAL FLAVOR WITH A NICE HIT OF LEMON. IT'S LIGHT AND NOT TOO SYRUPY SWEET...

TODAY SHOW

THIS ONE TASTES LIKE REAL TEA.

WE GOT WRITE-UPS IN SEVERAL INDUSTRY PUBLICATIONS AS WELL, THOUGH THERE WAS OFTEN AN IMPLICIT QUID PRO QUO.

BEVERAGEWORLD

FANCY FOOD SHOW

WE'VE BEEN GIVING YOU SO MUCH FREE PUBLICITY, CAN'T YOU BUY AN AD FROM US?

WE JUST DON'T HAVE ANY MONEY FOR ADS. BUT WE CAN OFFER YOU A RIDE BACK TO MIDTOWN IN OUR HAARLEM HONEYBUS.

BARRY NATHANSON, PUBLISHER OF *BEVERAGE AISLE*, WAS INFAMOUS FOR HIS ABILITY TO SELL AD SPACE.

FMG = BARRY NALEBUFF?

ACTUALLY, IT IS MY BAG. I GOT IT AT THE L.L. BEAN OUTLET AT A HUGE DISCOUNT AFTER SOME CUSTOMER HAD IT MONOGRAMMED AND THEN RETURNED IT.

WHOSE BAG IS THAT? THOSE AREN'T YOUR INITIALS.

WOW, YOU GUYS REALLY ARE HARD UP.

OK, I GUESS YOU DON'T HAVE TO BUY ANY ADS.

AND I MIGHT HAVE AN EXTRA BAG WITH A BN MONOGRAM FOR YOU.

SOLD!

WHEN YOU'RE RELYING ON FREE MARKETING, IT'S BEST TO REMEMBER LOUIS PASTEUR'S WORDS:

CHANCE FAVORS THE PREPARED MIND.

ON A SOUTHWEST FLIGHT FROM D.C.

ATTENTION, PASSENGERS. WE DON'T USUALLY DO THIS, BUT JAKE HERE IS A SUMMER INTERN ON HIS WAY TO MAKE HIS FIRST BIG SALES PRESENTATION. HE'S ASKED IF IT'S OK TO PRACTICE ON US.

HI, EVERYONE. I'M WITH HONEST TEA. WHAT MAKES OUR TEA HONEST? WE USE REAL TEA LEAVES AND NOTHING ARTIFICIAL. IT'S A GREAT-TASTING TEA WITH ONE-SIXTH THE SUGAR OF MOST BOTTLED TEAS...

AT A YOGA RETREAT IN CALIFORNIA

WHAT ARE THE ODDS...

OPRAH!

THAT'S GREAT YOU HAD TEA WITH YOU. HOW DID YOU KNOW OPRAH WOULD BE THERE?

I DIDN'T. I JUST ALWAYS HAVE TEA WITH ME.

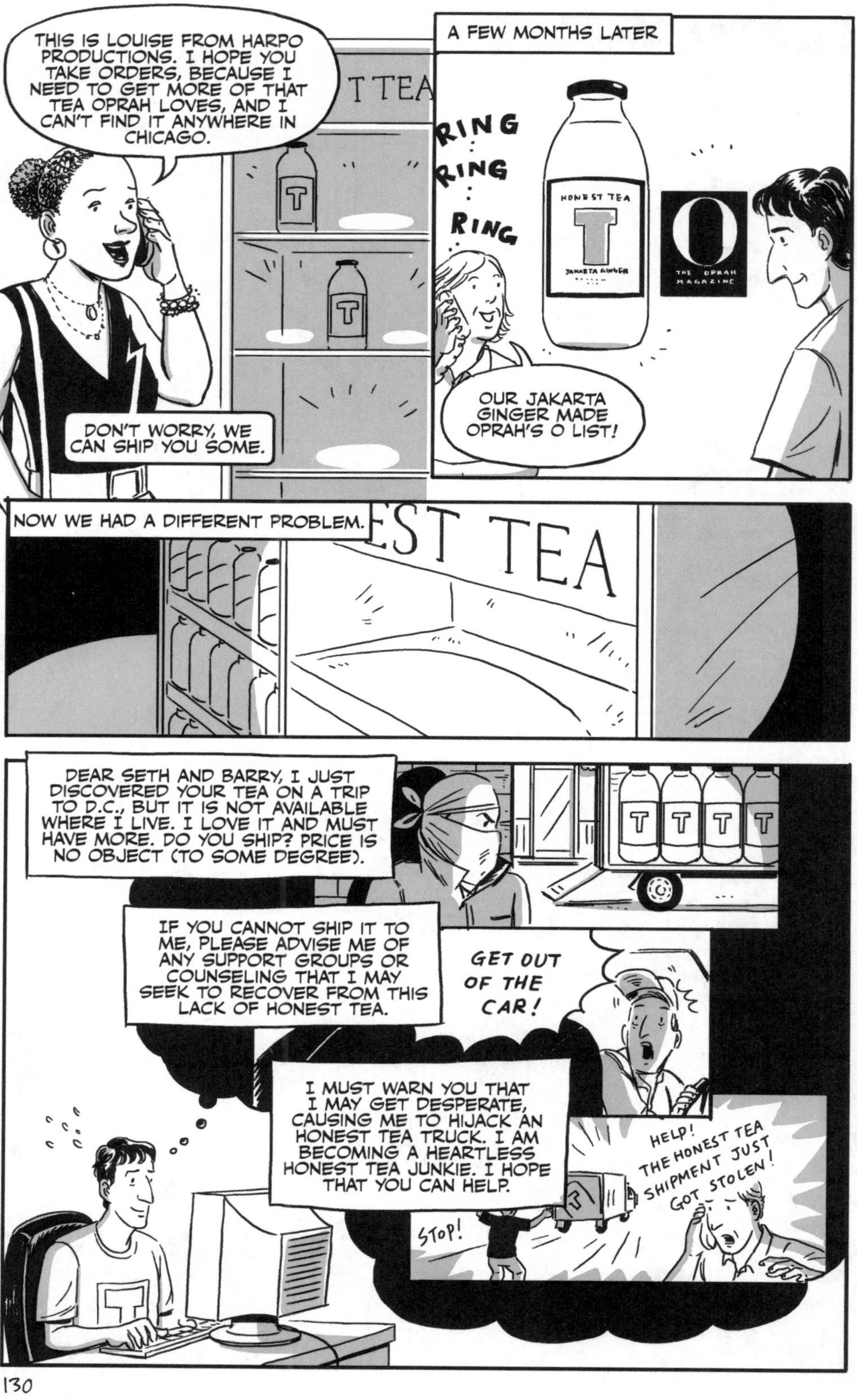
THIS IS LOUISE FROM HARPO PRODUCTIONS. I HOPE YOU TAKE ORDERS, BECAUSE I NEED TO GET MORE OF THAT TEA OPRAH LOVES, AND I CAN'T FIND IT ANYWHERE IN CHICAGO.
T TEA
DON'T WORRY, WE CAN SHIP YOU SOME.
A FEW MONTHS LATER
RING
RING
RING
HONEST TEA
T
JAKARTA GINGER
O
THE OPRAH MAGAZINE
OUR JAKARTA GINGER MADE OPRAH'S O LIST!
NOW WE HAD A DIFFERENT PROBLEM.
EST TEA
DEAR SETH AND BARRY, I JUST DISCOVERED YOUR TEA ON A TRIP TO D.C., BUT IT IS NOT AVAILABLE WHERE I LIVE. I LOVE IT AND MUST HAVE MORE. DO YOU SHIP? PRICE IS NO OBJECT (TO SOME DEGREE).
IF YOU CANNOT SHIP IT TO ME, PLEASE ADVISE ME OF ANY SUPPORT GROUPS OR COUNSELING THAT I MAY SEEK TO RECOVER FROM THIS LACK OF HONEST TEA.
GET OUT OF THE CAR!
I MUST WARN YOU THAT I MAY GET DESPERATE, CAUSING ME TO HIJACK AN HONEST TEA TRUCK. I AM BECOMING A HEARTLESS HONEST TEA JUNKIE. I HOPE THAT YOU CAN HELP.
HELP! THE HONEST TEA SHIPMENT JUST GOT STOLEN!
STOP!

HAVING GROWN 73% IN 2000, WE SAW EXCITING OPPORTUNITIES AHEAD. WE JUST NEEDED SOME MONEY TO TAKE ADVANTAGE OF THEM.

HOW MUCH DO WE NEED TO RAISE?

$2m

IDEALLY $2 MILLION, SO WE DON'T NEED TO WORRY ABOUT RAISING MONEY FOR AT LEAST TWO YEARS.

IF WE'RE RAISING ENOUGH CASH TO LAST TWO YEARS, WE SHOULD DO IT AT A VALUATION WE WON'T REGRET WHEN WE'RE MUCH LARGER.

LAST YEAR'S SALES WERE $1.9 MILLION; WHAT DO YOU THINK WE CAN DO IN 2001?

IF WE HAVE THE MONEY TO HIRE MORE PEOPLE AND DO MARKETING, I DON'T SEE WHY WE CAN'T REACH $7.5 MILLION.

THEN WE SHOULD ASK FOR A VALUATION TWICE THAT: $15 MILLION.

$7.5m

X2

MEETING WITH INVESTORS

I LIKE THE WAY THE BUSINESS IS DEVELOPING, BUT YOUR VALUATION IS A LITTLE RICH.

AND WITH ALL THOSE WARRANTS YOU'VE GOT, I'LL GET MORE DILUTED AS THE COMPANY GROWS.

IT'S ONE THING TO BASE YOUR VALUATION ON PAST YEARS' SALES; IT'S ANOTHER TO BASE IT ON SALES THAT HAVEN'T HAPPENED YET.

WE'RE CONFIDENT WE'LL HIT OUR TARGETS.

CONFIDENT ENOUGH TO GUARANTEE IT?

IF YOU HIT YOUR GOALS, THIS IS A FAIR OFFERING. BUT IF YOU DON'T, I'D LIKE TO SEE YOU PROTECT INVESTORS.

MEANING, IF OUR SALES FALL SHORT, WE WOULD GIVE UP SOME OF OUR SHARES TO JUSTIFY THE PROPOSED STOCK PRICE.

IF YOU DO THAT, I'M IN.

AS YOUR LAWYER, I DON'T RECOMMEND MAKING A GUARANTEE.

BUT IF WE DON'T, WE'LL HAVE TO LOWER THE VALUATION, AND WE'LL BE GIVING UP SHARES THROUGH DILUTION ANYWAY.

IT TURNED OUT 2001 WAS THE WRONG YEAR TO MAKE A GUARANTEE.

OH MY GOD.

THE NATION FINDS ITSELF PUSHED OVER THE EDGE INTO AN ALMOST CERTAIN RECESSION.

NASDAQ

AFTER 9/11, WE DECIDED TO CLOSE THE FUNDRAISING ROUND AT $1.6 MILLION, WELL SHORT OF OUR GOAL. WE STILL GREW AT NEARLY 70% IN 2001—NOT BAD, EXCEPT OUR $3.2 MILLION IN SALES WAS A FAR CRY FROM THE $7 MILLION WE GUARANTEED. AS A RESULT, WE HAD TO TRANSFER 125,000 OF OUR SHARES TO INVESTORS. *OUCH.*

ARE YOU SITTING DOWN?

WHAT NOW, GEORGE?

OCTOBER 2, 2001

WE'VE HAD TO SHUT DOWN THE PLANT.

HOW COME?

THREE RIVERS BOTTLING

WE GOT A CALL FROM DENVER POLICE THAT SOMEONE FOUND WHAT APPEARS TO BE A SEVERED PART OF THE MALE ANATOMY INSIDE A BOTTLE OF ORA POTENCY FRUIT PUNCH MADE AT OUR PLANT.

WHAT?!

I THOUGHT IT WAS SOME KIND OF PRANK, BUT THE POLICE ARE TAKING IT SERIOUSLY.

ENTER · POLICE · DO NOT

THE CORONER OUT THERE IS DOING TESTS AS WE SPEAK.

CSI

I'VE GOT TO CALL DENISE.

WHAT?!

EVERYTHING OK?

I DON'T KNOW. I'M PART OWNER OF A BOTTLING PLANT, AND A GUY IN COLORADO JUST FOUND SOMETHING IN ONE OF OUR BOTTLES.

A MALE SURPRISE?

HOW DO YOU KNOW ABOUT THAT!?

AND THE TOP NEWS TODAY: THERE'S A DRINK CALLED ORA POTENCY FRUIT PUNCH. AND THEY'RE NOT KIDDING. AFTER DRINKING MOST OF THE BOTTLE, JUAN SANCHEZ-MARCHEZ FOUND WHAT APPEARED TO BE 3" OF A SEVERED...

THE POLICE EXAMINED MR. SANCHEZ-MARCHEZ AND CONFIRMED THAT HE WASN'T MISSING ANY PARTS.

ACCORDING TO MR. SANCHEZ-MARCHEZ...

"IT'S A REALLY GOOD DRINK, BUT I'M NOT GOING TO DRINK IT ANYMORE."

IT'S ALL OVER THE WEB, TOO.

THE LARGEST ROADBLOCK IN THE INVESTIGATION IS THAT THE MISSING ITEM IS 3" LONG. IF THEY EVER DO FIND ITS OWNER, HE'S PROBABLY NOT GOING TO ADMIT IT'S HIS.

SETH, MORE BAD NEWS: KING SOOPERS HAVE PULLED THE PRODUCT FROM THEIR SHELVES, AND ORA IS RECALLING ALL ITS PRODUCTS IN COLORADO.

COULD SOMEONE HAVE PLANTED IT TO SET UP A LAWSUIT?

ANYTHING'S POSSIBLE. REGARDLESS, THIS COULD PUT OUR PLANT OUT OF BUSINESS.

HAVE YOU SEEN THE EVIDENCE?

I DON'T HAVE THE BOTTLE, BUT THE POLICE SENT ME A PICTURE. I'M FORWARDING IT TO YOU NOW.

THIS ISN'T HAPPENING.

CADAVER? VICTIM? ANIMAL?

TWO DAYS LATER

MOLD?!

IT WAS JUST A BROKEN SEAL. MOLD GOT INSIDE THE BOTTLE AND GREW INTO AN, AHEM, UNUSUAL SHAPE.

THAT'S GREAT NEWS! BUT I STILL WOULDN'T WANT IT IN MY DRINK.

NO KIDDING. THE ORA BRAND IS DEAD. AND THE RECALL AND PLANT SHUTDOWN ARE GOING TO COST US A FORTUNE.

RIP

ORA

PERHAPS SOMEDAY WE'LL BE ABLE TO LOOK BACK ON THIS AND LAUGH. YOU KNOW, IT COULD HAVE BEEN WORSE.

YEAH, IT COULD'VE BEEN IN A BOTTLE OF HONEST TEA.

EVEN WORSE. IT COULD'VE BEEN THE REAL THING.

HOW DO YOU DECIDE WHAT PRICE TO CHARGE?

IT'S A THREE-PART PROCESS. FIRST, WE NEED TO FIGURE OUT THE RELATIONSHIP BETWEEN OUR PRICE AND WHAT CONSUMERS PAY.

SAY WE WANT CONSUMERS TO SEE $1.39 AT THE REGISTER. SUPERMARKETS WORK ON A 30% MARGIN. THAT MEANS THE WHOLESALE PRICE HAS TO BE 97¢/BOTTLE.

$$\$1.39 \times 70\% = \$0.97$$

I THOUGHT SUPERMARKETS OPERATE ON A 2% MARGIN.

OVERALL, THEY DO. THEY MAKE 2% WHEN YOU TAKE INTO ACCOUNT ALL THEIR FIXED COSTS LIKE RENT, LABOR, UTILITIES, AND SPOILED PRODUCT. BUT WHEN YOU BUY SOMETHING PRICED AT $1.39, THEIR COST IS TYPICALLY 97¢.

DISTRIBUTORS ALSO WORK ON A 30% MARGIN. IF WE WANT THEM TO CHARGE RETAILERS 97¢, WE HAVE TO SELL TO THEM AT 68¢.

$$\$0.97 \times 70\% = \$0.68^*$$

SUPERMARKET — 42¢

DISTRIBUTOR — 29¢

HONEST TEA PROFIT — 23¢

HONEST TEA COST — 45¢

*HERE WE'VE ROUNDED NUMBERS TO THE NEAREST PENNY, BUT YOU SHOULDN'T—THOSE FRACTIONS OF A CENT ADD UP!

THE END PRICE IS MORE THAN DOUBLE WHAT YOU CHARGE.

68¢

23¢

45¢

YUP. 68¢ GOES TO $1.39.

SO HOW DID YOU PICK THE $1.39?

IN THE BEGINNING, WE CHOSE A PRICE BASED ON WHERE WE WANTED TO BE POSITIONED IN THE MARKET.

BUT HOW DO YOU KNOW $1.39 IS THE RIGHT PRICE TODAY?

THAT'S PARTS TWO AND THREE. IF WE RAISE OUR PRICE, WE HAVE TO THINK ABOUT WHAT THAT WOULD DO TO OUR MARGINS AND TO OUR SALES.

IF WE CHARGE AN EXTRA PENNY, OUR WHOLESALE PRICE GOES TO 69¢ OR UP 1.5%. BUT OUR PROFIT MARGIN GOES FROM 23¢ TO 24¢ A BOTTLE, A 4% INCREASE!

+ 1¢

23¢ → 24¢

HOW MANY THINK WE SHOULD RAISE THE PRICE?

HMMM... ABOUT TWO-THIRDS OF YOU.

NOT ME. THE PRICE INCREASE WILL SLOW YOUR SALES.

THAT EXTRA PENNY WOULD ADD 2¢ TO THE PRICE AT THE STORE.

1¢ = 1¢ 1¢

WE HOPE. BUT, STORES MIGHT BUMP UP THE PRICE BY A DIME SINCE $1.41 DOESN'T FIT THEIR NORMAL PRICING PATTERN.

99¢ $1.09 $1.19 $1.29
$1.39 $1.49

OUR SALES ARE GROWING AT 67%. IF THE PRICE INCREASE CUTS OUR GROWTH TO 60%, IT WOULD LOWER OUR PROFITS.

$$1.67 \times \$0.23 > 1.60 \times \$0.24$$

EVEN IF THE EXTRA PENNY INCREASED PROFITS TODAY, WE STILL MIGHT NOT DO IT. WE WANT TO DEMONSTRATE FAST GROWTH TO EXCITE DISTRIBUTORS AND INVESTORS.

1¢

THAT'S WHY WE STARTED OFF WITH FIELD-OF-DREAMS PRICING. WE'D NEVER REACH THE VOLUME TO BRING OUR COSTS DOWN UNLESS WE PRICED BASED ON COSTS FOR THE VOLUME WE HOPED TO ACHIEVE.

SALES GROWTH ALSO HELPS LOWER OUR COSTS, WHICH ALLOWS US TO LOWER OUR PRICE AND GROW EVEN FASTER. IT'S A VIRTUOUS CYCLE.

SALES GROWTH → LOWER COST → LOWER WHOLE-SALE PRICE → LOWER PRICE →

WHY DO STORES AND DISTRIBUTORS SET THEIR PRICE BASED ON FIXED MARGINS? SHOULDN'T THEY JUST ADD A FIXED AMOUNT PER BOTTLE?

THE 30% MARGIN IS A SIMPLE RULE OF THUMB, AND IT'S VERY EFFECTIVE AT STOPPING US (AND OTHERS) FROM CHARGING MORE. ANY PRICE INCREASE FROM US GETS DOUBLED. TO AVOID THE EXTRA LOSS IN SALES, WE DON'T RAISE PRICES AS MUCH.

WE LEARNED ABOUT THIS IN ECON. IT'S THE PROBLEM OF DOUBLE MARGINALIZATION.

ACTUALLY, WHEN YOU COUNT THE DISTRIBUTOR, WE HAVE TRIPLE MARGINALIZATION.

×3

UNFORTUNATELY, THE 30% MARGIN RULE IS UNFAIR TO US. STORES MAKE 30¢ WHEN THEY SELL A SNAPPLE, AND 42¢ WHEN THEY SELL AN HONEST TEA, EVEN THOUGH THE BOTTLES TAKE UP THE SAME AMOUNT OF SHELF SPACE.

WHAT WOULD YOU DO IF YOU OWNED THE STORE?

10% + 20¢

INSTEAD OF A FLAT 30%, I'D SET MARGINS AT 10% PLUS 20¢. THAT WOULD KEEP THE PRICE OF SNAPPLE AT 99¢ AND LOWER THE PRICE OF HONEST TEA TO $1.29.

YOU'RE JUST SAYING THAT BECAUSE YOU WANT TO HELP HONEST TEA.

Lowest Price!

Sale

IT ALSO HELPS THE STORE BY SHIFTING SALES TO HONEST TEA, WHERE IT MAKES 2¢ MORE A BOTTLE.

DING!

2¢ more

I THINK YOU'RE IN THE WRONG BUSINESS. DISTRIBUTORS ARE MAKING MORE THAN YOU DO— ALMOST $3.50 A CASE—JUST TO DROP OFF YOUR PRODUCT.

YOU'RE NOT THE FIRST TO THINK THAT.

QUAKER OATS THOUGHT THE SAME THING WHEN THEY BOUGHT SNAPPLE. THOMAS LEE, THE VENTURE CAPITALIST BEHIND THE DEAL, CAME TO OUR CLASS LAST YEAR TO EXPLAIN THE LOGIC.

HI, EVERYONE!

IN 1994, SNAPPLE SOLD 60 MILLION 24-PACK CASES. QUAKER FIGURED THEY COULD SAVE $3.50 A CASE BY BYPASSING DISTRIBUTORS AND SHIPPING DIRECTLY TO THE STORES, JUST LIKE THEY DO WITH GATORADE.

THAT'S $210 MILLION PRE-TAX, OR $126 MILLION AFTER TAX. A COMPANY WOULD VALUE THOSE SAVINGS AT $1.26 BILLION IN PRESENT DISCOUNTED VALUE.

EXACTLY. THAT'S WHY QUAKER THOUGHT $1.7 BILLION WAS A GOOD PRICE. NET OF COST SAVINGS, THEY WERE ONLY PAYING $440 MILLION FOR THE BRAND.

THEY DIDN'T REALIZE DISTRIBUTORS DO MORE THAN JUST DROP OFF THE PRODUCT. THE GOOD ONES MAKE SURE YOUR PRODUCTS ARE ON THE SHELVES AND NO ONE ELSE HAS STOLEN YOUR SPACE.

QUAKER DID SAVE A BOATLOAD ON DISTRIBUTION, BUT THEIR SALES PLUMMETED.

FIRING WENDY THE SNAPPLE LADY AND HOWARD STERN HURT SALES, TOO. 27 MONTHS LATER, QUAKER SOLD SNAPPLE FOR $300 MILLION AND UNFORTUNATELY QUAKER CEO BILL SMITHBURG LOST HIS JOB.

TRYING TO CUT OUT YOUR DISTRIBUTORS (AND SPOKESPEOPLE) CAN BE A REALLY BAD IDEA.

I DON'T SEE ANY HONEST TEA IN THE COOLER...

I'M DISAPPOINTED YOU AREN'T CARRYING HONEST TEA IN THE COLD CASE. ACCORDING TO THIS MARKET DATA, WE OUTSELL OTHER BRANDS YOU HAVE HERE BY 2 TO 1...

I KNOW ALL THAT.

WE USED TO CARRY IT THERE. BUT THE COOLER WAS EMPTY BY NOON. EVEN IF WE RESTOCKED IT THE DRINKS WEREN'T COLD. WE GOT LOTS OF COMPLAINTS.

THIS IS CRAZY! IF HIS BOSS KNEW WHAT WAS GOING ON, HE'D BE FIRED.

SO YOU'RE SAYING WE GOT TAKEN OUT BECAUSE WE SOLD TOO WELL?

THAT'S IT.

A COUPLE OF DAYS LATER

HERE'S A NEW HONEST TEA COOLER. NOW YOU DON'T HAVE TO WORRY ABOUT RUNNING OUT.

THANKS! IT'S PERFECT!

HONEST TEA

AFTER THE CRAZINESS OF 2001, THINGS WERE LOOKING BETTER BY EARLY 2002. WE WERE UP AND RUNNING WITH CANADA DRY POTOMAC, GIVING US TOP-TIER DISTRIBUTION IN OUR HOME MARKET, AND WE SAW GREAT RESULTS IN NEW YORK IN OUR FIRST YEAR WITH BIG GEYSER.

New York

WHILE SALES WERE GROWING AT NEARLY 70%, OUR PROFIT MARGIN WAS STILL UNDER 25%, AND WE FOUND OURSELVES PERPETUALLY SHORT ON CASH.

THUS, OUR SEARCH FOR INVESTMENT CAPITAL CONTINUED. MOST INVESTMENTS CAME IN ONE AT A TIME, AND IT USUALLY TOOK FIVE PROSPECTS TO LAND ONE NEW INVESTOR. IN THE HOPES OF INCREASING HIS YIELD, SETH DECIDED TO TRY PRESENTING TO INVESTMENT GROUPS.

I LIKE YOUR BRAND. MY WIFE EVEN LIKES THE TASTE OF IT.

AT THE DINNER CLUB, A NORTHERN VIRGINIA CLUB FOR TECH INVESTORS

BUT I'VE GOT A FRIEND LAUNCHING VAPOR-WEAR.COM. I DON'T QUITE UNDERSTAND HOW IT WORKS, BUT HIS EQUITY STRUCTURE IS STRAIGHTFORWARD.

AT THE INVESTORS' CIRCLE CONFERENCE, A GATHERING OF SOCIALLY RESPONSIBLE INVESTORS

LET ME GET THIS STRAIGHT: YOUR SALES IN 2001 WERE $3.2 MILLION, BUT YOU CLAIM YOUR COMPANY IS WORTH $13 MILLION?

WE'RE PROJECTING SALES OF $7.6 MILLION FOR 2002, SO THAT VALUATION IS LESS THAN TWICE SALES. SOBE JUST SOLD TO PEPSI FOR 2.2 TIMES SALES, AND WE'RE ONLY AT THE BEGINNING OF OUR GROWTH CURVE.

THAT TARGET SEEMS AMBITIOUS, AND THE VALUATION'S A LITTLE RICH FOR ME. PERHAPS I'D INVEST AT A VALUATION BELOW $10 MILLION, BUT, OF COURSE, I'D WANT PREFERRED STOCK.

HONEST TEA IS GOING TO BE WORTH EITHER A WHOLE LOT OR NOTHING. IF WE GO OUT OF BUSINESS, OUR ASSETS WILL BE STACKS OF LABELS, EMPTY BOTTLES, AND CASES OF TEA THAT COST MORE TO SHIP THAN THEY'RE WORTH.

BUT IF WE'RE ABLE TO BREAK THROUGH AS A NATIONAL BRAND, WE'LL BE WORTH WELL MORE THAN $13 MILLION, AND THIS QUIBBLING WILL SEEM FOOLISH.

GOOD LUCK. FOR NOW, I'LL BE PUTTING MY MONEY INTO ECO-PUPPETS.COM. BUT KEEP ME POSTED. LET ME KNOW IF YOU GET A LEAD INVESTOR—I MIGHT BE INTERESTED.

I NEED YOUR SUPPORT NOW, NOT WHEN I GET A LEAD INVESTOR.

HEY, SETH! HOW'S IT GOING?

REALLY WELL. WE JUST BECAME THE BESTSELLING TEA IN NATURAL FOODS. AND THAT'S DESPITE NOT YET BEING AUTHORIZED FOR ANY WHOLE FOODS MARKETS IN THE NORTHEAST.

GARY HIRSHBERG

YOUR TEA IS SELLING WELL AT OUR RESTAURANT, O'NATURALS. YOU'RE REALLY ONTO SOMETHING. MY WIFE, MEG, IS ADDICTED TO COMMUNITY GREEN.

THAT'S GREAT TO HEAR. I WISH THE INVESTORS' CIRCLE FOLKS SAW THE SAME POTENTIAL.

OH, YEAH, HOW DID IT GO INSIDE?

IT WAS ALL KUMBAYA— THEY SAY THEY ADMIRE WHAT WE'RE DOING, BUT I'M NOT SEEING ANY CHECKS.

WE SHOULD TALK. I JUST SIGNED A DEAL WITH GROUPE DANONE. THEY'RE BUYING 40% OF STONYFIELD FARM.

WOW! CONGRATULATIONS.

THANKS. PUTTING TOGETHER THE DEAL TOOK MORE THAN TWO YEARS, BUT I GOT A STRUCTURE THAT LETS ME KEEP CONTROL, AND MY EQUITY, TOO. PLUS, THEY WANT ME TO IDENTIFY FUTURE GROWTH OPPORTUNITIES FOR DANONE.

WELL, WE ARE TRYING TO RAISE $1.5 MILLION. WE'VE GOT VENTURE CAPITAL FIRMS OFFERING TO TAKE ALL OF IT, BUT THEY'RE BEATING US UP ON VALUATION.

I'M ABSOLUTELY CONVINCED THAT PURE FINANCIAL INVESTORS AREN'T WHO YOU NEED. LET ME SEE IF I CAN ARRANGE FOR STONYFIELD TO PARTICIPATE.

THAT WOULD BE AMAZING.

IF WE DO COME IN, WE'LL WANT TO BUY MOST OF THE AVAILABLE STOCK. MEG AND I WILL WANT TO INVEST PERSONALLY, AND I'LL WANT A BOARD SEAT—IF I CAN HELP YOU AVOID HALF THE MISTAKES I MADE, MY ADVICE WILL BE WORTH TWICE AS MUCH AS WE INVEST.

I'D BE HONORED.

OH, AND LET ME CHECK IN WITH TIM SPERRY, THE WHOLE FOODS BUYER IN THE NORTHEAST. HE'S MISSING OUT.

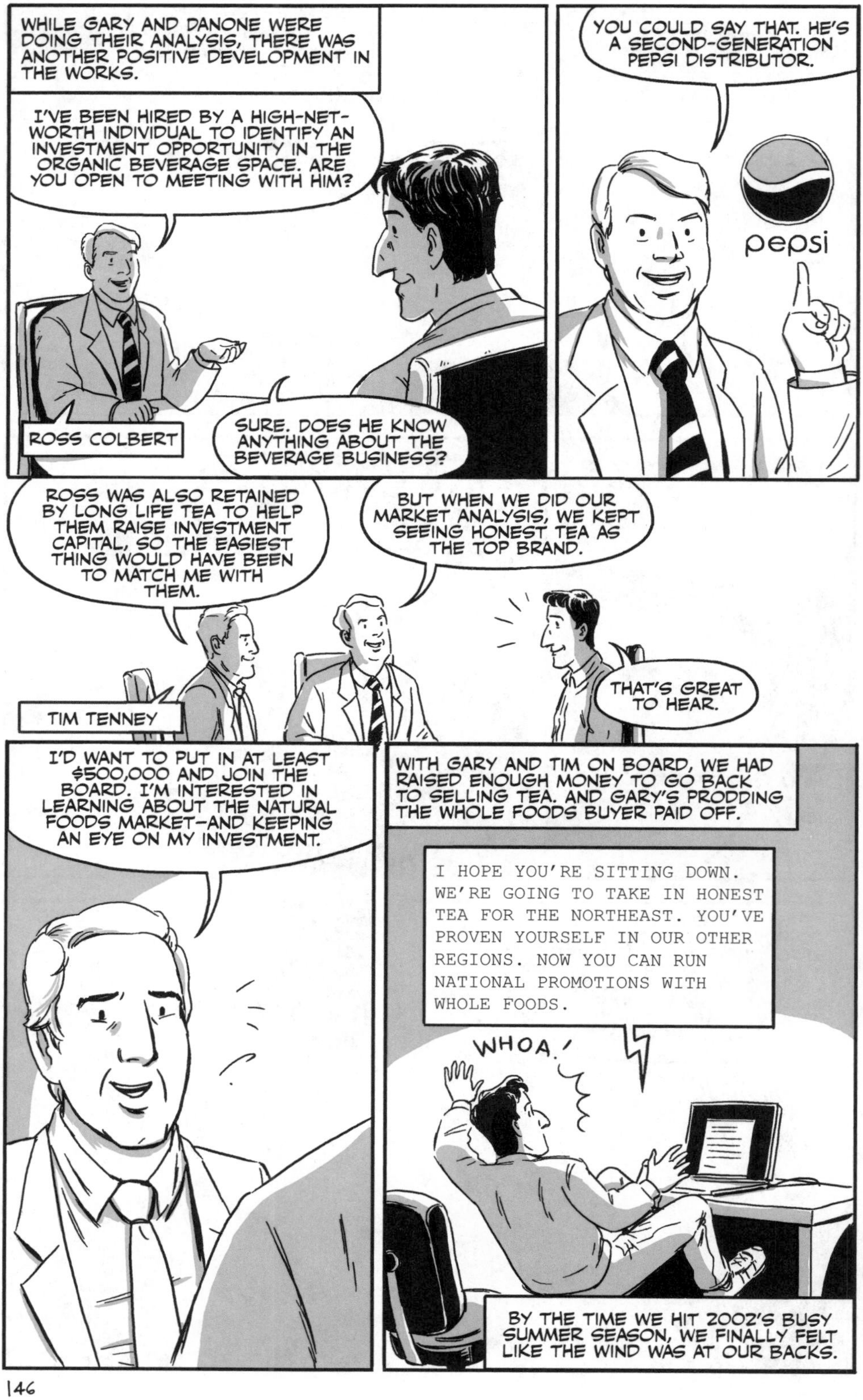

WHILE GARY AND DANONE WERE DOING THEIR ANALYSIS, THERE WAS ANOTHER POSITIVE DEVELOPMENT IN THE WORKS.
I'VE BEEN HIRED BY A HIGH-NET-WORTH INDIVIDUAL TO IDENTIFY AN INVESTMENT OPPORTUNITY IN THE ORGANIC BEVERAGE SPACE. ARE YOU OPEN TO MEETING WITH HIM?
ROSS COLBERT
SURE. DOES HE KNOW ANYTHING ABOUT THE BEVERAGE BUSINESS?
YOU COULD SAY THAT. HE'S A SECOND-GENERATION PEPSI DISTRIBUTOR.
pepsi
ROSS WAS ALSO RETAINED BY LONG LIFE TEA TO HELP THEM RAISE INVESTMENT CAPITAL, SO THE EASIEST THING WOULD HAVE BEEN TO MATCH ME WITH THEM.
BUT WHEN WE DID OUR MARKET ANALYSIS, WE KEPT SEEING HONEST TEA AS THE TOP BRAND.
TIM TENNEY
THAT'S GREAT TO HEAR.
I'D WANT TO PUT IN AT LEAST $500,000 AND JOIN THE BOARD. I'M INTERESTED IN LEARNING ABOUT THE NATURAL FOODS MARKET—AND KEEPING AN EYE ON MY INVESTMENT.
WITH GARY AND TIM ON BOARD, WE HAD RAISED ENOUGH MONEY TO GO BACK TO SELLING TEA. AND GARY'S PRODDING THE WHOLE FOODS BUYER PAID OFF.
I HOPE YOU'RE SITTING DOWN. WE'RE GOING TO TAKE IN HONEST TEA FOR THE NORTHEAST. YOU'VE PROVEN YOURSELF IN OUR OTHER REGIONS. NOW YOU CAN RUN NATIONAL PROMOTIONS WITH WHOLE FOODS.
WHOA!
BY THE TIME WE HIT 2002'S BUSY SUMMER SEASON, WE FINALLY FELT LIKE THE WIND WAS AT OUR BACKS.

NATURAL PRODUCT EXPO EAST, 2001

I WAS CONTACTED BY A SOUTH AFRICAN CO-OP THAT WANTS TO SELL US AN HERBAL TEA CALLED HONEYBUSH.

YOU MEAN ROOIBOS? WE ALREADY USE THAT IN OUR CINNAMON GOLD RUSH.

NO, HONEYBUSH. IT'S IN THE SAME PLANT FAMILY AS ROOIBOS, BUT IT HAS A SMOOTHER TASTE.

SOUNDS WORTH EXPLORING.

HI! I'M ELTON AND THIS IS DAWIE.

HI!

IT'S DEFINITELY DIFFERENT, BUT I LOVE IT.

IT HAS A SMOOTH, EARTHY FLAVOR WITH A HINT OF HONEY.

WITH HELP FROM A U.S. GOVERNMENT GRANT, OUR FARMERS CREATED A COOPERATIVE, BOUGHT THEIR OWN LAND, AND STARTED THE FIRST EVER COMMERCIAL PLANTING OF HONEYBUSH.

WHERE'S THE TEA GROWN?

HAARLEM, WITH TWO "A"S, AFTER THE DUTCH SPELLING.

WE'LL CALL IT HAARLEM HONEYBUSH!

AND LET'S JUST SELL IT AS IS— UNSWEETENED.

I'D LOVE TO LEARN MORE ABOUT HOW THE COMMUNITY PARTNERSHIP WORKS.

THEN YOU MUST COME VISIT.

WHO ARE WE GOING TO SEE AGAIN?

OUR PARTNERS IN SOUTH AFRICA WHO GROW THE HONEYBUSH FOR OUR NEW TEA.

BUT WE'VE BEEN TRAVELING FOR 25 HOURS. HOW COME YOU CAN'T JUST TALK TO THEM ON THE PHONE?

THEY DON'T REGULARLY ANSWER THE PHONE, THEY DON'T HAVE EMAIL, AND THERE'S ONLY ONE FAX MACHINE.

IF WE WANT TO BUILD A TRUSTING RELATIONSHIP, WE NEED TO MEET THEM IN PERSON.

I'M GLAD YOU'RE COMING, JONAH. IT'LL GIVE THEM A BETTER SENSE OF WHO I AM.

CAPE TOWN

WOW, THAT'S A GREAT VIEW OF TABLE MOUNTAIN.

WE'VE GOT TO CLIMB IT!

WAIT UP FOR ME, JONAH.

WHOA! I DIDN'T KNOW REAL PLACES COULD LOOK LIKE THIS.

THE NEXT DAY WITH DAWIE

THIS COOPERATIVE IS PART OF THE NEW SOUTH AFRICA. DURING APARTHEID, THE FARMERS OF HAARLEM COULD ONLY EARN MONEY AS DAY LABORERS FOR THE WHITE FARMERS.

ONLY 20% HAD REGULAR EMPLOYMENT. NOW THEY EACH OWN A HECTARE OF LAND AND RELY ONLY ON THEMSELVES AND THE LAND FOR THEIR LIVELIHOODS.

WELCOME TO LANGKLOOF, THE LONG VALLEY.

OUR FIRST STOP IS AUNT EVELYNE.

IS SHE YOUR AUNT?

NO, EVERYONE CALLS HER AUNT OUT OF RESPECT.

SHE'S THE LEADER OF THE COMMUNITY AND THE DRIVING FORCE BEHIND THE COOPERATIVE.

WELKOM!

KOM, LAAT EK JOU ROND WYS.

SHE IS GOING TO SHOW US AROUND.

BEFORE WE STARTED GROWING HONEYBUSH AS A CROP, WE USED TO PICK IT IN THE WILD.

WE ONLY KNEW WHICH PLANT TO PICK WHEN ITS BRIGHT YELLOW FLOWERS WERE IN BLOOM. IT WOULD TAKE EIGHT PEOPLE TWO TO THREE DAYS TO PICK ONE TON.

SINCE WE COULD ONLY CARRY 20 KILOS AT A TIME, WE HAD TO MAKE SEVERAL TRIPS UP AND DOWN THE HILLSIDE, DODGING SNAKES ALL THE WAY.

NOW WITH THE PLANTED CROP, EIGHT PEOPLE, USING SICKLES, CAN HARVEST THE SAME AMOUNT IN ONLY TWO HOURS. AND IT CAN BE CERTIFIED ORGANIC.

WHAT HAPPENED?

I HURT IT PLAYING RUGBY. THEY WERE BAREFOOT, SO I PLAYED BAREFOOT, TOO.

LOOKS LIKE YOUR FEET AREN'T QUITE AS TOUGH AS THEIRS.

JONAH, AUNT EVELYNE TELLS ME THAT YOU ARE THE FIRST AMERICAN CHILD TO EVER VISIT HAARLEM.

BYE-BYE, JONAH.

BACK IN BETHESDA

WE JUST SHIPPED OUR FIRST PRODUCTION RUN OF HAARLEM HONEYBUSH.

HONEST TEA

HAARLEM HONEYBUSH

IT'S A PERFECT PARTNERSHIP. THE LABEL EVEN USES A DRAWING FROM A HAARLEM ARTIST.

THERE'S ONLY ONE PROBLEM.

HMMM. TASTES FERMENTED.

I THINK THE HONEYBUSH WE RECEIVED WAS A LITTLE MOLDY.

THIS ISN'T THE IDEAL WAY TO LAUNCH A PRODUCT, BUT THE NEXT BATCH WILL TASTE BETTER. OUR PARTNERSHIP WITH THE CO-OP IS WHAT REALLY MATTERS.

WE'RE ASKING PEOPLE TO TAKE A PRETTY BIG LEAP FROM DRINKING SODA TO TRYING AN UNSWEETENED ORGANIC HERBAL TEA THEY'VE NEVER HEARD OF.

A FEW MONTHS LATER

I'M SEEING A LOT OF HAARLEM HONEYBUSH LEFT ON THE SHELF.

IT'S TAKING AWAY SHELF SPACE FROM OUR OTHER VARIETIES THAT SELL BETTER.

PEOPLE DON'T KNOW WHAT HONEYBUSH IS, AND HARLEM OR HAARLEM DOESN'T EXACTLY SOUND LIKE A PLACE THAT GROWS ORGANIC TEA.

MAYBE CONSUMERS JUST DON'T CARE ABOUT OUR PARTNERSHIP.

WE NEED TO DO A BETTER JOB MAKING THEM CARE. BUT FIRST WE NEED TO MAKE SURE THE DRINK TASTES GREAT.

I GUESS USING HONEYBUSH THAT ISN'T MOLDY WOULD BE A START.

AND ADDING A LITTLE SUGAR.

A FEW YEARS LATER

OUR POMEGRANATE RED TEA WITH GOJI BERRY IS NOW ONE OF THE TOP 10 BEVERAGES IN THE NATURAL FOODS INDUSTRY!

I'M GLAD WE GAVE HONEYBUSH A SECOND CHANCE.

CAFFEINE-FREE
HONEST TEA
POMEGRANATE RED TEA WITH GOJI BERRY
JUST A TAD SWEET

EVEN THOUGH IT ISN'T IN THE NAME, WE'RE BUYING MORE HONEYBUSH FROM HAARLEM FOR OUR RED TEA THAN WE EVER DID THE FIRST TIME AROUND.

EVEN WHEN YOU LAND A DISTRIBUTOR, YOU STILL HAVE TO FIGHT FOR THEIR ATTENTION. COMPANIES OFTEN TRY CONTESTS AND OTHER INCENTIVE SCHEMES TO GET ON THE SALES FORCE'S RADAR.

TODAY, WE HAVE PRESENTATIONS FROM THE FOLKS AT JONES SODA AND HONEST TEA.

SALES MEETING WITH G&G DISTRIBUTORS IN WALLINGFORD, CT

OUR WHOOPASS ENERGY DRINK IS REALLY WHOOPING ASS.

TO MOTIVATE YOU ALL TO SELL MORE WHOOPASS, WE'RE GOING TO SPONSOR A CONTEST.

WHOEVER SELLS THE MOST THIS MONTH GETS A $500 PRIZE. SECOND PLACE GETS $100.

THANKS. TURNING THE FLOOR OVER TO HONEST TEA, I THINK YOU ALL KNOW DAN FROM HIS DAYS AT NANTUCKET. BARRY IS THE COMPANY'S CO-FOUNDER AND LIVES IN NEW HAVEN.

HEY, GUYS. THIS DRINK IS AMAZING. IT DOESN'T TASTE LIKE ANYTHING YOU'VE EVER HAD.

HERE ARE THE INGREDIENTS FOR OUR BLACK FOREST BERRY.

CURRANTS

RASPBERRY

ELDER-BERRY

BLACKBERRY

HIBISCUS

TRY DOING THIS WITH YOUR OTHER DRINKS! HONEST TEA TASTES GREAT BECAUSE THE INGREDIENTS ARE SO GREAT.

MUNCH MUNCH

WOW!

I LOVE THE IDEA OF USING PRIZES TO MOTIVATE THE SALES TEAM. IN FACT, I WROTE MY THESIS ON CONTESTS AS AN INCENTIVE DEVICE.

WELL, CONTESTS DON'T WORK QUITE AS WELL AS YOU THINK THEY DO.

I'LL HAVE A STACK OF CHOCOLATE CHIP PANCAKES.

ME, TOO. AND COFFEE.

TWO EGGS, PANCAKES, AND BACON.

DO YOU HAVE SILVER DOLLARS?

STRAWBERRY PANCAKES FOR ME.

WHOSE TURN IS IT TO WIN THE SALES BONUS?

YOU WON LAST TIME, SO I'M UP NEXT.

AND I'LL TAKE THE $100 FOR SECOND PLACE.

OK. IT'S SETTLED.

SO MUCH FOR THE INCENTIVE EFFECT OF CONTESTS.

CONTESTS CAN WORK, BUT NOT FOR SALES REPS. IF THEY PLAY IT STRAIGHT, THE REPS WHO CONTROL THE BIGGEST ROUTES ALWAYS WIN.

THE OTHER REPS KNOW THEY DON'T HAVE A CHANCE, SO THEY DON'T EVEN TRY.

MOST COMPANIES IGNORE SALES MANAGERS, BUT THEY'RE THE ONES WHO SHOULD BE INCENTIVIZED. THEY KNOW WHICH ROUTES ARE PERFORMING AND CAN PUSH THEIR WHOLE TEAM TO SELL MORE.

LOOK WHO'S THE PROFESSOR NOW.

OUR FIRST BOTTLED TEAS WERE MADE WITH ORGANIC CANE SUGAR, BUT THE TEA LEAVES WERE NOT ORGANIC.

WHEN YOU WASH VEGETABLES, DO YOU DRINK THE WATER AFTERWARD?

SIP!

OF COURSE NOT.

ANUPA MUELLER, ONE OF OUR SUPPLIERS AND FOUNDER OF ECO-PRIMA TEA, HELPED EDUCATE US ABOUT THE BENEFITS OF ORGANIC TEA.

TEA LEAVES ARE NEVER RINSED. THE FIRST TIME THEY TOUCH WATER IS WHEN YOU BREW THEM, SO YOU ARE DRINKING THE WASH WATER.

SO ANY CHEMICALS SPRAYED ON THE LEAVES...

...END UP IN YOUR CUP.

OF COURSE, ORGANIC ISN'T JUST ABOUT KEEPING CHEMICALS OUT OF CONSUMERS' BODIES. THE TEA PLUCKERS WADE INTO THE BUSHES UP TO THEIR CHESTS. THEY INHALE ANY CHEMICALS SPRAYED ON THE BUSHES.

ORGANICS ALSO ENSURE THE ECOSYSTEMS AROUND THE TEA GARDENS MAINTAIN THEIR BIODIVERSITY.

I'M SOLD.

YOU HAD ME AT WASH WATER.

IN 1999, WE INTRODUCED THE WORLD'S FIRST ORGANIC BOTTLED TEA: FIRST NATION PEPPERMINT. THAT BEGAN OUR JOURNEY TOWARD MAKING EVERY VARIETY ORGANIC. IT WAS SLOW GOING, AND IT WASN'T ALWAYS EASY. SOMETIMES ORGANIC VERSIONS OF THE TEAS WE WANTED WEREN'T AVAILABLE IN A VIABLE QUANTITY, QUALITY, OR PRICE. OTHER TIMES, WE HAD TO CHANGE OUR RECIPES. HOWEVER, IN OCTOBER 2002 WE GOT A REASON TO SPEED THINGS UP.

THE U.S. DEPARTMENT OF AGRICULTURE IS CREATING A USDA ORGANIC SEAL. THIS WILL SET A COMMON DEFINITION FOR ORGANIC AND ENFORCE THE INTEGRITY OF THE STANDARD.

USDA ORGANIC

COULDN'T WE JUST PROMOTE OURSELVES AS "ALL NATURAL"? THAT SOUNDS MORE APPEALING THAN ORGANIC.

"NATURAL" = PRODUCT DOES NOT CONTAIN SYNTHETIC OR ARTIFICIAL INGREDIENTS.

FDA

FOOD AND DRUG ADMINISTRATION

ALMOST ANYTHING CAN BE CALLED NATURAL, INCLUDING PRODUCTS GROWN WITH CHEMICAL PESTICIDES AND HORMONES.

HORMONES

PESTICIDES

MALTODEXTRIN

FOR MANY YEARS, GENERAL MILLS SOLD ITS NATURE VALLEY BARS AS 100% NATURAL. TWO CALIFORNIA MOMS THOUGHT OTHERWISE.

THE INGREDIENTS INCLUDE HIGH-MALTOSE CORN SYRUP AND MALTODEXTRIN, WHICH ARE HIGHLY PROCESSED AND NOT FOUND IN NATURE.

NATURE VALLEY
100% NATURAL
Discover the different sides of the Valley.

100% Natural.
100% Delicious.

Our Chewy Trail Mix bars are made with delicious combinations of 100% natural ingredients like whole almonds, cranberries, peanuts and pomegranate.

UPDATE: NATURE VALLEY'S PACKAGING NO LONGER MAKES THE 100% NATURAL CLAIM.

OK, THEN. WHAT WOULD IT TAKE TO MAKE MOROCCAN MINT ORGANIC?

EVEN IF WE FOUND ORGANIC GUNPOWDER TEA, THERE'S NO ORGANIC PEPPERMINT OIL ON THE MARKET.

PEPPERMINT OIL

I'M NOT SURE WE SHOULD PLAY AROUND WITH OUR BESTSELLER.

TWO WEEKS LATER

HERE, TASTE THIS.

WOW! WHAT DID YOU DO?

INSTEAD OF MINT OIL, I ADDED ORGANIC PEPPERMINT AND SPEARMINT LEAVES AND BREWED THEM WITH THE TEA LEAVES. THOUGH IT COSTS A LITTLE MORE, IT'S ALL ORGANIC AND TASTES BETTER.

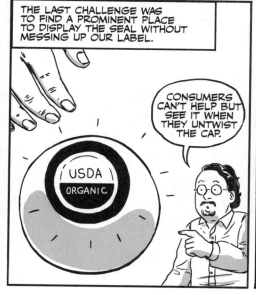

THE LAST CHALLENGE WAS TO FIND A PROMINENT PLACE TO DISPLAY THE SEAL WITHOUT MESSING UP OUR LABEL.

CONSUMERS CAN'T HELP BUT SEE IT WHEN THEY UNTWIST THE CAP.

USDA ORGANIC

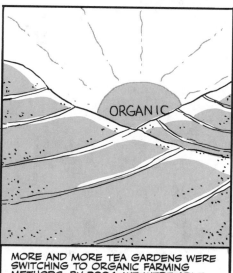

ORGANIC

MORE AND MORE TEA GARDENS WERE SWITCHING TO ORGANIC FARMING METHODS. BY 2004, WE WERE ABLE TO MAKE ALL OF OUR TEAS ORGANIC.

157

IN 2002, WE HELD A CONTEST FOR CUSTOMERS TO DESIGN THE LABEL FOR OUR NEWEST FLAVOR, A BLACK TEA WITH LEMON. ONE ENTRY SURPRISED US: IT HAD A SOBE LIZARD INSIDE THE "T." IT WAS FROM JOHN BELLO.

CLASS, PLEASE JOIN ME IN WELCOMING JOHN BELLO, THE FOUNDER OF SOBE. IN JUST FIVE YEARS, HE GREW THE COMPANY FROM $0 TO $225 MILLION IN SALES, AND THEN SOLD THE BUSINESS TO PEPSI FOR A REPORTED $370 MILLION.

ALL TRUE, BUT IN MY FIRST YEAR, I LOST $2 MILLION AND HAD TO MORTGAGE MY HOUSE.

WHAT WAS THE INSIGHT THAT LED YOU TO CREATE SOBE?

ONE OF THE SECRETS OF THE BEVERAGE INDUSTRY IS TO POSITION YOUR PRODUCT AS AN ELIXIR.

COCA-COLA WAS INVENTED BY A PHARMACIST AND MARKETED AS A BRAIN TONIC AND A CURE FOR HYSTERIA. 7UP ORIGINALLY CONTAINED LITHIUM, AND THERE'S A COMPANY TODAY THAT PRACTICALLY PROMISES YOU'LL LIVE FOREVER IF YOU DRINK THEIR POTION.

THAT'S WHY WE HAVE DRINKS WITH ST. JOHN'S WORT, GINKGO BILOBA, SELENIUM, ZINC, GINSENG, AND ECHINACEA.

I TAKE ST. JOHN'S WORT. BUT SHOULD MY DOSAGE REALLY DEPEND ON HOW THIRSTY I AM?

GIVEN THE TRACE AMOUNT OF ST. JOHN'S WORT IN THERE, I WOULDN'T WORRY ABOUT OVERDOSING.

SO IT'S MOSTLY A MARKETING PLOY.

WHAT ADVICE DO YOU HAVE FOR PROF. NALEBUFF AND HONEST TEA?

YOU SHOULD MARKET YOUR ORGANIC GREEN TEA AS AN ELIXIR.

AND FOR HEAVEN'S SAKE, PUT SOME MORE FREAKIN' ORGANIC SUGAR IN IT.

OUR TEAS ARE SELLING REALLY WELL IN NATURAL FOODS STORES, BUT NOT SO GREAT IN REGULAR GROCERY STORES AND DELIS.

HONEST TEA BOARD MEETING, 2003

OUR BOTTLES LOOK LIKE SNAPPLE'S, SO PEOPLE EXPECT OUR TEA TO BE JUST AS SWEET—AND END UP DISAPPOINTED.

IF, INSTEAD, THEY EXPECTED HONEST TEA TO BE A TASTY ALTERNATIVE TO WATER, THEY'D BE DELIGHTED. WE NEED TO FIND A WAY TO CREATE THE RIGHT EXPECTATION.

H_2O

HONEST TEA

WE ALSO HAVE TO MAKE SURE OUR DRINKS ARE RELEVANT TO GROCERY BUYERS.

WE USED TO SWEETEN STONYFIELD YOGURT WITH JUICE, BUT IT WAS EXPENSIVE. WHEN WE SWITCHED TO SUGAR, WE WORRIED OUR CUSTOMERS WOULD REBEL.

Stonyfield

SUGAR

THE OPPOSITE HAPPENED. OUR SALES TOOK OFF BECAUSE WE WERE ABLE TO LOWER OUR PRICES. TURNS OUT PEOPLE CARED MORE ABOUT THE YOGURT THAN WHICH SWEETENER WE USED.

Lower PRICE

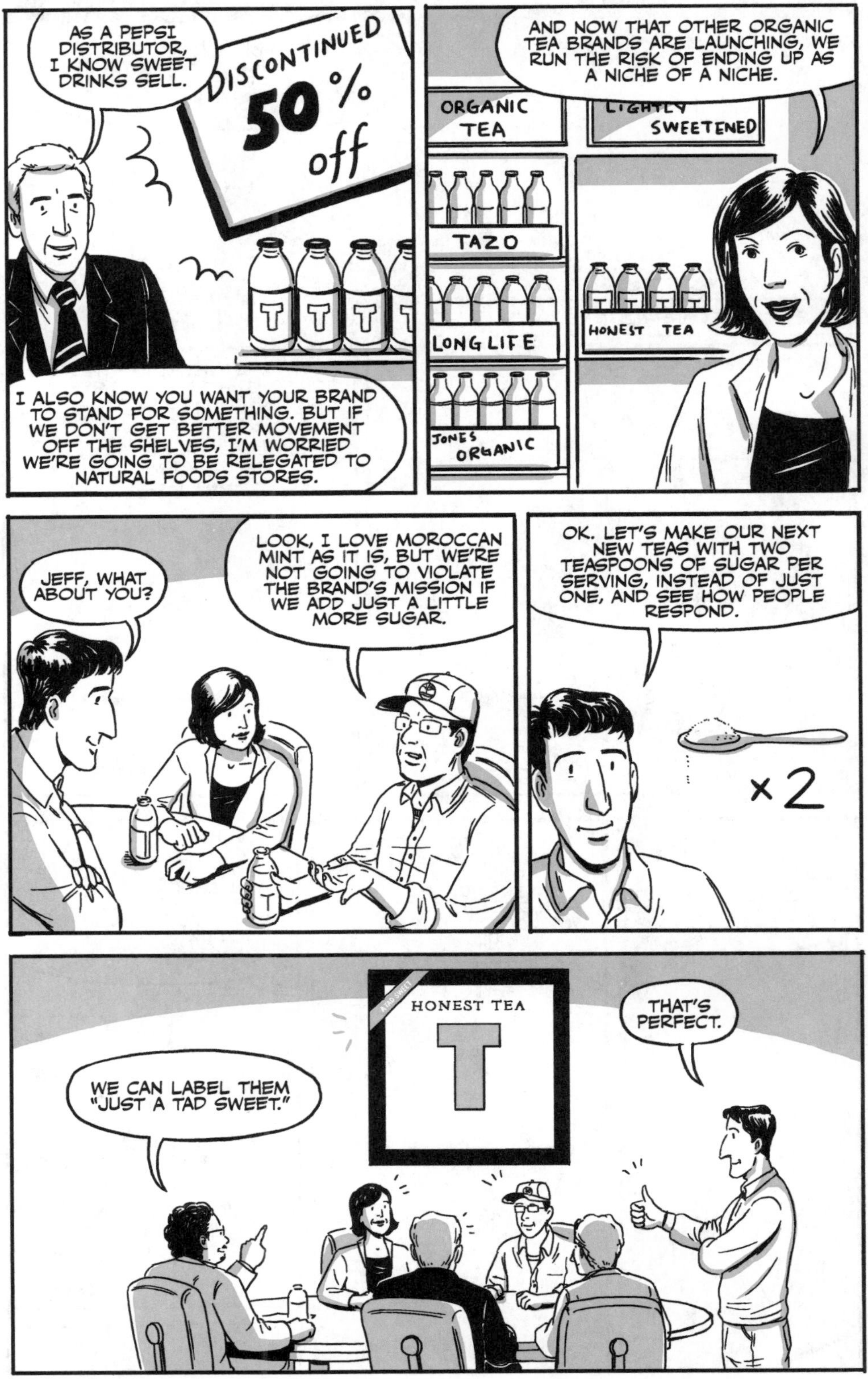
AS A PEPSI DISTRIBUTOR, I KNOW SWEET DRINKS SELL.
DISCONTINUED
50% off
I ALSO KNOW YOU WANT YOUR BRAND TO STAND FOR SOMETHING. BUT IF WE DON'T GET BETTER MOVEMENT OFF THE SHELVES, I'M WORRIED WE'RE GOING TO BE RELEGATED TO NATURAL FOODS STORES.
AND NOW THAT OTHER ORGANIC TEA BRANDS ARE LAUNCHING, WE RUN THE RISK OF ENDING UP AS A NICHE OF A NICHE.
ORGANIC TEA
LIGHTLY SWEETENED
TAZO
LONG LIFE
JONES ORGANIC
HONEST TEA
JEFF, WHAT ABOUT YOU?
LOOK, I LOVE MOROCCAN MINT AS IT IS, BUT WE'RE NOT GOING TO VIOLATE THE BRAND'S MISSION IF WE ADD JUST A LITTLE MORE SUGAR.
OK. LET'S MAKE OUR NEXT NEW TEAS WITH TWO TEASPOONS OF SUGAR PER SERVING, INSTEAD OF JUST ONE, AND SEE HOW PEOPLE RESPOND.
×2
HONEST TEA
T
WE CAN LABEL THEM "JUST A TAD SWEET."
THAT'S PERFECT.

I'LL BE THERE SOON FOR A *FORTUNE* PHOTO SHOOT. I HOPE THE PLANT LOOKS PRESENTABLE.

4:00 AM

YEAH. IN FACT, WE'RE RUNNING PRODUCT FOR ANOTHER ORGANIC TEA COMPANY, LONG LIFE.

YOU TOLD ME ABOUT THEM. ARE THEY MAKING THEIR TEA WITH A CONCENTRATE OR A POWDER?

UH, NO. ACTUALLY, THEY'RE BREWING WITH TEA LEAVES.

REALLY? HOW'D THEY FIGURE OUT HOW TO DO THAT?

I THOUGHT SINCE THREE RIVERS REALLY NEEDS THE BUSINESS, YOU'D BE OK IF THEY USED OUR BREWING SYSTEM.

WHAT?!! DON'T YOU THINK YOU SHOULD HAVE CHECKED WITH ME?

WELL, I DID HELP DESIGN THE SYSTEM.

BUT HONEST TEA PAID YOU TO DO IT, AND OUR GOAL ISN'T TO CREATE COMPETITION FOR OURSELVES.

LOOK, A LOT'S BEEN HAPPENING HERE, AND I'M TRYING TO KEEP THE PLANT AFLOAT. HOW ABOUT I TELL THEM THEY HAVE TO PAY HONEST TEA 25¢ A CASE FOR THE RIGHT TO USE THE SYSTEM?

WHAT IF I SAY NO?

THEN I'LL PROBABLY HAVE TO LAY OFF SOME PEOPLE.

WHAT IS LONG LIFE DOING FOR A WATER SOURCE?

YOU'RE NOT GOING TO LIKE THIS...

THREE RIVERS BOTTLING

FAR AWAY SPRINGS

YOU TOLD THEM ABOUT FAR AWAY SPRINGS?

WELL, I FIGURED...

OH... I'M TRYING.

TRY TO SMILE.

WHAT WAS GEORGE THINKING?!

IT GETS WORSE. I FOUND OUT THERE'S ANOTHER TEA COMPANY, SWEET LEAF FROM AUSTIN, THAT'S SET TO PRODUCE AT OUR PLANT.

AUSTIN? WE JUST HAD A POTENTIAL INVESTOR FROM THERE ASK FOR A COPY OF OUR BUSINESS PLAN.

IT'S THE SAME GUY. I GUESS WE WERE A LITTLE TOO HELPFUL.

BUT SWEET LEAF DIDN'T GET AS MUCH HELP FROM US AS LONG LIFE DID. NOT LONG AFTERWARD, GEORGE LEFT THE PLANT TO GO WORK FOR THEM AS A CONSULTANT, AND LATER BECAME THEIR CEO.

FANCY FOOD SHOW, JUNE 2003

ITO EN?

THEY'RE A HUGE TEA COMPANY IN JAPAN, AND THEY'VE JUST ENTERED OUR MARKET WITH AN UNSWEETENED BOTTLED TEA.

IT'S A BIT TOO GREEN FOR ME.

YOSUKE HONJO? I KNOW THERE ARE A LOT OF PEOPLE IN JAPAN, BUT WE HAPPEN TO HAVE AN INVESTOR WITH THAT NAME.

ACTUALLY... THAT INVESTOR IS ME.

YOU SAID YOU COULD CONNECT US WITH THE BEST JAPANESE TEA COMPANY. I SEE NOW YOU MADE THAT CONNECTION YOURSELF.

WE'RE GOING TO NEED YOU TO SELL YOUR SHARES.

IN 2003, WE STARTED GETTING INQUIRIES FROM MAJOR BRANDS. WE HOPED THESE WOULD PROVIDE OPPORTUNITIES TO BUILD OUR DISTRIBUTION.

WHAT DO WE KNOW ABOUT TETLEY?

THEY SELL A WHOLE LOT OF TEA BAGS. MANY OF THEIR CUSTOMERS ARE INSTITUTIONS LIKE SCHOOLS, HOSPITALS, EVEN PRISONS.

AND THEY WERE RECENTLY ACQUIRED BY TATA.

YES. APPARENTLY, MR. TATA DECIDED THERE WAS A BETTER BRAND NAME THAN TATA FOR TEA.

HI!

WE'VE WATCHED YOUR PROGRESS AND LIKE YOUR PRODUCTS VERY MUCH.

THANK YOU.

WE'D LIKE TO BRANCH OUT FROM TEA BAGS INTO BOTTLED TEA.

OKAY... AND HOW DO WE FIT IN?

WE HAVE GREAT RELATIONSHIPS WITH BUYERS AND RETAILERS. YOU HAVE A GREAT PRODUCT. TOGETHER, WE CAN CREATE THE LEADING BOTTLED TEA IN THE MARKET.

WE'D BE HAPPY TO WORK WITH YOU IN TERMS OF DISTRIBU- TION, BUT WE AREN'T LOOKING TO SELL THE COMPANY.

ARE YOU SURE?

YES. WE GREW NEARLY 50% LAST YEAR, AND I THINK WE'LL BREAK $6 MILLION IN SALES THIS YEAR. I'M AS EXCITED AND ENERGIZED TODAY AS I WAS AT THE START.

I HOPE YOU'LL RECONSIDER. YOU SHOULD KNOW THAT IF YOU DON'T SELL TO US, WE PLAN TO ENTER THE MARKET AND CRUSH YOU.

EVEN IF WE WERE LOOKING TO SELL, I DON'T THINK THAT'S THE BUYER WE'D WANT.

AND I'M NOT WORRIED ABOUT HAVING THEM AS A COMPETITOR. JUST AS WE'VE STRUGGLED WITH TEA BAGS, THEY'LL FIND OUT SELLING BOTTLED TEA ISN'T SO EASY.

WHEN IT CAME TO DEVELOPING NEW TEAS, OUR TEA SUPPLIERS OFTEN PAVED THE WAY FOR OUR INNOVATION.

YOU HAVE TO TRY OUR OOLONG TEA—IT HAS A RICH, ALMOST SMOKY TASTE.

I THOUGHT OOLONG TEAS CAME FROM CHINA AND TAIWAN.

OOLONG ISN'T THE NAME OF A REGION. IT'S THE WAY THE TEA IS PROCESSED.

GREEN TEA

TEA LEAVES ARE DRIED QUICKLY, RESULTING IN A LIGHTER HUE AND TYPICALLY LESS CAFFEINE.

OOLONG TEA

SEMI-FERMENTED (SOMEWHERE BETWEEN GREEN AND BLACK TEAS)

BLACK TEA

TEA LEAVES ARE LEFT TO WITHER AND OXIDIZE BEFORE DRYING.

OURS COMES FROM MAKAIBARI IN DARJEELING, ONE OF THE FIRST BIODYNAMIC AND FAIR TRADE TEA GARDENS IN THE WORLD.

DELICIOUS! WE'VE WANTED TO LAUNCH A PEACH TEA, AND THIS WOULD WORK PERFECTLY. HOW MUCH MORE WOULD IT COST TO BUY FAIR TRADE-CERTIFIED TEA?

ABOUT 20% MORE.

HMMM. LET ME LOOK AT THE NUMBERS.

TASTE THIS TEA. WE'VE BLENDED IT WITH ORGANIC BROWN RICE SYRUP AND ORGANIC PEACH PUREE.

SIP

SIP

FANTASTIC! IT'S ORIGINAL, BUT FAMILIAR ENOUGH TO BE ACCESSIBLE.

WE COULD MAKE THIS THE WORLD'S FIRST FAIR TRADE-CERTIFIED BOTTLED TEA. THE CERTIFICATION WILL THROW OUR MARGINS OFF A BIT, BUT I THINK WE CAN MAKE IT WORK.

ANY CHANCE WE CAN MAKE OUR ENTIRE LINE FAIR TRADE?

NOT ALL OUR TEA SUPPLIERS ARE FAIR TRADE CERTIFIED. EVEN WHERE THERE'S A FAIR TRADE OPTION, WE'D HAVE TO CUT OUR MARGINS OR RAISE PRICES.

BUT DON'T YOU THINK IT'S THE RIGHT THING TO DO?

THE RIGHT THING? YES, BUT AT THE WRONG TIME. AT THIS POINT, WE'RE STILL NOT BREAKING EVEN. IF WE CUT OUR MARGINS, WE'LL LOSE EVEN MORE MONEY.

MOST CUSTOMERS WON'T PAY A PREMIUM FOR FAIR TRADE, SO IF WE RAISE PRICES, WE'LL LOSE SALES. THAT WON'T HELP OUR SUPPLIER COMMUNITIES, AND IT'LL HELP THEM EVEN LESS IF WE GO OUT OF BUSINESS.

TOO EXPENSIVE!

I THINK WE NEED TO TAKE A LONGER-TERM APPROACH TOWARD FAIR TRADE.

IF WE WANT THIS TEA TO BE POPULAR, WE NEED A LABEL THAT SETS THE RIGHT TONE.

?

BERKELEY WHO?

MAYBE BERKELEY BREATHED WOULD HELP US OUT.

EMAIL TO SETH, CIRCA 1999

FINALLY I CAN FIND SOME REAL BOTTLED TEA—MY ONLY PURCHASED BEVERAGE. MY HEART RACED WHEN I SAW ACTUAL TEA FLOTSAM SWIRLING AROUND THE BOTTOM OF THE BOTTLE. FESS UP. YOU GUYS STICK THAT IN THERE AT GREAT EFFORT AFTERWARDS, DONCHA? WELL, YA NABBED ME.

-BerkeleyB

THE CREATOR OF *BLOOM COUNTY.* HIS PENGUIN, OPUS, IS ONE OF MY FAVORITE CARTOON CHARACTERS. HE AND HIS IN-LAWS WERE SOME OF OUR EARLIEST INVESTORS.

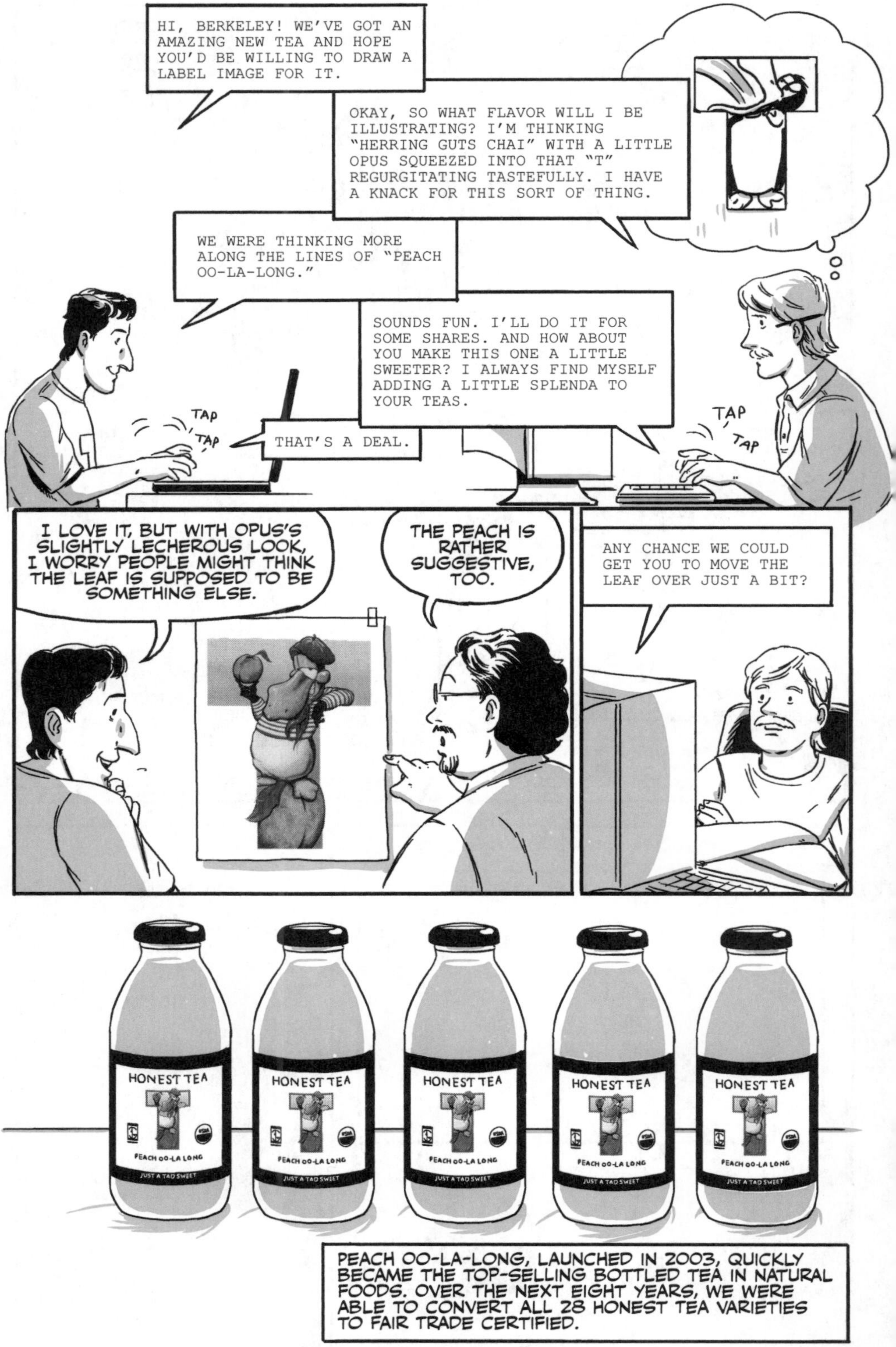
HI, BERKELEY! WE'VE GOT AN AMAZING NEW TEA AND HOPE YOU'D BE WILLING TO DRAW A LABEL IMAGE FOR IT.
OKAY, SO WHAT FLAVOR WILL I BE ILLUSTRATING? I'M THINKING "HERRING GUTS CHAI" WITH A LITTLE OPUS SQUEEZED INTO THAT "T" REGURGITATING TASTEFULLY. I HAVE A KNACK FOR THIS SORT OF THING.
WE WERE THINKING MORE ALONG THE LINES OF "PEACH OO-LA-LONG."
SOUNDS FUN. I'LL DO IT FOR SOME SHARES. AND HOW ABOUT YOU MAKE THIS ONE A LITTLE SWEETER? I ALWAYS FIND MYSELF ADDING A LITTLE SPLENDA TO YOUR TEAS.
TAP TAP
THAT'S A DEAL.
TAP TAP
I LOVE IT, BUT WITH OPUS'S SLIGHTLY LECHEROUS LOOK, I WORRY PEOPLE MIGHT THINK THE LEAF IS SUPPOSED TO BE SOMETHING ELSE.
THE PEACH IS RATHER SUGGESTIVE, TOO.
ANY CHANCE WE COULD GET YOU TO MOVE THE LEAF OVER JUST A BIT?
HONEST TEA
PEACH OO-LA LONG
JUST A TAD SWEET
PEACH OO-LA-LONG, LAUNCHED IN 2003, QUICKLY BECAME THE TOP-SELLING BOTTLED TEA IN NATURAL FOODS. OVER THE NEXT EIGHT YEARS, WE WERE ABLE TO CONVERT ALL 28 HONEST TEA VARIETIES TO FAIR TRADE CERTIFIED.

WE JUST GOT CALLS FROM TWO DIFFERENT WHOLE FOODS MARKETS. THEY EACH HAD A CUSTOMER FIND A PIECE OF GLASS INSIDE A BOTTLE OF HONEST TEA!

WAS ANYONE HURT?!

SUMMER 2003

THANK GOODNESS, NO. THE CHUNKS OF GLASS WERE SO LARGE, THERE WAS NO DANGER OF DRINKING THEM. BUT HOW DID THIS HAPPEN?

I DON'T KNOW, BUT I'M GOING TO FIND OUT.

HOW IS THIS POSSIBLE?

WHEN YOU FILL A GLASS BOTTLE WITH 190°F LIQUID, IT CAN BREAK. THAT'S THE NATURE OF GLASS.

190°F

CRACK

I KNOW GLASS BREAKS, BUT WHAT ABOUT OUR SAFETY PROCEDURES?

10'

WHENEVER A BOTTLE BREAKS, WE STOP THE LINE AND THROW AWAY ALL THE BOTTLES FIVE FEET BEFORE AND AFTER IT.

WE ALSO HAVE A SHIELD TO PREVENT BROKEN GLASS FROM LANDING IN BOTTLES BEFORE THEY'RE CAPPED.

THEN HOW DID WE END UP SHIPPING THIS?

IN JUNE, WE GOT A DELIVERY OF POORLY MADE BOTTLES. WE DIDN'T HAVE ANY OTHER INVENTORY, SO WE USED THEM. THEY BROKE A LOT MORE THAN USUAL.

FREAKS

SOFT BLISTERS

SPIKES

POP

CLEARLY, WHAT WE'RE DOING ISN'T ENOUGH.

IT DOESN'T HELP THAT WE USE A PRESSURE-FED FILLER—THE SAME KIND USED TO FILL SODA BOTTLES. IT FILLS THE BOTTLES QUICKLY, BUT IF A BOTTLE BREAKS, IT EXPLODES.

CRACK

POP

WHAT WE REALLY NEED IS A GRAVITY-FED FILLER. IT'S SLOWER, BUT IF A BOTTLE BREAKS, THERE'S NO FLYING GLASS.

THEN LET'S GET A GRAVITY FILLER *RIGHT AWAY.*

BUT WE DON'T HAVE THE MONEY.

$

WE DON'T HAVE A CHOICE.

WHOLE FOODS HAS A "THREE STRIKES AND YOU'RE OUT" POLICY. WE NOW HAVE TWO STRIKES.

WE NEED TO WITHDRAW EVERYTHING MADE IN JUNE FROM ALL WHOLE FOODS MARKETS.

I HATE TO SAY IT, BUT I THINK WE NEED TO PULL OUR JUNE PRODUCT FROM ALL STORES, NOT JUST WHOLE FOODS.

WE'VE BEEN USING THAT PRESSURE FILLER FOR YEARS. HOW DO WE KNOW THERE AREN'T ANY OLDER BOTTLES WITH GLASS OUT THERE?

YOU'RE BOTH RIGHT. WE NEED TO WITHDRAW ALL OUR PRODUCT MADE IN JUNE OR BEFORE. THIS IS GOING TO COST US HUNDREDS OF THOUSANDS. OUCH!

AND WE'LL HAVE TO PUT OUR SALES TEAM TO WORK PULLING PRODUCT OFF THE SHELVES INSTEAD OF PUTTING IT ON THEM.

SO MUCH FOR MY FIRST VACATION IN THREE YEARS...

I KNOW THIS DOESN'T FEEL GOOD, BUT IF WE SURVIVE, AT LEAST WE'LL HAVE LIVED UP TO OUR NAME.

HOW WILL WE PREVENT THIS FROM HAPPENING AGAIN?

ALONG WITH THE GRAVITY FILLER, WE'VE SWITCHED GLASS SUPPLIERS AND HIRED A NEW QUALITY CONTROL MANAGER AT THE PLANT.

WE SHOULD ALSO THINK ABOUT GETTING INTO PLASTIC BOTTLES.

CAN'T WE SUE SOME- ONE TO COMPENSATE US FOR THE LOST PRODUCT, LOST SALES, AND DAMAGED REPUTATION?

I WISH. THE GLASS COMPANY SAYS THE BOTTLING PLANT DIDN'T HANDLE THE GLASS PROPERLY. THE PLANT SAYS THEY RECEIVED DEFECTIVE GLASS. SO HONEST TEA GETS STUCK WITH THE BILL.

POSTSCRIPT: ANOTHER COMPANY, ABOUT OUR SIZE, RECEIVED THE SAME DEFECTIVE GLASS WITH THE SAME RESULTS. THEY DIDN'T WITHDRAW THEIR PRODUCT AND WENT OUT OF BUSINESS SOON AFTER.

49. ONE WORD: PLASTICS

BIG GEYSER JUST SOLD A FULL PALLET INTO WESTERLY MARKET. LOOK AT THE DISPLAY!

4 for $5.00

WOW. THAT'S AMAZING!

A MONTH LATER

YOU'VE GOT TO SEE THIS DISPLAY WE SET UP AT WESTERLY.

I KNOW. I'VE SEEN IT.

REALLY? WE JUST SOLD IT IN.

4 for $5.00

A FEW WEEKS LATER

I JUST GOT A CALL FROM GEYSER. THEY LOST WESTERLY TO A NATURAL DISTRIBUTOR. THEY'RE PISSED.

YOU COULD SAY THAT. LISTEN TO THIS VOICEMAIL FROM ONE OF THEIR ROUTE GUYS.

YO, MIKE, THIS IS LOUIE. YOU CAN TAKE YOUR #@$%!! HONEST TEA AND STICK IT UP DAN CAVANAUGH'S BIG FAT #@$%!!. %$%^*# YOU, #@$%!! HONEST TEA.

WHAT'S GOING ON?

A STORE ON HIS ROUTE BUYS FROM GEYSER WHEN THEY HAVE US ON DEAL, AND THEN SWITCHES TO THE NATURAL DISTRIBUTOR WHEN THEY HAVE US ON SALE.

HONEST TEA

HONEST TEA

AS LONG AS OUR DRINKS ARE IN THE STORE, SHOULDN'T WE BE HAPPY?

BUT OUR DISTRIBUTORS AREN'T.

AND MORE OF OUR SALES ARE ON DISCOUNT, WHICH IS KILLING OUR MARGINS.

I DON'T MIND COMPETITION, BUT LET'S NOT COMPETE AGAINST OURSELVES. WE NEED TO FOCUS ON CAPTURING SHELF SPACE FROM OTHER BRANDS.

DISTRIBUTORS NEED TO FEEL LIKE THEY OWN THE BRAND. I'VE TRIED TO EXPLAIN TO GEYSER THAT THE OVERLAP IS ONLY 10% OF ACCOUNTS, BUT YOU'RE GOING TO BE HEARING IT FROM LEWIS.

SURE ENOUGH...

I LOVE HONEST TEA. WE CAN MAKE IT ONE OF THE TOP BRANDS IN NEW YORK CITY. BUT WE NEED EXCLUSIVE RIGHTS.

MY GUYS CAN'T GET BEHIND YOU 100% IF THEY SEE SOMEONE ELSE SELLING IT, LET ALONE SELLING IT FOR A LOWER PRICE.

MEETING BACK AT HQ

IF WE DON'T GIVE GEYSER EXCLUSIVITY, WE WON'T BE ABLE TO SELL BEYOND NATURAL FOODS STORES.

BUT WE CAN'T ABANDON UNITED NATURAL. THEY'RE OUR BIGGEST DISTRIBUTOR AND GIVE US NATIONAL COVERAGE.

WHAT IF WE CREATE A SEPARATE PRODUCT LINE FOR DSD* GUYS LIKE GEYSER TO SELL?

NEW PRODUCT

*DIRECT STORE DELIVERY

YOU MEAN THE SAME BRAND AND CALORIE PROFILE, JUST A DIFFERENT PACKAGE?

SURE. GIVEN THE RECALL WE JUST WENT THROUGH, IT WOULD BE GREAT NOT TO BASE ALL OUR BUSINESS ON GLASS.

WITH A PLASTIC BOTTLE WE COULD SELL IN SCHOOLS, CAMPS, AND OTHER PLACES WHERE GLASS ISN'T ALLOWED.

I JUST MET WITH A SUPPLIER WHO HAS A NEW PANEL-LESS PLASTIC BOTTLE.

PANEL-LESS?

IT DOESN'T HAVE THE RIBS AND EXPANSION PANELS YOU SEE ON SPORTS DRINK BOTTLES. IT LOOKS A LOT LIKE GLASS, BUT WEIGHS $\frac{1}{7}$ AS MUCH.

THAT MEANS WE COULD PUT 33% MORE PRODUCT ON A TRUCK WITHOUT GOING OVER WEIGHT. THAT'S A HUGE SAVINGS.

JONATHAN CLARK, CFO

25,344 GLASS BOTTLES

33,696 PLASTIC BOTTLES

IN 2004, WE INTRODUCED OUR NEW PLASTIC BOTTLES, FILLED WITH OUR TOP-SELLING FLAVORS. THIS DIDN'T CLEAR UP CONFUSION AND FRUSTRATION THE WAY WE'D HOPED.

HONEST TEA — LORI'S LEMON TEA
HONEST TEA — GREEN DRAGON TEA
HONEST TEA — BLACK FOREST BERRY
HONEST TEA — PEACH-OO-LA LONG
HONEST TEA — LORI'S LEMON TEA

WE LEARNED OUR LESSON AND QUICKLY DEVELOPED NEW FLAVORS JUST FOR THE PLASTIC LINE. HEAVENLY HONEY GREEN BECAME OUR BESTSELLING TEA, EVEN MORE SO AFTER WE SIMPLIFIED THE NAME TO HONEY GREEN TEA. DSD GUYS, LIKE BIG GEYSER, WERE HAPPIER WITH PLASTIC BECAUSE THERE WAS LESS BREAKAGE, AND EVERYONE WAS HAPPIER WITH EXCLUSIVE TERRITORIES. AT LONG LAST, WHEN WE REACHED OUT TO NEW DSD DISTRIBUTORS, THEY STARTED RETURNING OUR CALLS.

People often ask, "What was the hardest part?" In fact, everything was hard: raising money, brewing and bottling, writing label copy, marketing, hiring, firing, selling. If it were easy, someone else would have done it. If it were easy, we would have succeeded with tea bags.

That said, as someone who comes from the world of academia, two areas were particularly challenging for me. One was operations: making and delivering the product. The other was dealing with people, many of whom didn't get it.

MANAGING OPERATIONS IS ESPECIALLY HARD.

Although we splurged on the highest-quality tea leaves, we didn't invest enough in our operations. It took us 10 years to find someone who was excellent at running it. We should have let some people go a lot earlier. WE DIDN'T KNOW WHAT WE DIDN'T KNOW.

The cost of making a mistake here was enormous, far more than what we paid the person running operations. We lost product, lost sales, and damaged our reputation. Altogether, we lost more than $1 million due to production problems: mismatched labels, the 2003 glass withdrawal, moldy honeybush, and dented bottles. At least as damaging were dozens of less-than-perfect batches we put on the market because we didn't have other product to sell. Those batches were some people's first and last impression of Honest Tea.

MISTAKES ADD UP. You might think that having dents in 1% of your plastic bottles doesn't really affect the other 99%. OK, I thought that. The problem is those dented bottles end up sticking around on the shelves. Pretty soon, 20% of the bottles on the shelf are dented and customers start to think your product is defective. Sales slow down as customers pick their way around the deformed bottles.

Before long, 50% of the bottles left on the shelf are deformed. In short, a 1% problem can rapidly become a 100% problem.

EVERY CHANGE CREATES RIPPLES. As an ideas guy, I always had lots of suggestions for small changes that would lead to incremental improvements. Yet it rarely seemed to work out that way. We moved to a new label material, and it crinkled. We moved to a new, lighter bottle, and the old label didn't quite fit. The problem is that it takes time to iron out the kinks. Creative people like to tinker; operations people like a routine. Anything that disrupts that routine is much more costly than you imagine.

DON'T DABBLE. We obviously made mistakes with the tea bag line. On the other hand, we didn't lose sight of the bottled-tea line, and that was what really mattered. With hindsight, we should have either stayed out of the tea bag business or spent more money to have someone who knew about production help us.

GO SLOW. Entrepreneurs naturally want to grow fast and take advantage of every opportunity. We are inspired by Robert Browning's verse: "A man's reach should exceed his grasp." Entrepreneurs (and academics) should think big and stretch boundaries. But when it comes to distribution, this is a really bad idea.

In 2001, we paid for an opportunity to go national with the cafés inside Barnes & Noble. In markets where we already had a presence and thus some awareness, we did fine. But in new markets, we found customers weren't looking to experiment with new drinks at a bookstore. In other markets, we couldn't deliver, literally. We didn't have any distribu-

tors within 250 miles of the bookstore in New Orleans, and dozens of other cities. When Barnes & Noble calculated our average sales per store, we got tagged as a failure. It was one strike and we were out. As painful as it is to pass up a chance to grow, it's much better to wait until your distribution catches up to your ambition.

PEOPLE ARE CHALLENGING, TOO.

As a game theorist, I encourage people to truly understand the other party's perspective. When you put yourself in their position, it isn't what you would do wearing their shoes, it's what they would do wearing their shoes. No surprise, but that's much easier said than done, especially when their shoes don't fit your feet or your worldview.

PEOPLE ACT STUPIDLY. You're not going to change that. You have to figure out how to solve their problems. When a store didn't stock our tea because it sold out too quickly, I wanted to get the guy fired. But that wouldn't sell more tea. Instead, we solved his problem by getting the store a bigger cooler.

UNDERSTAND YOUR BUYER, WHICH ISN'T AS OBVIOUS AS IT SEEMS. Your buyer is not the customer who pays for your product at the cash register. It is the distributor and the category manager at the retailer. You have to make the sale to them. They've seen it all before and are often quite cynical. Each thinks he or she (though it's typically a he in this business) is the key to your success. Worse still, these buyers often can't imagine anyone would like a beverage with very little sugar.*

*At one large chain, the tea buyer was a Mormon and wouldn't drink any tea, so it was particularly challenging to help him appreciate how our product was different and better.

Honest Tea wasn't designed for this person. Our board and our sales team pushed us to make slightly more mainstream options, ones with 30 to 40 calories rather than

9 to 17. The new products still didn't please most buyers' palates, but they could at least imagine someone else might like them.

AVOIDABLE ERRORS

With the benefit of hindsight, what might we have done differently? Our lawyer would say we shouldn't have guaranteed our 2001 sales. Indeed, he said it at the time. So why didn't we listen?

It is always worth looking for the root cause of a mistake. We pushed for an unreasonably high valuation, and when investors pushed back, we were forced to guarantee our results.

And what was the cause of our overambitious valuation? I don't think it was greed. I think it was the entrepreneur's preternatural optimism. That optimism was reflected in our track record of missing projected sales targets.

We could try to blame these misses on how hard it is to forecast sales when growing at 50% or more. Much of our growth was coming from new accounts and new distributors, and they typically came on board slower than we would have liked. Even so, the fact remains that we were consistently overoptimistic.

Why didn't we learn better? Because it helped us to believe. Our optimism was tied to our ambition. As John McEnroe said, "I'll shoot for the stars, and I'll settle for the moon and I'll give it a hell of a try." Even when we didn't hit our forecasts, we still delivered growth that kept us and our investors excited about the future.

The real root cause of our costly guarantee was the fact that we had lost objectivity. We think it's fine, even desirable, to focus on the upside when leading a start-up. But don't forget you're drinking the Kool-Aid. When your objective lawyer warns you about making guarantees, you should listen.

Surprisingly, our biggest mistake wasn't predictions, production, or people. It was a strategic blunder. It was getting distracted by projects not directly related to selling Honest drinks in bottles. The tea bag line and the bottling plant depleted our cash and our energy, and, perhaps most important, distracted Seth from building our sales and our brand.

Why did we err? In the case of the tea bag line, we were seduced by what looked like an easy win. Customers were asking us for it. Our sales team could sell it. We saw an opportunity to make a tea bag that was different and better. We forgot the fact that nothing is easy, especially when you're doing something different.

Our mistake with the plant was more complicated. It wasn't that we hadn't anticipated the risks. We knew there would be challenges. We knew running a plant wasn't our strength and would be a distraction. So what was behind our decision to buy the plant? We thought we had a much more pressing problem to solve: getting access to production (during apple cider season) and getting access to the plant to experiment. We feared we might succeed in the market and yet lose it all because we didn't have enough production capacity to meet demand. To avoid one potentially fatal risk, we created another.

With hindsight, a better solution would have been to compensate our original bottling plant for better access. At our size, we were too small a customer to get the attention we needed. Had we offered to pay $25,000 for better access, I suspect we could have gotten our phone calls returned and more time at the plant. In short: right diagnosis, wrong solution.

Sometimes the mistakes compounded. If we hadn't bought Three Rivers, we never would have shared our tea-brewing technology with our competition. There was a lot of pressure to let our plant produce for direct competitors. The plant was bleeding money, and our partners pushed us hard. Even so, we should have held firm. Our plant made some money manufacturing for our rivals, and they would have been in the market even if we hadn't given them access to our plant. But their product would not have been nearly as good without access to our tea-brewing equipment. We know. It took us years of experimenting to figure out the best way to brew real tea leaves.

WE'RE NOT QUITE AS DUMB AS WE SOMETIMES LOOK. Keep in mind that we're emphasizing our mistakes. My colleague Sharon Oster likes to say that you learn more from your mistakes than your successes. We're trying to share the learning part.

We haven't told you all our mistakes (like when we staged a Boston Tea Party and no one came) or all our successes. If we got the chance for a do-over, I think we could get to $5 million in sales a little quicker and for a lot less money.

How did we survive our mistakes? We had passion. We had investors who believed in us. And we had the big picture right. There were some key mistakes we *didn't* make. We never risked losing control of the company. We never strayed from keeping the product Honest.

Looking back over the first six years, there are two lessons that seem so obvious in hindsight but weren't nearly as apparent when I was knee-deep in tea leaves.

SALES ARE (ALMOST) ALL THAT COUNTS.

Without sales, nothing else is possible. Even for a company like ours, which emphasizes a social and environmental mission of making organic and Fair Trade tea, our impact is marginal if we don't sell truckloads of tea.

So, besides having a great product, how do you make sales happen?

DEGREES DON'T SELL—PEOPLE DO. Many of our top salespeople never went to college, but they know how to communicate and gain respect from key decision makers, many of whom also didn't go to college. War stories about old beverage brands, shared experiences raising children, and insights on Notre Dame's offensive line all help develop personal relationships that lead to sales success.

Every Honest Tea employee, including our accountants, goes out on a sales call at least a few times a year.

Early on, we had one salesman with an MBA who put together an impressive spreadsheet full of tabs that displayed where all of our sales were going to come from. But spreadsheets aren't reality. This "salesperson" spent too much time behind a computer and not enough on the street. It's very easy to paint a picture of sales growth on a spreadsheet, but someone has to turn the projections into a reality.

DISTRIBUTION, DISTRIBUTION, DISTRIBUTION. Ralph Waldo Emerson promised that if you build a better mousetrap, the world will beat a path to your door—but if you're selling something better that's heavy and made of glass, they may not be able to carry it home. Web entrepreneurs don't have this problem. The rest of us need distributors.

HOW DO I BRING THIS HOME?

The problem is distributors don't think they need you and are rarely interested in taking on a new brand unless they see it selling. It's a catch-22: until you have sales, they don't want you; but without a distributor, it is hard to generate sales.

So how do you start from nowhere? Though I didn't realize it at the time, my formative years as a Red Sox fan—I was 10 years old in 1975, when the Sox came heartbreakingly close to reversing their World Series curse—helped me navigate this most difficult early phase. Here are three things the Red Sox taught me:

MANUFACTURE RUNS. In 2004, when the Red Sox were three outs from being eliminated from the American League Championship Series, they found a way, not necessarily a pretty way (Big Papi's single in the 14th inning), to win. When we couldn't get beverage distributors to take an interest in us, we found other ways to get to the shelf—cheese distributors, corned beef distributors, charcoal distributors—until beverage distributors started paying attention. Once we got our first real distributor on board, we made the most of it.

THERE'S ALWAYS APRIL. An entrepreneur has to constantly overcome disappointments and setbacks. In our first few years, we were turned down by stores, distributors, restaurants, investors—you name it. Most people would have given up after the first 10 rejections, but as a Red Sox fan I have always understood that "no" really means "not yet." Despite four years of bimonthly rejections from Canada Dry Potomac, I always found another reason to hope. Pure persistence (OK, some might say it was more like stalking) kept us in the game. Sox fans quickly develop the ability to regenerate hope in the face of setbacks or in the face of Bucky Dent. For us, a change in management at Canada Dry Potomac created a new opportunity, and because we hadn't hung up our spikes, we were able to seize it.

YOU GOTTA WIN IN NEW YORK. Sox fans know September is going to come down to Boston and New York. For Honest Tea to become a national brand, we had to develop a presence in the Big Apple. We invested much more money in New York than we made on our sales there, but it paid off there and elsewhere. The best way to convince a distributor your brand has traction, that consumers get it, is to take them on a tour of New York City and let them see what is possible firsthand. Once we could demonstrate success in that most competitive of marketplaces, we were able to take our brand to distributors in other cities.

To speed up the process, it sometimes helps to develop a flagship account by giving a store a deal they can't refuse, even if it means losing money to make it happen. Then the store becomes your ally and helps persuade the distributor that you are worthy of being carried.

THE OTHER THING THAT COUNTS IS MONEY.

You need to raise enough money so that you don't run out of cash, but not so much that you feel flush. When you don't have much cash, you watch every penny. The challenge is maintaining that same level of attention when you don't think you need to.

Early on, when we could least afford it, we had some unexpected expenses.

CUSTOMERS DON'T ALWAYS PAY. I was amazed the first time a customer didn't pay for something he bought. Where was that in my accounting class? OK, I know it's called "bad debt," but that first incident was still a bit of a shock. It feels just like you've been robbed—which you were—except you don't get to call the police. You can try to take legal action, but that's a costly distraction that rarely pays off—you have a business to run. As our business grew, we were able to graduate up the distributor food chain so nonpayment became less of a problem, but in the beginning it was a real challenge. We had to write off almost 10% of our revenue. Remember what I said about manufacturing runs. In order to get to market, we had to take chances on distributors, and the result wasn't always pretty.

TRACK YOUR CASH. Make sure your operating plan tracks your cash flow—how much money you have in the bank—and not just your profits. It's actually possible to grow yourself out of business. Your profit statement looks great, but there's no cash to meet payroll. The faster we grew, the less money we seemed to have on hand, as receivables built up and we needed to spend money on inventory.

The first step is to anticipate your cash flow. Then find ways to stretch what you have. Being able to pay suppliers in 60 days rather than 30 days is like getting a free loan. Using a local bank—ours was around the corner—instead of mailing in deposits means your money is available more quickly.

> Lack of money
> is no obstacle.
> Lack of an idea
> is an obstacle.
>
> Ken Hakuta

Ken Hakuta is the man behind the Wacky WallWalker fad, and an Honest Tea investor.

LACK OF MONEY ISN'T ALWAYS AN OBSTACLE. This is a good thing, given we didn't have much money and our customers didn't always pay. Limited resources forced us to find creative ways to achieve our goals. We couldn't afford to advertise on the TODAY show, but our national field-marketing director, Patrick Jammet, found another way to gain visibility with that audience. He showed up on TODAY's outdoor set at 3:00 a.m. and positioned himself perfectly for Matt Lauer's interview with Ellen Page, the star of *Juno*.

Creating opportunities can be expensive, but it's cheap to take advantage of ones that randomly come your way. As the Boy Scouts say: "Be prepared." I'm always surprised when I meet an entrepreneur who doesn't have a sample product in his or her shoulder bag. (I'll understand if the product is bigger than a bread box, but even then I'll want to see a picture or video.) If you run into Oprah, you want to be ready.

TOO MUCH MONEY CAN MAKE YOU STUPID. Until you've got the business figured out, more money just means more costly mistakes. We knew we didn't know what we were doing. Fortunately, we launched our line in the natural foods channel, where customers seek out new products and are (slightly) more willing to overlook product imperfections. By starting on a smaller local stage, we were able to contain our mistakes.

One last thought before we return to our story: I remember thinking in business school that a good manager doesn't have to fire people. But any fast-growing organization is bound to make mistakes, to experience situations where good people don't fit or, even more painful, aren't able to grow with the enterprise. Though I still hate doing it, I've gotten better at firing people, because being clear and decisive is a better strategy for you and the employee than slowly and painfully trying to ease someone out.

Looking back, how did we survive? A Red Sox fan—and any self-respecting entrepreneur—has to be comfortable as the underdog. We went up against companies literally 1,000 times our size with marketing budgets that dwarfed our sales. We knew things wouldn't happen overnight, and we knew there would be setbacks. But we also knew there would always be next April.

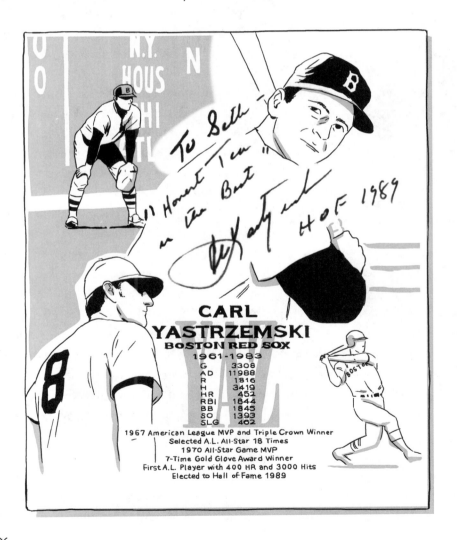

III. A BRAND EMERGES: 2004–2008

SETH, I'D REALLY LIKE YOU AND YOUR FAMILY TO VISIT MAKAIBARI, THE ESTATE WHERE WE SOURCE YOUR OOLONG TEA.

NEW DELHI

WOW! SO MANY PEOPLE!

WHERE ARE THE TEA BUSHES?

NOT HERE. WE'VE GOT MORE TRAVELING TO DO TOMORROW.

DARJEELING

PEOPLE IN INDIA SEEM RELAXED AND EASYGOING—EXCEPT WHEN THEY GET BEHIND THE WHEEL.

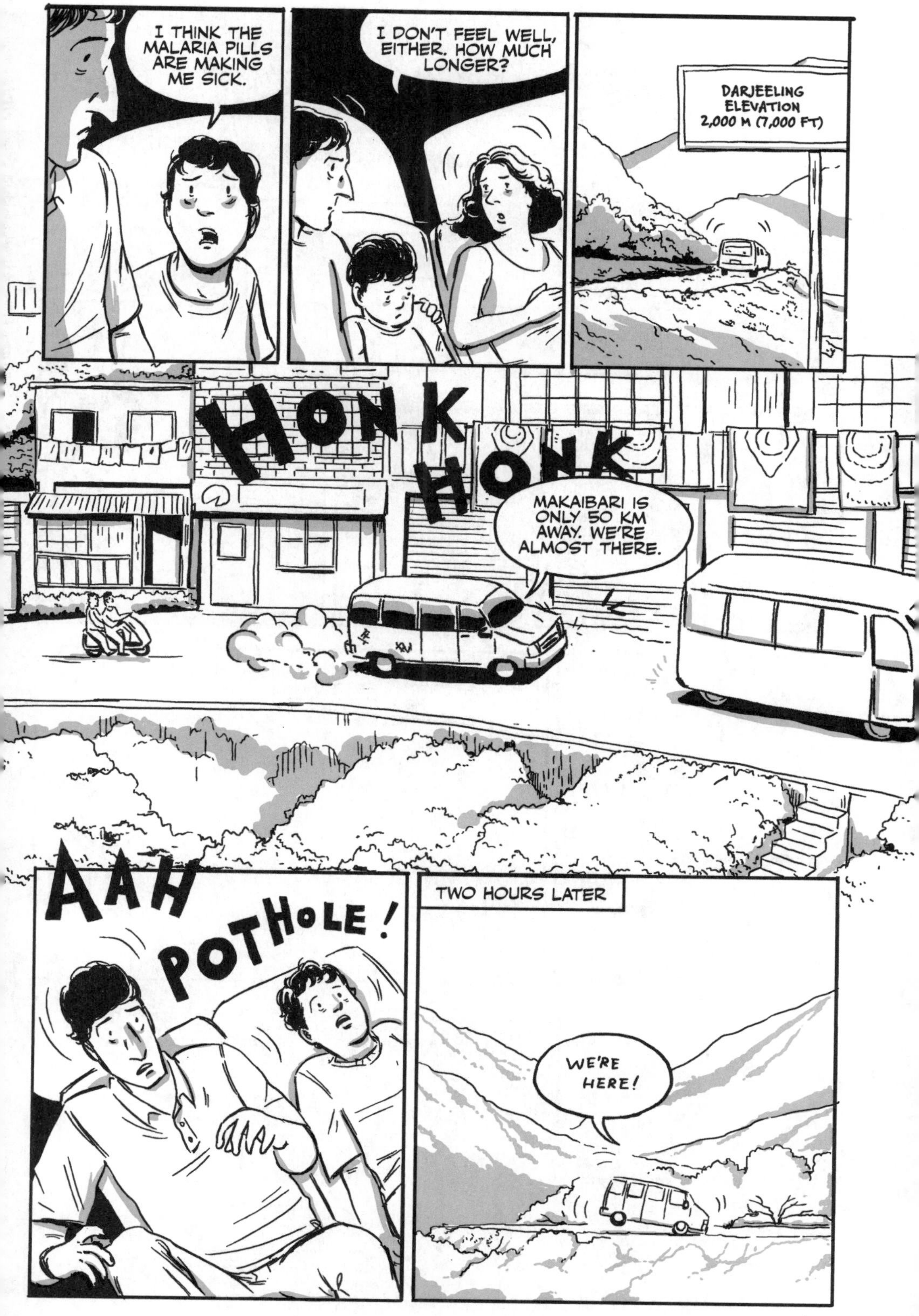
I THINK THE MALARIA PILLS ARE MAKING ME SICK.
I DON'T FEEL WELL, EITHER. HOW MUCH LONGER?
DARJEELING ELEVATION 2,000 M (7,000 FT)
HONK HONK
MAKAIBARI IS ONLY 50 KM AWAY. WE'RE ALMOST THERE.
AAH POTHOLE!
TWO HOURS LATER
WE'RE HERE!

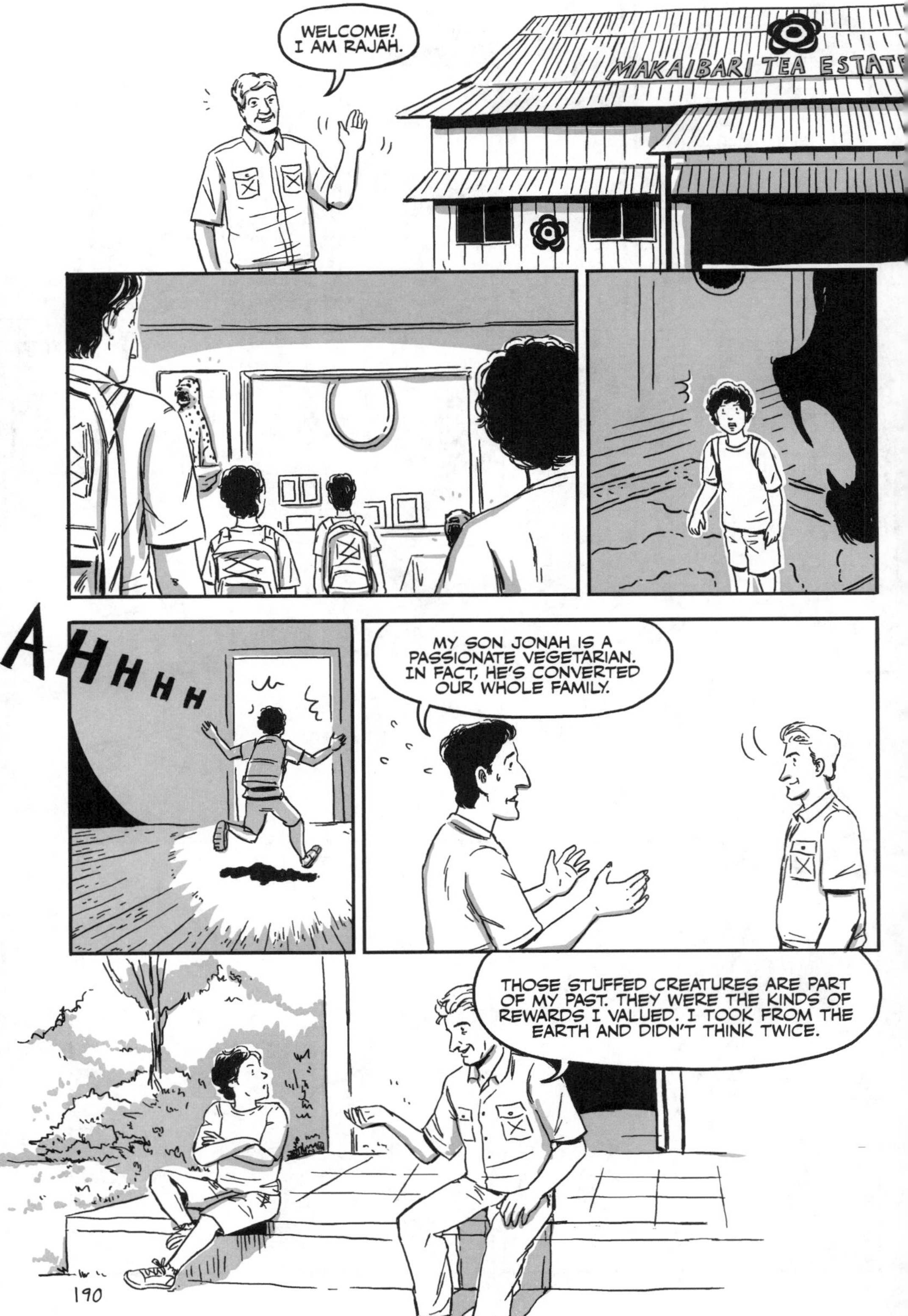
WELCOME! I AM RAJAH.
MAKAIBARI TEA ESTATE
AHHHHH
MY SON JONAH IS A PASSIONATE VEGETARIAN. IN FACT, HE'S CONVERTED OUR WHOLE FAMILY.
THOSE STUFFED CREATURES ARE PART OF MY PAST. THEY WERE THE KINDS OF REWARDS I VALUED. I TOOK FROM THE EARTH AND DIDN'T THINK TWICE.

MY FAMILY HAS RUN THIS GARDEN SINCE 1859.

I WENT TO UNIVERSITY IN ENGLAND AND ENJOYED THE WESTERN LIFESTYLE. I HARDLY CONSIDERED COMING BACK TO LIVE HERE.

THIS CAUSED MY FATHER A GREAT DEAL OF WORRY.

BUT MAN PROPOSES AND GOD DISPOSES.

ONE DAY, I WAS OUT RIDING NEAR THE GARDEN.

A WILD BOAR CROSSED MY PATH AND I WAS THROWN FROM MY HORSE.

AS I LAY ON THE GROUND UNABLE TO MOVE, I MADE A VOW.

IF I EVER MANAGE TO WALK AGAIN, I WILL LEAD A DIFFERENT LIFE.

AND I HAVE. I MADE MAKAIBARI THE FIRST ORGANIC GARDEN IN INDIA,

AND THE FIRST FAIR TRADE TEA GARDEN IN THE WORLD,

RESPECTING THE EARTH, INSTEAD OF JUST TAKING FROM IT.

THAT'S GOOD AND ALL, BUT I'M NOT SURE THAT STUFFED TIGER INSIDE WOULD BE SO IMPRESSED.

MAKAIBARI IS A NATURAL MIRACLE.

MOST TEA GARDENS ARE MONOCULTURES—FORESTS ARE CLEARED AND RE-PLACED WITH TEA BUSHES.

THOUGH THIS MAKES CUL-TIVATION MORE EFFICIENT, WHENEVER ONE SPECIES TAKES OVER, IT ALTERS THE REST OF THE ENVIRONMENT.

DIVERSITY DIMINISHES, AND WITH IT THE ECO-SYSTEM'S ABILITY TO COPE WITH THREATS LIKE DROUGHT, FUNGUS, AND INSECTS.

IT'S LIKE HOW AN ATHLETE WHO TRAINS FOR ONLY ONE SPORT BECOMES MORE PRONE TO INJURY.

WE SAW A LOT OF TEA GARDENS ON THE DRIVE UP HERE. THEY LOOKED VERY GREEN AND... ORDERLY.

YES, BUT IF YOU LOOKED CLOSER, YOU WOULD HAVE SEEN LANDSLIDES WHERE THE SOIL HAD BECOME TOO DRY AND THIN TO CATCH THE RAINWATER.

AND MORE IMPORTANT, YOU WOULDN'T HAVE SEEN ANY OTHER SIGNS OF LIFE—NO BIRDS OR BUTTERFLIES OR ANIMALS OF ANY KIND.

MAKAIBARI IS A MENAGERIE. MORE THAN TWO-THIRDS OF THE LAND HERE IS RAIN FOREST AND NATURAL VEGETATION, SUPPORTING INCREDIBLE PLANT AND ANIMAL DIVERSITY.

AND LOTS OF BUGS, TOO.

INDEED, THEY MAY HAVE EVEN DISCOVERED A NEW SPECIES HERE: THE TEA DEVA. ITS BODY MIMICS A TEA LEAF!

THIS IS THE BEST TEA I'VE EVER HAD!

YOU'RE NOT ALONE IN THINKING SO. ONE OF OUR TEAS RECENTLY SOLD AT AUCTION FOR $391/KG. A NEW RECORD!

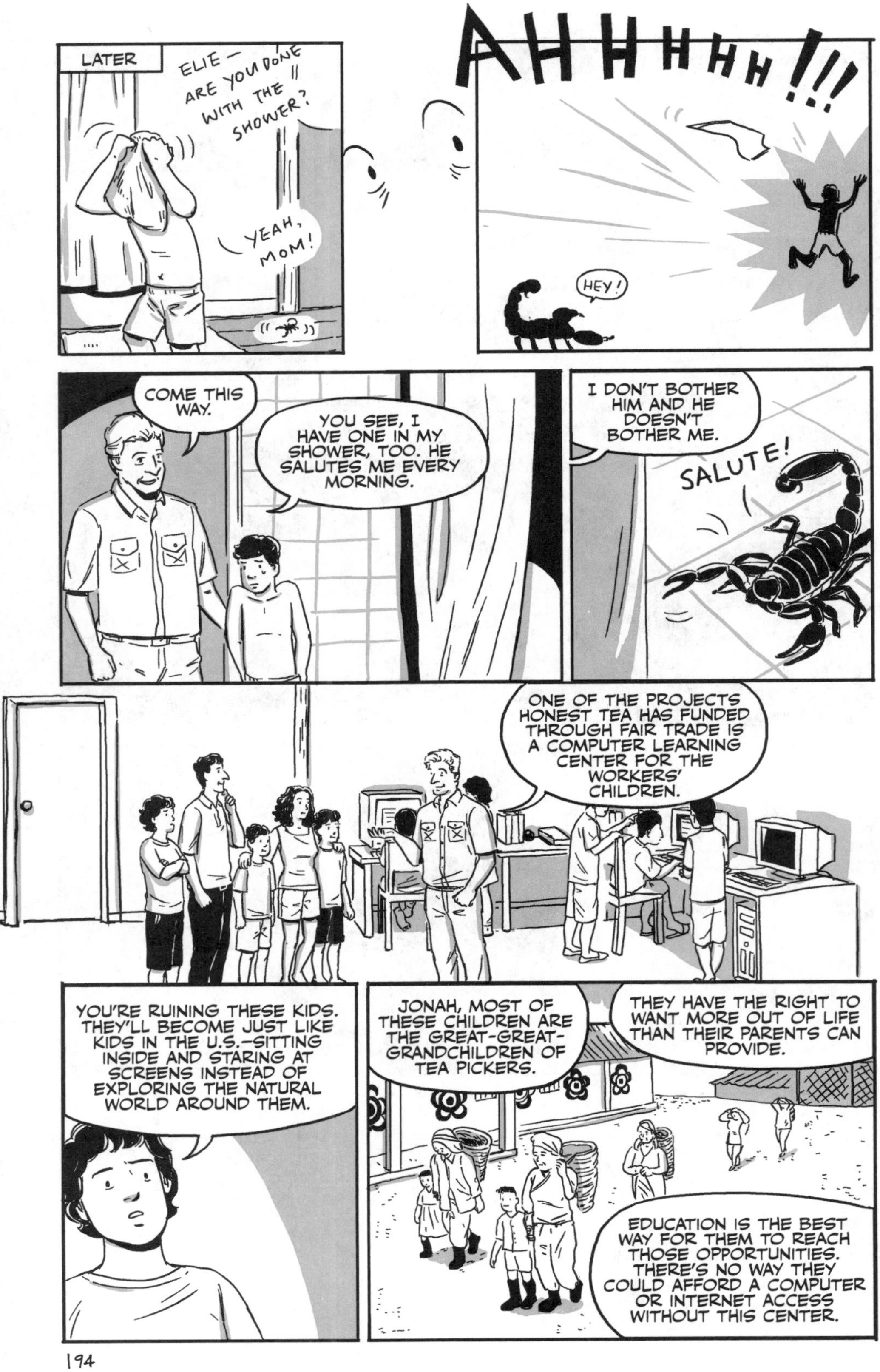
LATER
ELIE — ARE YOU DONE WITH THE SHOWER?
YEAH, MOM!
AHHHHHH!!!
HEY!
COME THIS WAY.
YOU SEE, I HAVE ONE IN MY SHOWER, TOO. HE SALUTES ME EVERY MORNING.
I DON'T BOTHER HIM AND HE DOESN'T BOTHER ME.
SALUTE!
ONE OF THE PROJECTS HONEST TEA HAS FUNDED THROUGH FAIR TRADE IS A COMPUTER LEARNING CENTER FOR THE WORKERS' CHILDREN.
YOU'RE RUINING THESE KIDS. THEY'LL BECOME JUST LIKE KIDS IN THE U.S.—SITTING INSIDE AND STARING AT SCREENS INSTEAD OF EXPLORING THE NATURAL WORLD AROUND THEM.
JONAH, MOST OF THESE CHILDREN ARE THE GREAT-GREAT-GRANDCHILDREN OF TEA PICKERS.
THEY HAVE THE RIGHT TO WANT MORE OUT OF LIFE THAN THEIR PARENTS CAN PROVIDE.
EDUCATION IS THE BEST WAY FOR THEM TO REACH THOSE OPPORTUNITIES. THERE'S NO WAY THEY COULD AFFORD A COMPUTER OR INTERNET ACCESS WITHOUT THIS CENTER.

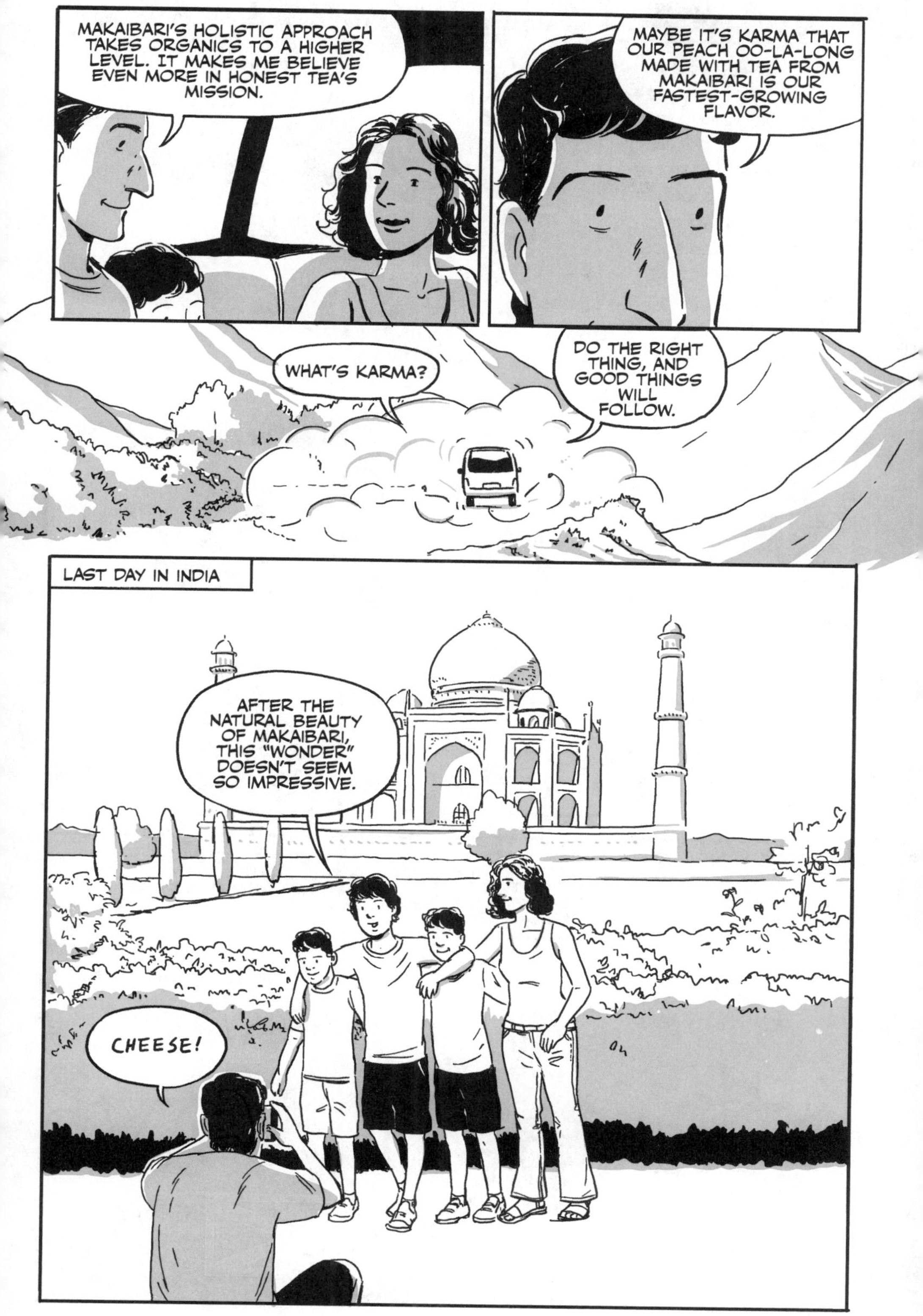
MAKAIBARI'S HOLISTIC APPROACH TAKES ORGANICS TO A HIGHER LEVEL. IT MAKES ME BELIEVE EVEN MORE IN HONEST TEA'S MISSION.
MAYBE IT'S KARMA THAT OUR PEACH OO-LA-LONG MADE WITH TEA FROM MAKAIBARI IS OUR FASTEST-GROWING FLAVOR.
WHAT'S KARMA?
DO THE RIGHT THING, AND GOOD THINGS WILL FOLLOW.
LAST DAY IN INDIA
AFTER THE NATURAL BEAUTY OF MAKAIBARI, THIS "WONDER" DOESN'T SEEM SO IMPRESSIVE.
CHEESE!

WE'D HAD ALL KINDS OF COMPANY VEHICLES OVER THE YEARS, BUT NONE REALLY FIT. FIRST WE BOUGHT A USED GREEN DODGE CARAVAN AND PASTED TWO BOTTLE STICKERS ON IT. IT WAS EFFECTIVE AS A DELIVERY VEHICLE BUT DIDN'T CONVEY THE IMAGE OF A PREMIUM BEVERAGE.

IN 2001, WE RENTED AN RV FOR OUR EAST COAST SAMPLING TOUR.

THIS IS GREAT! WHAT WE'RE SAVING ON LODGING WILL MORE THAN MAKE UP FOR THE COST OF THE RV.

OUT OF ORDER

WC

SO MUCH FOR BEING COST-EFFECTIVE. IN THE END, WE HAD TO GET HOTEL ROOMS FOR OUR INTERNS.

IN 2002, WE HAD THE HAARLEM HONEYBUS, WHICH WAS ONLY MILDLY MORE SUCCESSFUL THAN THAT TEA VARIETY. IT WAS NICE BRANDING BUT EXPENSIVE, SO WE ONLY KEPT IT FOR ONE SEASON.

WE NEEDED TO FIND A VEHICLE TO TRANSPORT OUR TEA THAT ALSO CONNECTED WITH OUR BRAND.

WHAT ABOUT THE TOYOTA PRIUS?

IT ISN'T PRACTICAL FOR US. WE NEED TO CARRY AT LEAST 50 CASES OF TEA, AND A PRIUS CAN BARELY HOLD 20.

ARE ANY AMERICAN CAR COMPANIES COMING OUT WITH A HYBRID?

I HEARD FORD IS MAKING A HYBRID VERSION OF THEIR SMALL SUV. MY BROTHER IS A REPORTER IN DETROIT AND COULD GET THE NAME OF THE PERSON LEADING THE PROJECT.

Ford

LET'S REACH OUT TO THEM. MAYBE WE CAN GET A DISCOUNT ON THE HYBRIDS. IT'S WORTH A TRY.

WHERE ARE YOU GOING?

DETROIT, TO MEET EXECUTIVES AT FORD.

I'M NEVER GOING TO DRIVE A CAR. IF EVERYONE RODE A BIKE, WE'D ALL BE A LOT HEALTHIER AND USE A LOT LESS GAS.

YOU'RE RIGHT, JO. BUT REMEMBER THAT TIME I TRIED TO BIKE HOME WITH A CASE OF TEA?

OOPS

SOMETIMES YOU NEED A CAR TO CARRY STUFF AROUND.

WE CAN BE YOUR AMBASSADOR TO THE NATURAL FOODS WORLD. OUR CONSUMERS ARE CONSUMERS YOU WANT TO CONNECT WITH.

OUR VEHICLES APPEAR AT HUNDREDS OF EVENTS ON THE EAST AND WEST COASTS—FILM FESTIVALS, ROAD RACES, AND CONCERTS—PLUS ALL THE BIG NATURAL FOODS STORES.

OUR TEAM OF SUMMER INTERNS GIVES OUT TENS OF THOUSANDS OF SAMPLES TO ENVIRONMENTALLY CONSCIOUS AND HEALTH-CONSCIOUS CONSUMERS.

THAT'S ALL GREAT, BUT HAS ANYONE ACTUALLY HEARD OF HONEST TEA?

Ford
3.5 million VEHICLES

T
7.8 million BOTTLES

WHILE WE MAY BE SMALL IN TERMS OF DOLLARS, WE HAVE A PRESENCE IN THE MARKET. LAST YEAR, WE SOLD TWICE AS MANY UNITS AS FORD IN THE U.S.

WE CAN INTRODUCE YOU TO YOUR TARGET AUDIENCE IN A WHOLE NEW WAY. WORKING TOGETHER, THE ESCAPE HYBRID CAN BE THE NEW "MODEL TEA."

A FEW MONTHS LATER, AT THE LOHAS (LIFESTYLE OF HEALTH AND SUSTAINABILITY) CONFERENCE IN CALIFORNIA

WHAT AM I DOING HERE WITH FORD MOTOR COMPANY? IT'S HARD TO IMAGINE THAT TWO COMPANIES COULD BE MORE DIFFERENT.

FORD IS 25,000 TIMES LARGER THAN HONEST TEA. IF FORD WANTED TO TELL PEOPLE ABOUT THE ESCAPE HYBRID, SHOULDN'T THEY HAVE PARTNERED WITH SOMEONE THEIR OWN SIZE, LIKE FINLAND?

AUTO SALES
$138 BILLION

GDP
$142 BILLION

IN THE SAME WAY WE CHOSE TO MAKE OUR TEA ORGANIC, FORD IS MOVING IN A MORE SUSTAINABLE DIRECTION. IT'S NOT BECAUSE OF GOVERNMENT MANDATES OR LAWSUITS, BUT BECAUSE OF SOMETHING EVEN MORE POWERFUL— CONSUMER DEMAND.

OUR HOPE IS THAT THE ESCAPE HYBRID WILL REPLACE MILLIONS OF NON-HYBRID SUVS, STRENGTHENING OUR ECOSYSTEM AND MAKING OUR NATION MORE ENERGY INDEPENDENT.

IT IS MY DELIGHT TO PRESENT TO YOU THE GREAT TEA ESCAPE!

WHY DIDN'T WE GO WITH THE NAME MODEL TEA? IT WAS PERFECT!

THEY WANTED "ESCAPE" IN THE NAME. THEY GAVE US THE CARS, SO THEY GOT TO PICK THE NAME.

IT WAS TIME TO RAISE MONEY YET AGAIN. IN DECEMBER 2004, WE MET WITH SOLERA CAPITAL, A WOMEN-LED VENTURE CAPITAL FIRM IN NEW YORK.

AS INVESTORS IN ANNIE'S HOMEGROWN, WE UNDERSTAND YOUR SPACE.

I LOVE ANNIE'S.

WE'D LIKE TO INVEST $8 MILLION IN HONEST TEA. THERE'S JUST ONE ISSUE.

WHAT'S THAT?

YOUR PROPOSED VALUATION OF $20.5 MILLION IS TOO HIGH. WITH SALES AT $5.9 MILLION AND NO PROFITS, WE THINK A $12 MILLION PRE-MONEY VALUATION IS GENEROUS.

$$\frac{\$8m}{(\$12m + \$8m)} = 40\%$$

THEY'LL OWN 40% OF THE COMPANY. YIKES.

BUT WE WERE ONLY LOOKING TO RAISE $2 MILLION. WE THINK THAT'S ENOUGH TO TAKE THE BRAND TO THE NEXT LEVEL.

WITH YOUR NEW PLASTIC LINE, WE THINK THIS IS THE TIME TO ACT.

THE COMPETITION IS HEATING UP. STARBUCKS IS PUSHING TAZO, AND PEPSI IS PUSHING SOBE. YOU HAVE TO BE AGGRESSIVE WITH SLOTTING.

YOU NEED TO HIRE MORE SALESPEOPLE AND REGIONAL MANAGERS. YOU SHOULD START ADVERTISING. AND YOU'LL NEED WORKING CAPITAL.

I'M NOT SURE WE COULD REALLY SPEND $8 MILLION WISELY.

THINK BIG! THIS IS A CRUCIAL MOMENT— YOU NEED TO PROVE YOU CAN BE A PLAYER. AND GIVEN THE SIZE OF OUR FUND, WE CAN'T JUSTIFY SPENDING THE TIME ON SMALL INVESTMENTS.

OUR TOTAL PAYROLL, MARKETING, AND RENT DON'T ADD UP TO $2.5 MILLION.

MOLLY MIGHT BE RIGHT ABOUT SPENDING MORE MONEY, BUT FIRST WE NEED TO GROW SALES ENOUGH TO JUSTIFY A HIGHER VALUATION.

PLUS, THEY WANT REDEMPTION RIGHTS, LIQUIDATION PREFERENCES, TWO BOARD SEATS... WE'D BE GIVING UP CONTROL.

THAT CONCERNS ME, ESPECIALLY SINCE IT SEEMS LIKE THE FOUNDERS ARE NO LONGER WITH THEIR COMPANIES AFTER SOLERA GETS CONTROL.

WAY TO GO, ELIE!

IT'S NICE TO HAVE INTEREST FROM PRIVATE EQUITY, BUT IT FEELS LIKE A HIGH PRICE TO PAY.

FOR YOU AND ME BOTH—MY SHARES WOULD GO DOWN IN VALUE. WITH THE WAY THE COMPANY IS GROWING, YOU SHOULDN'T FEEL FORCED TO TAKE THAT KIND OF OFFER.

I KNOW I'D PUT MORE MONEY IN. WHY DON'T YOU REACH OUT TO YOUR INVESTORS AND SEE IF THEY CAN BEAT SOLERA'S OFFER? IF THEY CAN'T, THEN TAKE IT.

RIGHT AWAY, OUR INVESTORS OFFERED TO PUT IN $400,000.

WE HAVE ENOUGH TO TIDE US OVER. BUT WHAT ARE WE GOING TO DO FOR WORKING CAPITAL? OUR INVENTORIES AND RECEIVABLES ARE OVER $1.5 MILLION AND GROWING.

IT LOOKS LIKE WE'LL GET APPROVED FOR AN $800,000 LINE OF CREDIT FROM CITY FIRST BANK OF D.C.

THAT'S GREAT.

BUT THERE'S A CATCH. THEY REQUIRE BOTH OF US TO PERSONALLY GUARANTEE THE FULL AMOUNT.

I DON'T THINK WE HAVE A CHOICE.

SALE

CAN YOU TELL ME SOME GOOD NEWS?

BUSINESS IS GREAT. WE'RE SENDING THREE VARIETIES TO OVER 1,000 TARGET STORES.

WE GOT APPROVED FOR A TEST WITH CRACKER BARREL; THAT'S A 500-STORE CHAIN.

Cracker Barrel
Old Country Store

ALL SIX OF OUR VARIETIES AT SAFEWAY ARE IN THEIR TOP 30 NATURAL BEVERAGES, SO THEY'RE TAKING IN THREE MORE VARIETIES.

SAFEWAY®

I THINK WE COULD HIT $10 MILLION IN SALES NEXT YEAR!

THANKS. I NEEDED TO HEAR THAT.

WITHIN A FEW MONTHS, WE RAISED THE REST OF THE $2 MILLION, MOSTLY FROM OUR EXISTING INVESTORS. OUR SALES IN 2005 GREW 62% TO $9.6 MILLION AND IN 2006 WERE HEADING TOWARD $13.5 MILLION. AT THAT POINT, WE FELT WE COULD WISELY SPEND MORE MONEY TO ACCELERATE OUR GROWTH. THE HIGHER SALES WOULD JUSTIFY A HIGHER VALUATION, SO DILUTION WOULD BE LESS OF AN ISSUE.

THAT FALL, WE MET A VERY WEALTHY PRIVATE INVESTOR, WHOM WE'LL CALL BILL.

I LOVE YOUR PRODUCTS. I THINK YOU'RE PERFECTLY POSITIONED AS THE COUNTRY MOVES TO HEALTHY, ORGANIC CHOICES.

WE'RE LOOKING FOR INVESTORS WHO CAN BOOST OUR GROWTH.

HELP US UNDERSTAND WHAT YOU BRING TO THE TABLE.

I CAN GET YOU INTO PROPERTIES ALL OVER THE COUNTRY AND INTRODUCE YOU TO THE CEOS AT WALMART, COSTCO, TARGET, SAFEWAY, TRADER JOE'S, AND FOOD SERVICE DISTRIBUTORS LIKE HOST MARRIOT AND ARAMARK.

I HAVE A GREAT TRACK RECORD IN THE HEALTH AND WELLNESS SPACE.

$80 million

CRACK!

AS LEAD INVESTOR, I HELPED ONE COMPANY GROW FROM $500,000 TO $80 MILLION IN SALES.

I UNDERSTAND YOU ARE LOOKING FOR AN OPERATIONS PERSON.

MY NETWORK CAN HELP YOU IDENTIFY AND ACCESS SOME GREAT CANDIDATES.

AND, UNLIKE THE PRIVATE EQUITY GUYS, WE ARE PATIENT CAPITAL.

HOW MUCH ARE YOU LOOKING TO RAISE?

$10 MILLION. THOUGH I HATE TO SAY NEVER, WITH THAT AMOUNT WE SHOULDN'T NEED TO DO ANY MORE FUNDRAISING ROUNDS.

AND WHAT DO I GET FOR THAT?

24% OF THE COMPANY. WE'RE RAISING MONEY AT A $31 MILLION PRE-MONEY VALUATION.

HOW DO YOU JUSTIFY THAT NUMBER?

THAT'S THREE TIMES OUR LAST 12 MONTHS' SALES, PLUS TAX-LOSS CARRYFORWARDS, NET OF DEBT. AND IT'S 1.3 TIMES OUR FORECASTED SALES FOR 2007.

THAT'S PRICEY, BUT I'M IN.

MY ONE REQUIREMENT IS THAT YOU INCREASE THE EQUITY POOL FOR EMPLOYEES. I WANT YOU TO HAVE 12% AVAILABLE.

BACK AT THE OFFICE

THE ONLY THING I DON'T GET IS THE EQUITY POOL. WE ALREADY HAVE A GREAT SENIOR TEAM AND PLENTY OF EQUITY INCENTIVES. OUR EMPLOYEES HAVE OPTIONS ON 5% OF SHARES, AND YOU HAVE OPTIONS ON 15%.

THERE'S GOTTA BE SOMETHING ELSE GOING ON.

PERHAPS, BUT IT ISN'T A BIG PROBLEM IN TERMS OF DILUTION. IF WE CREATE A 12% OPTION POOL, WE JUST HAVE TO GIVE BILL 12% MORE SHARES, WHICH COULD INCREASE HIS STAKE FROM 24% TO 26.5%.

OK. I'LL SIGN THE TERM SHEET.

204

AND OF COURSE, WE'LL BE GETTING PARTICIPATING PREFERRED STOCK.

BILL'S LAWYER

THAT ISN'T IN THE TERM SHEET WE SIGNED.

HONEST TEA'S LAWYER, GEORGE LLOYD

PARTICIPATING PREFERRED STOCK MEANS THEY GET THEIR $10 MILLION BACK BEFORE ANYONE ELSE GETS ANYTHING. AND THEN, ON TOP OF THAT, THEY GET THE FULL VALUE OF THEIR SHARES. IT'S AS IF YOU RETURN AN ITEM TO A STORE, ONLY YOU GET YOUR MONEY BACK AND GET TO KEEP THE ITEM.

PREFERRED STOCK COLOGNE

I'm all yours!

GIVEN HOW MUCH MONEY WE'RE INVESTING, WE DESERVE PARTICIPATING PREFERRED STOCK.

IT ISN'T A QUESTION OF WHAT YOU DESERVE. IT'S WHAT WE AGREED TO. YOU AGREED TO BUY COMMON STOCK JUST LIKE EVERYONE ELSE.

THAT'S NOT HOW WE DO BUSINESS—WE ALWAYS GET PARTICIPATING PREFERRED.

HAVE YOU SPOKEN TO BILL ABOUT THIS?

HE'S AWAY ON HIS HONEYMOON. I'M THE ONE HANDLING THIS CONTRACT.

WE'LL HAVE TO LOOK AT OTHER OPTIONS.

YOU UNDERSTAND WE HAVE A 21-DAY LOCKUP. YOU AREN'T ALLOWED TO NEGOTIATE WITH ANYONE ELSE DURING THAT TIME.

I'M NOT SURE WE CAN WAIT 21 DAYS AND THEN START FROM SCRATCH.

I WOULDN'T DO BUSINESS WITH YOU EVEN IF YOU GOT RID OF THAT DEMAND! I DON'T TRUST YOU!

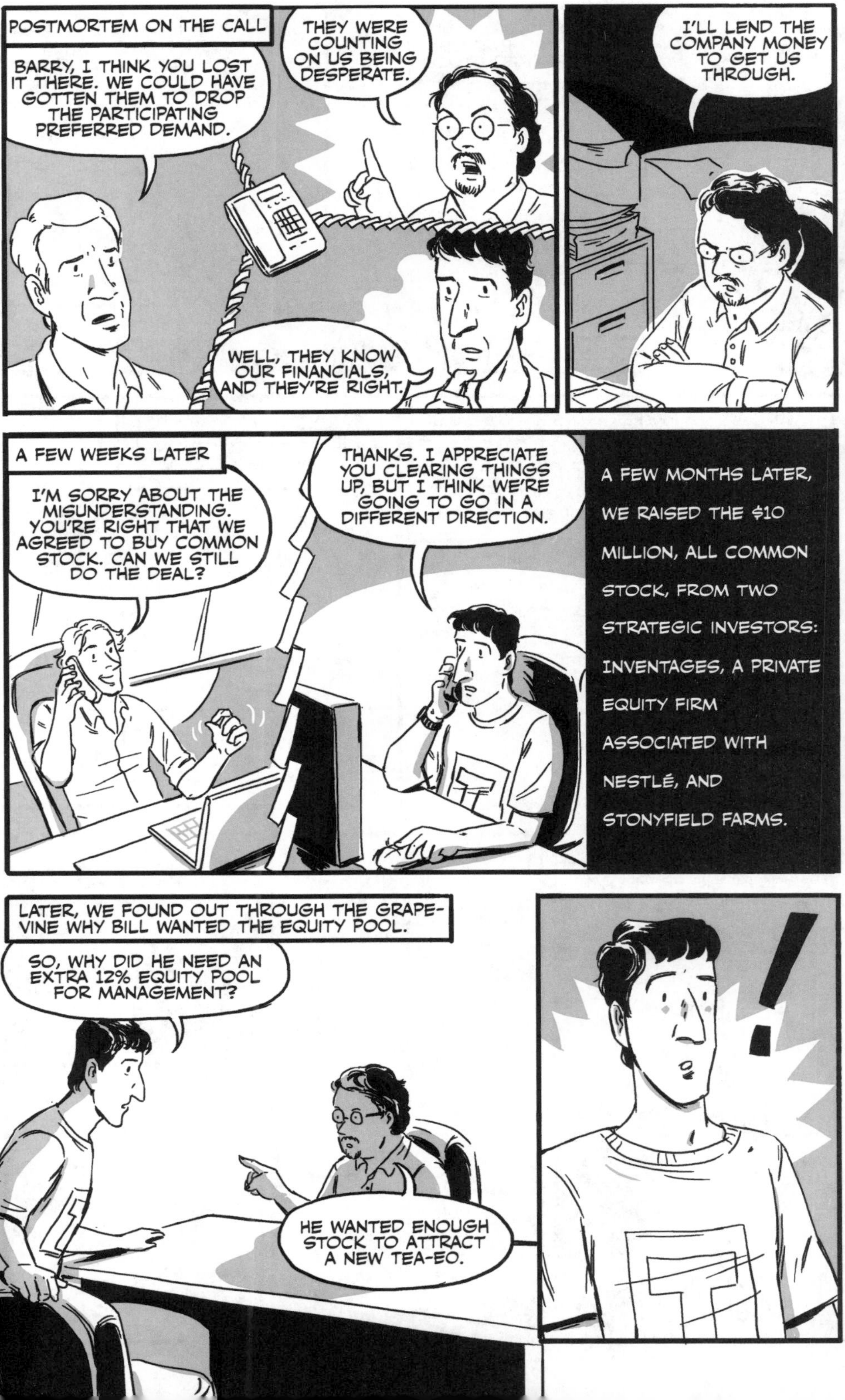
POSTMORTEM ON THE CALL
BARRY, I THINK YOU LOST IT THERE. WE COULD HAVE GOTTEN THEM TO DROP THE PARTICIPATING PREFERRED DEMAND.
THEY WERE COUNTING ON US BEING DESPERATE.
WELL, THEY KNOW OUR FINANCIALS, AND THEY'RE RIGHT.
I'LL LEND THE COMPANY MONEY TO GET US THROUGH.
A FEW WEEKS LATER
I'M SORRY ABOUT THE MISUNDERSTANDING. YOU'RE RIGHT THAT WE AGREED TO BUY COMMON STOCK. CAN WE STILL DO THE DEAL?
THANKS. I APPRECIATE YOU CLEARING THINGS UP, BUT I THINK WE'RE GOING TO GO IN A DIFFERENT DIRECTION.
A FEW MONTHS LATER, WE RAISED THE $10 MILLION, ALL COMMON STOCK, FROM TWO STRATEGIC INVESTORS: INVENTAGES, A PRIVATE EQUITY FIRM ASSOCIATED WITH NESTLÉ, AND STONYFIELD FARMS.
LATER, WE FOUND OUT THROUGH THE GRAPE-VINE WHY BILL WANTED THE EQUITY POOL.
SO, WHY DID HE NEED AN EXTRA 12% EQUITY POOL FOR MANAGEMENT?
HE WANTED ENOUGH STOCK TO ATTRACT A NEW TEA-EO.
!

IN 2005, THE CHICKEN OUT ROTISSERIE RESTAURANT CHAIN ASKED US TO DEVELOP A PRIVATE-LABEL LINE OF TEAS FOR THEM. WHILE WE WERE WORKING ON RECIPES, THEY ASKED US TO INCLUDE A LEMONADE. WE COULDN'T SEE ANY REASON WHY NOT, SO WE DEVELOPED AN AMAZING CRANBERRY LEMONADE THAT WASN'T TOO SWEET. IN THE END, CHICKEN OUT DIDN'T TAKE OUR TEAS OR THE LEMONADE. BUT WE'D CREATED A GREAT PRODUCT, AND IT GOT US THINKING OUTSIDE THE "T."

CHICKEN OUT ROTISSERIE

NOT EVERYONE DRINKS TEA. WE SHOULD HAVE A LINE FOR THOSE PEOPLE.

LIKE WHAT?

THE CRANBERRY LEMONADE, FOR STARTERS.

DOES IT MATTER THAT IT ISN'T BREWED?

NOT REALLY. IT'S AN "HONEST" PRODUCT: IT'S ORGANIC AND A LOT LESS SWEET THAN ANYTHING ELSE OUT THERE.

WHAT YOU'RE SAYING IS WE ARE REALLY "HONEST BEVERAGE." OUR FIRST PRODUCTS WERE TEAS, BUT WE DON'T HAVE TO LIMIT OURSELVES.

EXACTLY. THERE'S A HUGE OPPORTUNITY HERE. BUT TO SUCCEED, WE NEED A WHOLE LINE, NOT JUST ONE FLAVOR.

ANYTHING WITH POMEGRANATE IS RED-HOT RIGHT NOW.

POMEGRANATE JUICE IS CRAZY EXPENSIVE. AND IT'S REALLY SWEET.

SO DILUTE IT. THAT'S WHAT WE DO WITH OUR KIDS' APPLE JUICE.

HOW ABOUT A LIME RICKEY? THAT WAS ALWAYS MY FAVORITE GROWING UP.

‹ LIME RICKEY ›

1 LIME

8 OZ CARBONATED WATER

1.5 OZ RASPBERRY SYRUP

WHAT DO WE CALL THE LINE?

IN ENGLAND, THEY CALL A DILUTED FRUIT DRINK A "SQUASH."

I DON'T THINK THE NAME HONEST SQUASH WILL WORK OVER HERE. PEOPLE WILL THINK WE'RE JUICING ZUCCHINI.

LIMEADE, LEMONADE, WHY NOT HONEST ADE?

SHOULD IT BE HONEST ADE OR AID?

NO! AID

WE CAN'T CALL THE LINE HONEST AIDS.

HONEST ADE IT IS!

THE FLAVORS CAME EASILY. WE STARTED WITH THE CRANBERRY LEMONADE AND A LIMEADE, LATER ADDING A POMEGRANATE BLUEBERRY AND AN ORANGE MANGO. THE HARDER PART WAS DESIGNING A LABEL THAT CONNECTED WITH THE TEA LINE BUT HAD ITS OWN IDENTITY.

CRANBERRY LEMONADE

ORANGE MANGO

POMEGRANATE BLUEBERRY

LIMEADE

WITHOUT "TEA" IN THE NAME, DOES IT MAKE SENSE TO USE ART INSIDE A "T" ON THE LABEL?

WHAT IF WE PLAY WITH THE IDEA OF THIS BEING A "THIRST ADE"?

WE COULD MOVE THE BAR DOWN ON THE "T" TO MAKE A PLUS SIGN.

THAT'S STRIKING, BUT TOO MUCH LIKE THE RED CROSS.

HOW ABOUT WE TURN THE "T" UPSIDE DOWN AND MAKE IT LOOK LIKE A STOVEPIPE HAT? IT'LL BE A VISUAL PUN ON "HONEST ABE."

THAT'S TOO CUTE BY HALF. WE NEED MORE HELP. LET'S ASK OTHER DESIGNERS FOR IDEAS.

LET'S TRY OUR MARKETING DIRECTOR'S SISTER VANESSA. SHE'S A GRAPHIC DESIGNER AND HAS WANTED TO WORK WITH US.

hi!

WHAT DO YOU THINK OF THIS? I'M EMPHASIZING THE "HONEST" RATHER THAN THE "ADE."

A BIT TOO MUCH LIKE HARVARD FOR ME. THE "H" REALLY ISN'T AS CONDUCIVE TO ART INSIDE AS A "T."

WHAT ABOUT THE LETTER "A"?

SAME PROBLEM.

I'M NOT SURE YOU SHOULD GIVE UP ON USING THE LETTER "A."

THESE ARE BETTER, BUT WE SHOULD CONSIDER SOMETHING ELSE BESIDES LETTERS.

OTHER DESIGNER

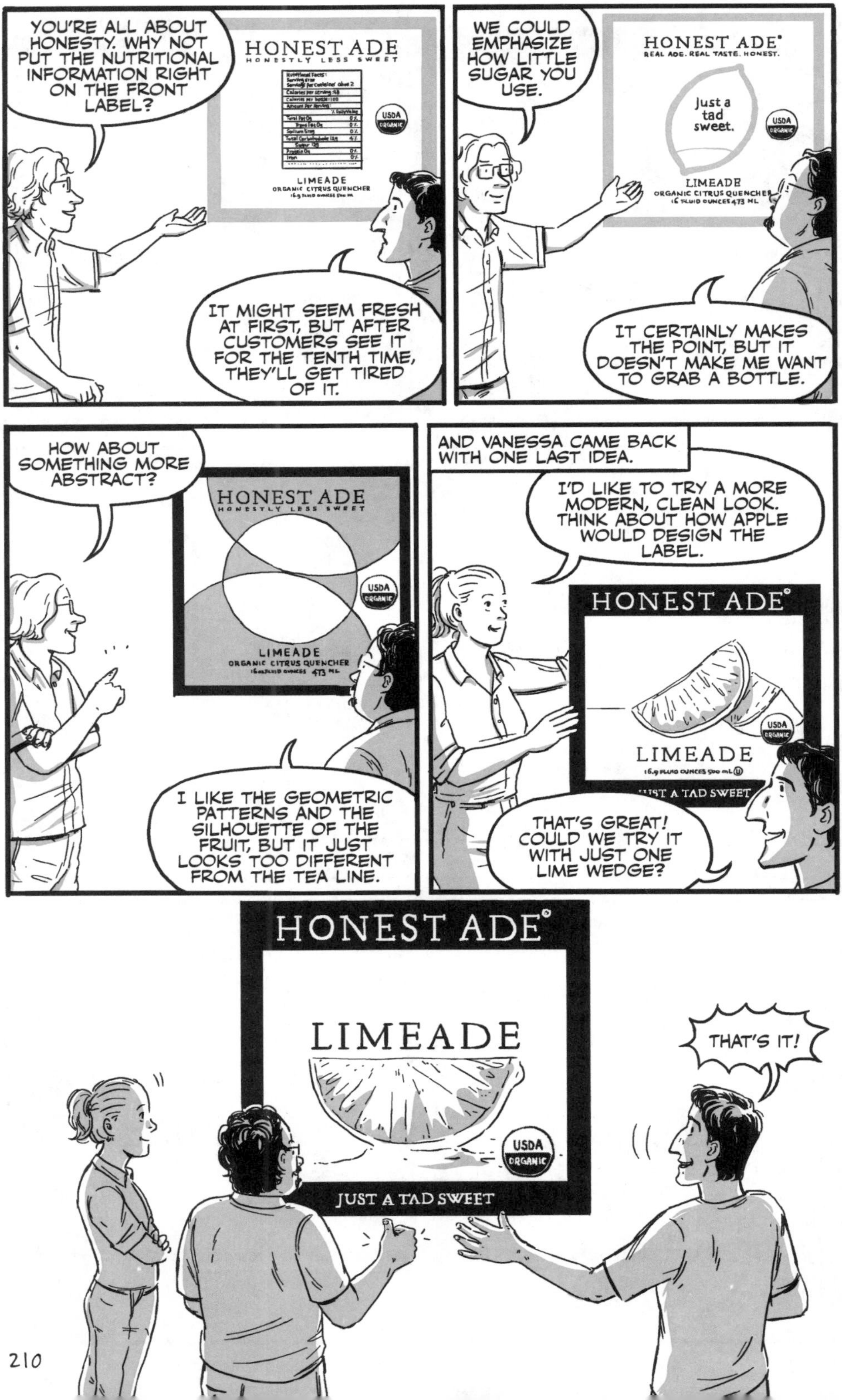

YOU'RE ALL ABOUT HONESTY. WHY NOT PUT THE NUTRITIONAL INFORMATION RIGHT ON THE FRONT LABEL?
HONEST ADE
HONESTLY LESS SWEET
USDA ORGANIC
LIMEADE
ORGANIC CITRUS QUENCHER
IT MIGHT SEEM FRESH AT FIRST, BUT AFTER CUSTOMERS SEE IT FOR THE TENTH TIME, THEY'LL GET TIRED OF IT.
WE COULD EMPHASIZE HOW LITTLE SUGAR YOU USE.
HONEST ADE
REAL ADE. REAL TASTE. HONEST.
Just a tad sweet.
USDA ORGANIC
LIMEADE
ORGANIC CITRUS QUENCHER
16 FLUID OUNCES 473 ML
IT CERTAINLY MAKES THE POINT, BUT IT DOESN'T MAKE ME WANT TO GRAB A BOTTLE.
HOW ABOUT SOMETHING MORE ABSTRACT?
HONEST ADE
HONESTLY LESS SWEET
USDA ORGANIC
LIMEADE
ORGANIC CITRUS QUENCHER
I LIKE THE GEOMETRIC PATTERNS AND THE SILHOUETTE OF THE FRUIT, BUT IT JUST LOOKS TOO DIFFERENT FROM THE TEA LINE.
AND VANESSA CAME BACK WITH ONE LAST IDEA.
I'D LIKE TO TRY A MORE MODERN, CLEAN LOOK. THINK ABOUT HOW APPLE WOULD DESIGN THE LABEL.
HONEST ADE
USDA ORGANIC
LIMEADE
16.9 FLUID OUNCES 500 mL
THAT'S GREAT! COULD WE TRY IT WITH JUST ONE LIME WEDGE?
HONEST ADE
LIMEADE
USDA ORGANIC
JUST A TAD SWEET
THAT'S IT!

YOU LANDED OUR FIRST COKE DISTRIBUTOR!

THEY'RE SMALL, AND BUFFALO ISN'T EXACTLY THE ICED TEA CAPITAL OF THE U.S., BUT YES.

MAY 2006

BUFFALO

EXCEPT THERE'S A CATCH: THEY INSIST ON A PERPETUAL CONTRACT.

WE CAN'T DO THAT. IF THEY DO A BAD JOB, WE'LL BE STUCK FOREVER.

THEY SAY THEY NEED A PERPETUAL CONTRACT TO JUSTIFY THEIR INVESTMENT IN BUILDING OUR BRAND. WE DON'T HAVE A CHOICE.

IF WE GIVE THEM A PERPETUAL CONTRACT, THERE HAS TO BE SOME PERFORMANCE STANDARD.

THEY'LL NEVER AGREE TO A VOLUME TARGET.

VOLUME TARGET
$1 million SALES

WHAT ABOUT A GROWTH TARGET?

WE'RE GROWING AT 50%. WE CAN'T REQUIRE THEM TO GROW AT 50%, OR EVEN 10%, FOREVER.

GROWTH TARGET
50% GROWTH

HMMM...

OK. LET'S REQUIRE THEM TO BE IN THE TOP HALF OF OUR DISTRIBUTORS IN TERMS OF PER CAPITA SALES.

AS A COKE DISTRIBUTOR, THEY HAD BETTER BE ABOVE AVERAGE.

TOP HALF

DISTRIBUTORS

THAT'S WHY I THINK THEY'LL AGREE TO IT. PLUS, IT FITS INTO A BEHAVIORAL ECONOMICS BIAS WHERE PEOPLE OVERESTIMATE THEIR ABILITY RELATIVE TO OTHERS.

think they're above average

80%

IT'S LIKE LAKE WOBEGON, WHERE ALL THE CHILDREN ARE ABOVE AVERAGE.

LAKE WOBEGON

EXACTLY. I DON'T LIKE THE IDEA OF HITCHING UP FOREVER, BUT IF THEY END UP BEING BELOW AVERAGE, AT LEAST WE'LL HAVE A WAY OUT.

56. A DAY IN THE LIFE

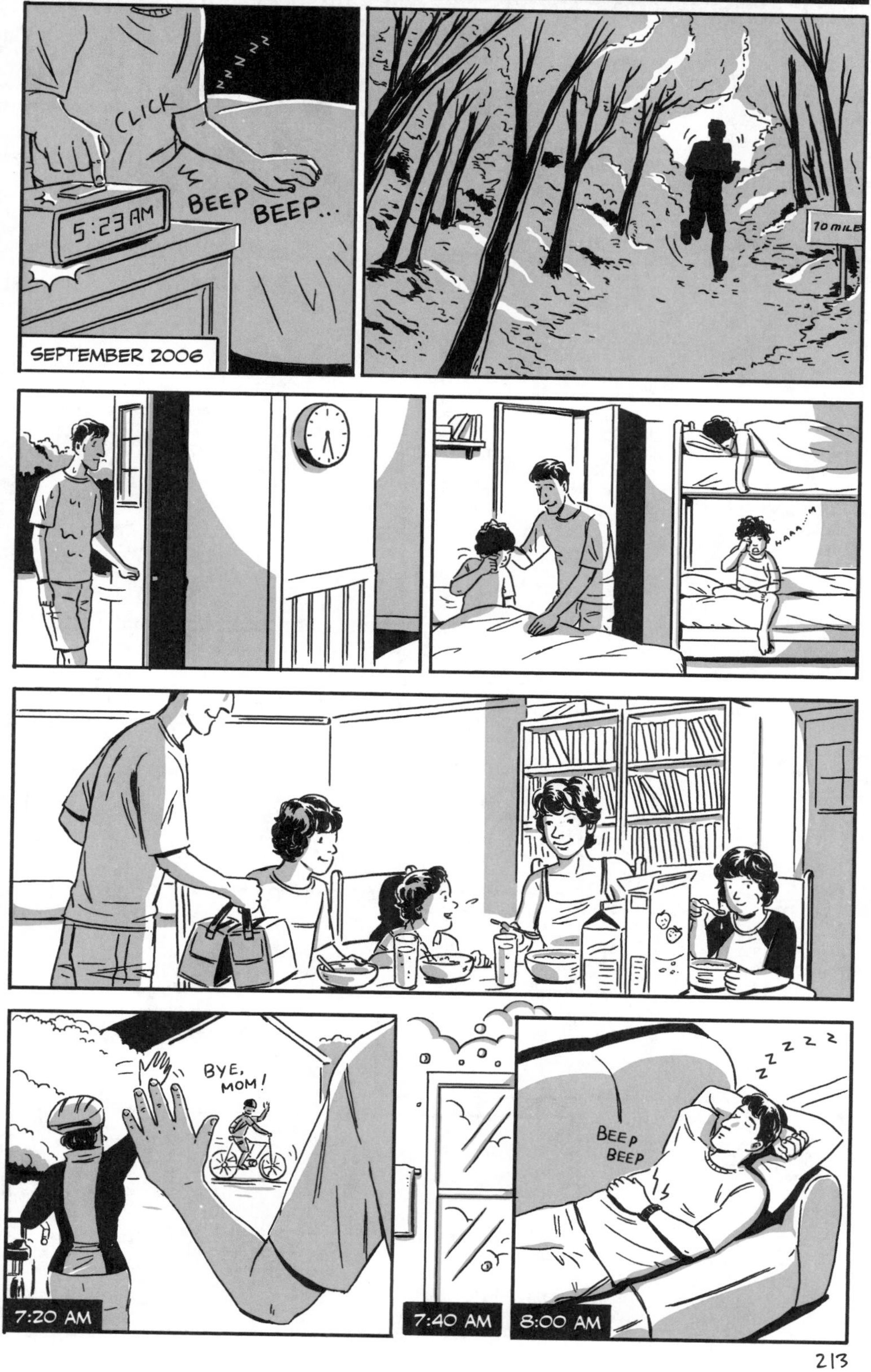

CLICK
Z Z Z Z
5:23 AM
BEEP BEEP...
SEPTEMBER 2006
10 MILE
WAAA...M
BYE, MOM!
7:20 AM
7:40 AM
BEEP BEEP
Z Z Z Z Z
8:00 AM

BEST PARKING
SPOT IN
BETHESDA.

8:10 AM

From: Laurence S.
Subject: Honest Tea has changed my life

Dear Seth and Barry,

I love your teas. I have weaned myself off the sugary Starbucks mochas thanks to your efforts. But more important, your teas are delicious—the Gold Rush Cinnamon is disgustingly good. My other favorite is Heavenly Honey Green. I'm a student at Penn, and I frequently walk all the way to the one campus cafeteria that sells your teas. I had to ask them to order a larger quantity every week because they always ran out by lunch. Let me just say that you two are drink geniuses—this drink is more than a tea. It's an all-body experience. Unbelievable that no one ever figured how to make delicious tea in a bottle without sweetener. Gratefully yours,

Laurence S.

TAP...
TAP

Hi Laurence!

Thanks for a wonderful, and truly gratifying, note. Responses like yours are just what we hoped for when we launched Honest Tea. Don't be afraid to request Honest Tea at other locations on campus so you don't have to walk so far—not that that's always a bad thing, but hopefully more people will be able to buy the tea more easily. Enjoy, and please help spread the word—we're a small company and that's the best way for us to grow! Honestly yours, Seth

From: Steve S.
Subject: The Label

Dear Seth and Barry,

Love the product. But why is the label yucky plastic instead of nice paper?

Hi Steve,

Fair question. We had paper labels originally but as the bottles sweat and occasionally get dipped in ice, the paper starts to degrade, wrinkle, and look bad. It's not an easy tradeoff, but we've erred on the side of making sure our product is sellable. Also, the plastic melts down as part of the recycling process and does not contaminate the waste stream. Regards, Seth

TAP
TAP

CONFERENCE CALL WITH BOTTLING PLANT

OUR TEST RUN OF THE NEWLY DESIGNED PLASTIC BOTTLES SHOWS 20% OVALIZATION.

8:30 AM

CALL WITH A PROSPECTIVE DISTRIBUTOR IN MASSACHUSETTS

WE'VE HEARD GOOD THINGS FROM THE FOLKS AT LESCO IN CAPE COD. WE'VE DECIDED TO GIVE HONEST TEA A TRY.

YES! MAYBE MY MOM WILL BE ABLE TO FIND HONEST TEA IN STORES SOMEDAY SOON.

9:30 AM

SALES BOARD

WE SIGNED UP ATLAS DISTRIBUTING IN CENTRAL MASS.

WEEKLY CALL TO THE BUYER AT HAPPY HARRY'S, A DELAWARE DRUGSTORE CHAIN

HI, JOHN, THIS IS SETH GOLDMAN FROM HONEST TEA. I'M FOLLOWING UP ABOUT DOING A TEST AT YOUR STORES. WE'RE SEEING STRONG SALES AT WAWA IN YOUR MARKET AND WOULD LOVE TO BRING OUR ORGANIC DRINKS TO YOU...

BEEP!

10:30 AM

IT'S BITTERSWEET TO LEAVE OUR LONGTIME BANK, BUT OUR LINE-OF-CREDIT NEEDS HAVE GROWN BEYOND WHAT A SMALL, LOCAL BANK CAN PROVIDE.

PROVIDENT BANK

10:45 AM

MARKET RESEARCH

CAFE X-PRESS
DELI - CAFE

HONEST TEA

11:30 AM–1:30 PM

WHAT DOES THE WORD ZEROGANIC MEAN TO YOU?

?

HOW IS THE TASTE?

BACK TO THE DRAWING BOARD.

MORE SHELF SPACE?

1:40 PM

BACK AT HQ

2:00 PM

LOTS OF BILLS

		Due	Pay
Payroll		$65,468	$65,468
Zuckerman-Honickman	Bottle supplier	$139,046	$53,959
Castle Co-Packers	East Coast production	$30,690	$12,748
H.A. Rider	West Coast production	$2,673	$889
Eco-Prima	Tea supplier	$21,700	$3,465
Q Trade	Tea supplier	$2,618	$2,618
Goodwin Procter	Law firm	$6,192	$0
Gamse Lithographing	Labels	$16,880	$2,167
New Connections	Sales support	$1,793	$1,793
Smurfit-Stone	Cardboard cases	$9,936	$9,936
Wholesome Sweeteners	Organic sugar	$7,275	$7,275
Total		$304,271	$160,318

AND OTHER GOODIES

EXPENSIVE LAWYERS
POM WONDERFULL
HONEST TEA
BETHESDA .....

IT HAS COME TO OUR ATTENTION THAT YOU ARE CONSIDERING THE NAME POM BLUE. POM WONDERFUL CLAIMS EXCLUSIVE RIGHTS TO THE WORD "POM."

THE NAME POMEGRANATE BLUE IS SOUNDING BETTER EVERY DAY.

3:00 PM

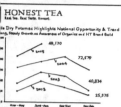

TAP TAP

I CAN'T BELIEVE I'M FLYING TO BOSTON TOMORROW TO MEET WITH A BUYER AT HIS OFFICE IN QUINCY, EVEN THOUGH HE LIVES IN VIRGINIA AND BUYS FOR A CHAIN IN MARYLAND. I GUESS THAT'S WHAT HAPPENS WHEN YOUR CHAIN MERGES WITH ONE BASED IN NEW ENGLAND—STOP & SHOP.

4:30 PM

HI, DAD!

5:15 PM

HEE HEE

7:00 PM

217

7:45 PM

TAP TAP

9:00 PM

I LIKE MY DIET SNAPPLE BETTER.

9:15 PM

THAT'S GREAT ABOUT GETTING DISTRIBUTION IN MASSACHUSETTS.

YOU'RE MAKING MY MOM VERY HAPPY.

9:45 PM

HOW LARGE A LINE OF CREDIT CAN WE GET AT THE NEW BANK?

$3 MILLION. BUT THEY WANT EACH OF US TO ISSUE A PERSONAL GUARANTEE.

OK. IT'S NOT LIKE WE HAVE A CHOICE.

CUSTOMERS DIDN'T GET THAT "ZEROGANIC" MEANT A NO-CALORIE, ORGANIC DRINK.

ZERO
+
ORGANIC
=
ZEROGANIC

HONEST TEA

10 calories

TANGERINE GREEN TEA

THE DRINK REALLY HAS FOUR CALORIES, NOT ZERO, SO HOW ABOUT WE ADD A GRAM OF SUGAR AND MAKE IT HONEST 10? IT'S A NICE PLAY ON A PERFECT 10.

THAT'LL WORK

SIP

10:15 PM

11:00 PM

ZZZZ...

11:04 PM

WHY EXACTLY AM I LEARNING HOW TO DRIVE A STICK SHIFT?

THAT WAY, IF YOUR BOYFRIEND WANTS TO DRIVE THE CAR, HE WON'T KNOW HOW.

MARCH 2007

BUT I DON'T HAVE A BOYFRIEND.

THANK GOODNESS.

LET'S STOP AT THE WHOLE FOODS IN HADLEY. IT'S ONLY 10 MINUTES OUT OF OUR WAY.

DAD, WE'RE ON A COLLEGE TOUR, NOT A STORE CHECK TOUR. BESIDES, WE ALREADY STOPPED AT THE WHOLE FOODS IN HARTFORD.

ACTUALLY, THERE ARE TWO IN HARTFORD. WE'LL CATCH THE OTHER ONE ON THE WAY HOME.

WHOLE FOOD

HI, I'M BARRY, CO-FOUNDER OF HONEST TEA. I REALLY APPRECIATE YOUR CARRYING OUR TEAS. CAN I HELP YOU RESTOCK?

OH... OKAY

YOU CAN PRETEND YOU DON'T KNOW ME, BUT IF YOU HELP ME RESTOCK, IT'LL GO A LOT QUICKER.

WE'RE ALMOST THERE. TAKE A LEFT ON HURON.

CHICAGO, JULY 2007

MELANIE, I'M SENDING YOU A PICTURE. WE REALLY NEED MORE FACINGS AT WHOLE FOODS' GOLD COAST STORE.

TELL ME ABOUT YOUR INTEREST IN THE UNIVERSITY OF CHICAGO.

WELL, I LIKE THE QUIRKINESS. I LIKE THAT PEOPLE TAKE THEIR CLASSES SERIOUSLY...

IT WAS PRETTY WEIRD. THE GUY WAS DRINKING HONEST TEA THE WHOLE TIME.

DID YOU MENTION THE CONNECTION?

NO. THIS ISN'T ABOUT *YOU*.

GOOD POINT.

STILL, IT WAS KINDA FUNNY! THERE ARE PEOPLE OUTSIDE OUR IMMEDIATE FAMILY BUYING HONEST TEA.

221

EARLY 2007

WHY ARE WE GOING TO CHICAGO AGAIN?

THERE'S AN EXHIBIT WITH PICTURES OF GRANDPA'S FAMILY AT THE ELGIN MUSEUM.

WHY ARE WE WAITING AT THE GATE? WE FINISHED BOARDING AGES AGO.

THAT'S BARACK OBAMA!

LADIES AND GENTLEMEN, I'VE JUST HEARD WE'LL BE ON THE GROUND FOR ANOTHER 30 MINUTES, SO FEEL FREE TO WALK ABOUT THE CABIN. OUR YOUNGER PASSENGERS ARE WELCOME TO VISIT THE COCKPIT.

LET'S GO.

DO WE HAVE TO?

LOOK AT ALL THOSE BUTTONS!

HI, SENATOR OBAMA. I'M SETH GOLDMAN, CO-FOUNDER OF HONEST TEA. WE HEARD FROM YOUR OFFICE THAT YOU LIKE OUR DRINKS.

I DO! I WAS JUST HAVING A BOTTLE OF COMMUNITY GREEN ON MY WAY TO THE AIRPORT.

THAT'S GREAT TO HEAR. THESE ARE MY BOYS, JONAH, ELIE, AND ISAAC.

HEY, FELLAS.

SENATOR, I DREW THIS PICTURE OF YOU. WOULD YOU SIGN IT FOR ME?

2008 PRESIDENTIAL CAMPAIGN

HI, THIS IS REGGIE LOVE FROM THE OBAMA CAMPAIGN. CAN YOU HELP ME FIND HONEST TEA FOR THE SENATOR?

HONEST TEA HQ

HE WANTS TO GIVE YOUR CAFFEINE-FREE FLAVORS A TRY. THERE'S ENOUGH GOING ON TO KEEP HIM AWAKE.

TRY BLACK FOREST BERRY. HERE'S WHERE YOU CAN BUY SOME.

HE LIKES IT. THANKS! —REGGIE LOVE

ONLY CELEBRITIES LIKE BARACK OBAMA DEMAND BOTTLES OF A HARD-TO-FIND ORGANIC BREW, BLACK FOREST BERRY HONEST TEA, AND WORRY ABOUT THE PRICE OF ARUGULA.

RICK DAVIS, MCCAIN CAMPAIGN MANAGER

I DO HAVE TO ASK MY OPPONENT: IS THAT THE BEST YOU CAN COME UP WITH? IS THAT WHAT IS WORTHY OF THE AMERICAN PEOPLE?

Newsweek

SMACKDOWN

The Elitism Index

Obama is Honest Tea and protein bars, McCain doughnuts and Diet Coke. —

	Ivory Tower	Old-School Ties	Home/Homes	Hollywood Pals
John McCain				
Barack Obama				
Winner				

CAN YOU BELIEVE WE'VE BECOME AN ISSUE IN THE CAMPAIGN?

I'D UNDERSTAND IF OBAMA WERE DRINKING EVIAN, BUT WE'RE AN ALL-AMERICAN COMPANY.

THE PUBLICITY IS ALL GOOD, BUT WHY DID DAVIS HAVE TO ADD THAT WE'RE HARD TO FIND?

I'M AFRAID THAT'S TRUE.

PRESIDENTIAL INAUGURATION, JANUARY 20, 2009. A VERY LIMITED EDITION OF BARACK FOREST BERRY IS DELIVERED TO OBAMA.

CAFFEINE-FREE

HONEST TEA

USDA ORGANIC

BARACK FOREST BERRY

SHOULD WE BE WORRIED THAT OUR PRODUCT MIGHT GET TOO ASSOCIATED WITH ONE PARTY?

WELL, JELLY BELLY BENEFITTED FROM BEING A FAVORITE OF REAGAN'S. BESIDES, I'VE HEARD SEVERAL PROMINENT REPUBLICANS DRINK HONEST TEA, TOO.

HI, THIS IS NAVY PROCUREMENT. WE ARE LOOKING TO STOCK UP ON HONEST TEA FOR THE WHITE HOUSE.

FRIDGE AT WHITE HOUSE

225

DAD, YOU'RE ALL ABOUT HEALTHY DRINKS, SO I DON'T GET WHY YOU PUT SUPER-SWEET DRINKS IN MY LUNCH.

SETH, THERE'S 100 CALORIES IN THIS 6.7 OZ POUCH. THAT'S MORE SUGAR THAN THEY PUT IN SODA.

IT'S NOT SUGAR—IT'S HIGH-FRUCTOSE CORN SYRUP.

GOOD QUESTION.

CAPRI SUN HAS THE KIDS' JUICE MARKET ALMOST TO ITSELF. WE SHOULD MAKE AN HONEST KIDS' PRODUCT.

I GET IT. PUT HONEST ADES INTO A POUCH.

WE COULD CUT THE CALORIES OF CAPRI SUN IN HALF.

OR MAYBE EVEN MORE.

SINCE IT'S MOMS WHO BUY IT, WE WANT TO CUT THE SUGAR AS MUCH AS POSSIBLE, SUBJECT TO THE CONSTRAINT THAT KIDS ARE STILL WILLING TO DRINK IT.

ALWAYS THE PROFESSOR.

TEST PANEL OF SETH'S KIDS AND THEIR FRIENDS

60 cal
SOME LIKE IT, WHILE OTHERS THINK IT IS A BIT TOO SWEET.

50 cal
EVERYONE REALLY LIKES THIS ONE. LOTS OF THUMBS UP AND SMILES.

40 cal
THIS ONE PASSES THE TEST, TOO, ALBEIT WITH LESS ENTHUSIASM.

30 cal
GETTING SOME RESISTANCE. SOME KIDS THINK IT IS BOOOORING.

20 cal
TONGUES OUT, THUMBS DOWN, TOO WATERY.

FORTY CALORIES IT IS. WE'LL USE SUGAR FOR THE SWEETENER, AND MAKE IT ALL ORGANIC.

AND DOUBLE THE PRICE.

WE DON'T HAVE TO GO THAT FAR. WE CAN MAKE GOOD MARGINS AT 25¢ A POUCH.

WHAT SHOULD WE CALL IT? WE'VE BEEN USING THE NAME HONEST KIDS.

KIDS DON'T WANT TO BE CALLED KIDS. IT ISN'T COOL.

I THINK OUR TARGET MARKET IS TOO YOUNG TO CARE.

AND REMEMBER, KIDS DON'T BUY THE PRODUCT— THEIR MOMS DO.

BESIDES, WE DON'T HAVE ANY OTHER NAMES THAT WORK BETTER.

CAN WE USE A RECYCLABLE POUCH?

I'M AFRAID NOT. THE POUCH MATERIAL IS MADE OF RECYCLABLE PLASTIC, BUT THE FOIL LINER AT THE BOTTOM CAN'T BE SEPARATED.

foil

POUCHES USE FAR LESS MATERIAL THAN ANY OTHER OPTION.

Stonyfield

liquid   pouch
98%   2%

MOST RECYCLABLE PACKAGES DON'T GET RECYCLED. THAT'S WHY "REDUCE" IS THE MOST IMPORTANT STEP IN "REDUCE, REUSE, RECYCLE."

TRUE, BUT I'M NOT GIVING UP ON THE RECYCLING PART.

GOOD. YOU DON'T WANT TO CREATE LITTER AND LANDFILL, ESPECIALLY WITH YOUR BRAND ON IT.

WHAT ABOUT UPCYCLING? TERRACYCLE IS GREAT AT FINDING NEW USES FOR DISCARDED ITEMS.

WE'VE NEVER DONE ANYTHING LIKE THIS, BUT IF YOU SEND US THE POUCHES, WE COULD SEW THEM TOGETHER AND MAKE PENCIL CASES, TOTE BAGS, AND THE LIKE.

TERRACYCLE™

NEATEST KIDS

TOM SZAKY

IT DOESN'T MAKE SENSE FOR KIDS TO INDIVIDUALLY SEND IN THEIR USED POUCHES. LET'S ASK SCHOOLS TO COLLECT THEM. WE'LL REWARD THE SCHOOLS BY DONATING 2¢ FOR EACH POUCH THEY SEND IN.

I'M NOT SURE HOW MUCH DEMAND THERE WILL BE. HOW ABOUT WE START THE BRIGADE WITH 100 COLLECTION LOCATIONS?

WITHIN 24 HOURS OF THE PROGRAM LAUNCH, ALL 100 LOCATIONS WERE SIGNED UP.

WE'RE HAVING MORE DEMAND FOR THE UPCYCLED PRODUCTS THAN WE HAVE POUCHES TO MAKE THEM. I THINK WE'VE REALLY COME UP WITH SOME GREAT PRODUCTS.

AUGUST 2007

UPCYCLING GOES UPMARKET: CONCERT PIANIST SOYEON LEE MADE HER CARNEGIE HALL DEBUT WEARING A GOWN, DESIGNED BY NINA VALENTI, MADE FROM MORE THAN 5,000 HONEST KIDS GOODNESS GRAPENESS POUCHES.

The New York Times

And What About the Straws?

FEBRUARY 14, 2008

THE POUCH UPCYCLING IS WORKING GREAT. I KNOW IT'S EXCLUSIVE TO HONEST TEA, BUT HOW WOULD YOU FEEL IF I WERE TO APPROACH KRAFT ABOUT USING THEIR CAPRI SUN POUCHES?

IF WE'RE SERIOUS ABOUT MAKING A CHANGE, OUR IDEAS NEED TO GO MAINSTREAM. I'D RATHER HELP CREATE SOMETHING THAT TAKES A BILLION POUCHES OUT OF THE WASTE STREAM THAN OWN AN IDEA THAT CAPTURES A MILLION. GO FOR IT.

BY 2012, OVER 140 MILLION JUICE POUCHES HAD BEEN UPCYCLED BY TERRACYCLE FROM 67,000 COLLECTION LOCATIONS.

WHILE WE'RE PROUD OF OUR ORGANIC AND FAIR TRADE INITIATIVES IN CHINA, INDIA, AND SOUTH AFRICA, WE DIDN'T SEE WHY THOSE PRINCIPLES SHOULD ONLY APPLY OVERSEAS. HERE ARE A FEW OF THE WAYS WE INVEST IN OUR EMPLOYEES AND THE ENVIRONMENT CLOSER TO HOME.

BEYOND THE STANDARD HEALTH, DENTAL, AND LIFE INSURANCE, WE WANT TO SUPPORT OUR EMPLOYEES' WELL-BEING.

SINCE MOST OF US ARE ON THE ROAD, WHERE IT'S HARD TO FIND HEALTHY FOOD OPTIONS, WE BARTER WITH LIKE-MINDED FOOD COMPANIES FOR HEALTHY SNACKS.

WE HAVE A WELLNESS COACH TO HELP EMPLOYEES MEET THEIR PERSONAL HEALTH GOALS.

WE MAKE OUR CORPORATE LADDER EASIER TO CLIMB BY AGGRESSIVELY PROMOTING FROM WITHIN.

MORE THAN 10% OF OUR STAFF STARTED AS INTERNS, INCLUDING THE DIRECTORS OF FIELD MARKETING, WEST DIVISION SALES, AND NATIONAL FOODSERVICE.

WE WANTED TO CREATE A SENSE OF OWNERSHIP ACROSS THE COMPANY. WE PROVIDED STOCK OPTIONS TO EVERY EMPLOYEE AFTER 12 MONTHS.

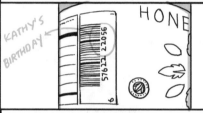

WHEN WE BRING OUT A NEW DRINK, WE LET AN EMPLOYEE SELECT THE LAST FIVE DIGITS OF THE UPC CODE—SOME CHOOSE A BIRTHDAY, OTHERS AN ANNIVERSARY.

TO REDUCE OUR IMPACT ON THE ENVIRONMENT, WE BOUGHT JAMIS BIKES FOR ALL EMPLOYEES AND INSTALLED A SHOWER IN THE OFFICE TO MAKE IT EASIER TO RIDE TO WORK.

WE SUBSIDIZE PARKING FEES BUT GIVE THE SAME ALLOWANCE TO THOSE WHO COME TO WORK VIA METRO, ON FOOT, OR BY BIKE, SO WE AREN'T FAVORING CAR DRIVERS.

IN 2007, WE CO-FOUNDED BETHESDA GREEN, A LOCAL INITIATIVE TO PROMOTE A GREENER ETHOS IN OUR HOMETOWN.

WE INSTALLED RECYCLING BINS IN HEAVY-FOOT-TRAFFIC AREAS AND HELPED LOCAL RESTAURANTS CONVERT THEIR GREASE INTO BIODIESEL, GENERATING HUNDREDS OF GALLONS OF FUEL PER MONTH.

WE CAN'T TELL OUR STORY WITHOUT SHINING A LIGHT ON THE TEA-M DOING THE HARD, OFTEN PHYSICAL WORK TO MAKE IT HAPPEN—THE PEOPLE WHO CONVERT OUR CONCEPTS INTO CASES ON THE SHELF DAY AFTER DAY. HERE ARE TWO OF THE UNSUNG HEROES OF HONEST TEA.

MIKEY P—THE ULTIMATE STREET SALESMAN
DSD Salesperson, New York City & New Jersey
Employee since 2004

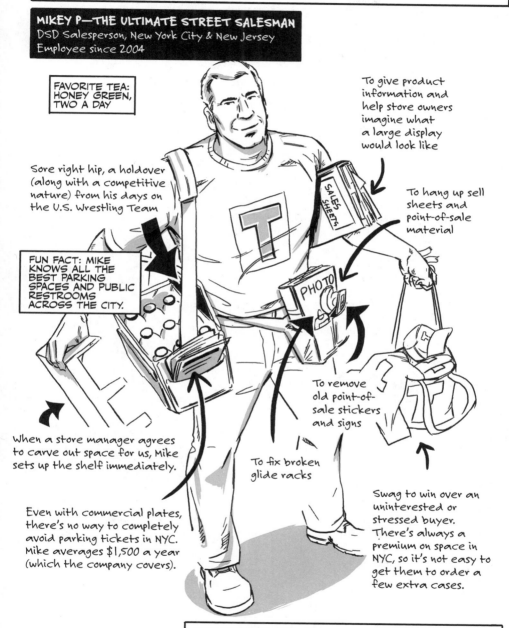

FAVORITE TEA: HONEY GREEN, TWO A DAY

To give product information and help store owners imagine what a large display would look like

Sore right hip, a holdover (along with a competitive nature) from his days on the U.S. Wrestling Team

To hang up sell sheets and point-of-sale material

SALES SHEETS

FUN FACT: MIKE KNOWS ALL THE BEST PARKING SPACES AND PUBLIC RESTROOMS ACROSS THE CITY.

PHOTO

To remove old point-of-sale stickers and signs

When a store manager agrees to carve out space for us, Mike sets up the shelf immediately.

To fix broken glide racks

Even with commercial plates, there's no way to completely avoid parking tickets in NYC. Mike averages $1,500 a year (which the company covers).

Swag to win over an uninterested or stressed buyer. There's always a premium on space in NYC, so it's not easy to get them to order a few extra cases.

MIKE HITS THE STREETS BY 6:00 AM TO SIGN NEW ACCOUNTS. FROM 11:30 AM ON, HE REWORKS DISPLAYS, SINCE DELI OWNERS ARE TOO BUSY TO PLACE ORDERS DURING LUNCHTIME. HE SETS SHELVES, GRABS SPACE, AND DEVELOPS RELATIONSHIPS WITH NOT JUST STORE OWNERS BUT THE GUYS WHO STOCK THE SHELVES.

BECCA—EMPRESS OF THE CENTRAL U.S.
Natural Foods Salesperson, from Minnesota to Texas
Employee since 2007

FUN FACT: SHE ALWAYS HAS SOME KNITTING AND PICTURES OF HER TWO CATS WITH HER.

To snap pictures (with permission, of course) of store employees in Honest Tea shirts and families drinking Honest Tea or Honest Kids

To black out UPC codes so that samples aren't mixed up with store inventory

For sampling Honest Kids and as an airline-friendly box cutter

FAVORITE TEA: JUST GREEN TEA

No high heels or short skirts; she's got to be ready to help stock shelves or dig deep into the stockroom.

To clean up the inevitable broken bottles

Coupons to hand out to customers drinking Honest Tea, or buying a basketful

$1 OFF

She's a vertically challenged individual—a step stool helps her safely reach bottles on pesky top shelves.

Vitamin C and Oscillococcinum
Neuro Optimizer
Lavender Essential Oil
Peppermint Essential Oil

BECCA MAINTAINS AN ALL-ORGANIC DIET, MAKING HER AN IDEAL NATURAL FOODS AMBASSADOR. SHE TRAVELS ALMOST EVERY WEEK, MEETING WITH RETAILERS, BROKERS, AND DISTRIBUTORS, AS WELL AS MAKING SALES AT TRADE SHOWS AND NATURAL FOODS STORES.

THE STOCK MARKET VALUE OF JONES SODA JUST BROKE $800 MILLION!

WHAT'S THE STORY? HAVE THEIR SALES EXPLODED?

NOPE, THEY'RE AT $39 MILLION, ABOUT TWICE WHERE WE ARE.

YOU MEAN THEY'RE TRADING AT OVER 20 TIMES REVENUE?! THAT'S INSANE.

APRIL 2007

JIM CRAMER HAS BEEN TALKING UP THE STOCK ON *MAD MONEY*.

JONES SODA (JSDA) COULD BE THE NEXT HANSEN'S NATURAL (HANS)

HANSEN'S MONSTER ENERGY DRINK MADE THAT COMPANY WORTH OVER $5 BILLION.

I DON'T THINK WE'RE ANYWHERE NEAR READY TO GO PUBLIC, BUT THESE VALUATIONS MAKE ME WONDER: ARE WE MISSING SOMETHING?

I'M AFRAID NOT. JONES IS MAKING MONEY, WE AREN'T. AFTER THE DOT.COM CRASH, YOU CAN'T GO PUBLIC UNTIL YOU DEMONSTRATE PROFITABILITY.

BESIDES, THE COSTS AND DISTRACTION OF BEING PUBLICLY HELD ARE TOO HIGH FOR A COMPANY OUR SIZE.

233

JONES' STOCK PRICE HAS TRIPLED IN THE LAST THREE MONTHS.

WITHOUT ANY BIG CHANGE IN SALES.

—JSDA (Daily) 31.54

THAT'S BECAUSE EVERYTHING IS BASED ON RUMOR AND SPECULATION.

AND PRESS RELEASES. THEY'VE BEEN ANNOUNCING LOTS OF HIGH-PROFILE DEALS.

THEY JUST SIGNED A CONTRACT WITH THE SEATTLE SEAHAWKS TO OUST COKE AS THE EXCLUSIVE SODA AT QWEST FIELD.

I'M SURE THAT WAS PRICEY.

THEY ALSO DID A SEVEN-YEAR DEAL WITH THE NEW JERSEY NETS THAT WILL COST THEM $1.7M ANNUALLY.

OUR ENTIRE MARKETING BUDGET IS UNDER $1 MILLION!

IT SOUNDS LIKE THEY'RE BUSY SELLING STOCK AND PUMPING UP THE PRICE FOR THE NEXT QUARTERLY REPORT, INSTEAD OF SELLING CASES TO BUILD LONG-TERM VALUE.

THEY'RE DOING A PRETTY GOOD JOB SELLING STOCK, THOUGH—$800 MILLION IS A LOT OF MONEY!

BUT IT DOESN'T BUY THEM DISTRIBUTION.

LOOK AT THEIR POURING RIGHTS DEAL WITH THE NEW JERSEY NETS. THERE ARE 42 HOME GAMES AND THE AVERAGE ATTENDANCE IS 17,000.

JONES WHOOPASS est 96

Beer PREMIUM

other Beverages

IF A THIRD OF THE FANS BUY A JONES SODA, THAT'S 238,000 UNITS SOLD.

THEY'LL ALSO GET A MARKETING BENEFIT BECAUSE PEOPLE WILL BE EXPOSED TO THE BRAND.

BUT JONES IS PAYING $1.7 MILLION A YEAR. THAT COMES TO OVER $7 FOR EVERY BOTTLE SOLD!

THAT'S WHY WE WON'T BE DOING THOSE DEALS.

ONE MONTH LATER, MAY 2007

COKE JUST BOUGHT VITAMIN WATER FOR $4.1 BILLION!

THAT'S AMAZING. WHAT WERE THEIR SALES?

BEVERAGE WORLD HAS THEM AT $355 MILLION LAST YEAR.

THAT'S 12 TIMES SALES. THIS IS GOOD FOR US, RIGHT?

NOT ENTIRELY. MANY OF OUR INDEPENDENT DISTRIBUTORS ARE LOSING THEIR KEY BRANDS. IN THE PAST YEAR ALONE, IZZE, FUZE, AND NOW VITAMIN WATER HAVE BEEN BOUGHT UP. SOME DISTRIBUTORS ARE STRUGGLING TO SURVIVE.

I GUESS THE GOOD NEWS IS WE'VE BECOME, BY DEFAULT, A KEY BRAND FOR OUR DISTRIBUTORS. NOW THEY'LL PAY MORE ATTENTION TO US.

OUR DISTRIBUTION NETWORK STILL HAD LARGE HOLES. WHILE SALES WERE GROWING AT 70%, SIGNING NEW DISTRIBUTORS WAS BECOMING MORE AND MORE OF A CHALLENGE.

HEY, BOSS, WE HAVE A PROBLEM. I THOUGHT WE WERE ABOUT TO SIGN UP A COKE DISTRIBUTOR IN THE NORTHEAST, BUT THE DEAL IS DEAD.

WHAT HAPPENED?

TO GET VITAMIN WATER, COKE DISTRIBUTORS HAD TO AGREE NOT TO TAKE ON ANY OTHER NEW BRANDS. COKE WANTS THEM FOCUSED ON VITAMIN WATER.

AND ANOTHER THING, SNAPPLE DISTRIBUTORS HAVE STOPPED ANSWERING MY CALLS.

I THINK I KNOW WHY. SNAPPLE JUST SENT A LETTER TO ITS DISTRIBUTORS THREATENING TO TERMINATE THEIR CONTRACTS IF THEY CARRY US.

ONE OF OUR DISTRIBUTORS SENT US A COPY OF THE LETTER. SNAPPLE CLAIMS WE ARE AN "IMITATIVE" PRODUCT AND SO DISTRIBUTING HONEST TEA IS A VIOLATION OF THEIR CONTRACT.

HOW DID HE RESPOND?

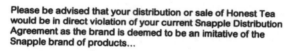
Cadbury Schweppes
AMERICAS BEVERAGES

May 21, 2007

**VIA CERTIFIED MAIL
RETURN RECEIPT REQUESTED**

███████████████████████

Re: Honest Tea

███████████████████████

Please be advised that your distribution or sale of Honest Tea would be in direct violation of your current Snapple Distribution Agreement as the brand is deemed to be an imitative of the Snapple brand of products...

Any such sale of the Imitative Product will result in us exercising our rights and remedies, up to and including termination of your distribution rights for the Snapple brand of products.

Sincerely,

███████████

IT WAS CLASSIC.

I HAVE BEEN A LOYAL, COOPERATIVE, AND TOP-PRODUCING SNAPPLE DISTRIBUTOR FOR OVER 16 YEARS, AND I AM APPALLED AT THE ACCUSATION THAT A BRAND IN MY PORTFOLIO, HONEST TEA, IS A THREAT TO THE SNAPPLE BRAND IN MY TERRITORY. YOU CLAIM HONEST TEA IS AN "IMITATIVE" PRODUCT TO SNAPPLE. HOW DO YOU FIGURE? ...

TAP TAP

HE THREATENED TO FILE A COMPLAINT WITH THE FTC IF THEY DIDN'T RETRACT THEIR LETTER.

IT'S GOOD OUR EXISTING DISTRIBUTORS ARE FIGHTING FOR US, BUT I DON'T SEE NEW ONES TAKING A CHANCE.

237

IN 2007, COKE AND NESTLÉ REVISED THE TERMS OF THEIR U.S. JOINT VENTURE TO MARKET NESTEA. FOR THE FIRST TIME IN 15 YEARS, BOTH COKE AND NESTLÉ WERE FREE TO PURSUE TEA VENTURES ON THEIR OWN.

KIM JEFFERY, CEO OF NESTLÉ WATERS NORTH AMERICA, REACHED OUT TO SEE IF WE WERE INTERESTED IN BEING PART OF HIS PORTFOLIO. WE ALREADY KNEW HIM WELL; HE HAD BEEN INSTRUMENTAL IN ARRANGING THE $5 MILLION INVESTMENT FROM INVENTAGES.

BEFORE RESPONDING, WE FIRST NEEDED TO CONSIDER IF NESTLÉ WAS A GOOD FIT.

LET'S START WITH THE PLUSES.

I LIKE KIM AND HIS TEAM. THEY'RE NOT JUST INTELLIGENT AND TALENTED, THEY ARE DECENT PEOPLE I CAN TRUST.

GOOD.

KIM IS THE ONE WHO BROUGHT PERRIER TO THE U.S. HE'S AN ENTREPRENEUR AT HEART.

AGREED.

NESTLÉ IS GOING TO BUY A TEA BUSINESS, WHETHER IT IS OURS OR SOMEONE ELSE'S. WE WILL EITHER BE WITH THE WORLD'S LARGEST FOOD AND BEVERAGE COMPANY, OR COMPETING AGAINST IT.

I'D RATHER BE WITH IT.

GIVEN THEIR $4 BILLION IN VOLUME, THEY ARE VERY WELL CONNECTED WITH DISTRIBUTORS.

ALTHOUGH A LOT OF THAT VOLUME GOES THROUGH WAREHOUSE DISTRIBUTION. THERE'S NO SALESPERSON TO MAKE SURE IT'S MERCHANDISED AND SOLD THE RIGHT WAY.

STILL, THEY COULD GET US INTO THOUSANDS OF NEW STORES AND EVERY FOOD CART IN NEW YORK CITY.

DOES IT BOTHER YOU THAT THEY'RE THE LARGEST SELLER OF BOTTLED WATER IN THE U.S.?

H_2O

PEOPLE COMPLAIN ABOUT THE ENVIRONMENTAL IMPACT OF BOTTLED WATER, BUT AT LEAST IT'S A HEALTHY ZERO-CALORIE BEVERAGE.

OF COURSE, PEOPLE SHOULDN'T BE DRINKING FROM A BOTTLE WHEN THERE'S TAP WATER NEARBY, BUT NESTLÉ HAS BEEN VERY INNOVATIVE IN REDUCING THE WEIGHT OF THEIR BOTTLES.

16 fl. oz

0.4 oz

THEIR 16 FL OZ BOTTLE WEIGHS 0.4 OZ WHEN EMPTY, 70% LESS THAN OURS!

WHY CAN'T WE DO THAT?

I KNOW WHAT YOU'RE THINKING. WE CAN'T DO THAT BECAUSE OUR BOTTLES NEED TO STAND UP TO 190°F WATER.

TEA

190°F

AND KIM HAS BEEN A BIG ADVOCATE FOR MORE RECYCLING.

n p r

EVERY PLASTIC CONTAINER THAT'S RECYCLABLE SHOULD HAVE SOME DEPOSIT ON IT.

5¢ 5¢ 5¢

AND THE DOWNSIDES?

WE MAY BE THE TOP BRAND IN THE NATURAL FOODS CHANNEL, BUT MOST AMERICANS HAVE YET TO DISCOVER US. OUR BRAND STILL NEEDS A LOT OF HAND-HOLDING.

I JUST DON'T THINK WE'RE READY TO SELL YET.

THAT'S A BIGGIE.

OK. WE SHOULD ONLY TAKE AN OFFER THAT'S TOO GOOD TO REFUSE.

I'LL LET YOU HANDLE THE NEGOTIATION.

WHILE I WANT TO BUY THE COMPANY TODAY, I DON'T HAVE AUTHORIZATION TO MAKE YOU AN OFFER. YOU'RE JUST TOO SMALL.

THAT SAID, I'D LIKE THE OPTION TO BUY THE COMPANY FOR $150 MILLION IF WE CAN HELP YOU GET TO $50 MILLION IN SALES NEXT YEAR. I THINK THAT'S VERY DOABLE.

I DON'T THINK WHAT YOU PROPOSE WILL WORK FOR US OR OUR INVESTORS.

WHILE WE APPRECIATE YOUR INTEREST AND CONFIDENCE, THERE'S TOO MUCH UNCERTAINTY AND THE PRICE IS TOO LOW.

WHAT WOULD WORK FOR YOU?

WELL, HOW ABOUT...

HE DIDN'T COUNTER. HE JUST SAID NO.

I KNOW KIM IS DISAPPOINTED AND UPSET. I HOPE WE MADE THE RIGHT DECISION.

ME, TOO. WHEN I SPOKE TO HIM AFTERWARD, HE SEEMED TO THINK YOU HAD SERIOUS DELUSIONS ABOUT WHAT THE COMPANY IS WORTH.

HE EVEN SUGGESTED YOU MAY HAVE SCREWED THINGS UP FOR ME AND MY FAMILY.

HE STILL WANTS TO BUY HONEST TEA AND ASKED TO KEEP IN TOUCH. HE'S CONVINCED THIS CAN BE A GREAT COMPANY BUT WARNS THAT OUR NEXT CHAPTER MAY NOT BE EASY.

NEGOTIATING FOR OURSELVES IS HARD. WE'VE GOT SO MUCH AT STAKE, IT'S IMPOSSIBLE TO BE TOTALLY OBJECTIVE.

BUT LET'S TRY TO LOOK AT THE BIG PICTURE. THE BUSINESS IS GOING GREAT. AND WE DIDN'T REALLY WANT TO SELL.

HONEST TEA

I JUST WISH THINGS HADN'T ENDED ON SUCH A SOUR NOTE. THIS HAS ALL BEEN VERY DISTRACTING. I NEED TO GET BACK TO SELLING TEA.

241

THAT SUMMER, WE HEARD REPORTS COCA-COLA WAS LOOKING TO ADD A TEA BRAND TO ITS PORTFOLIO.

July 5, 2007: ATLANTA (AP) — Coca-Cola (KO) is exploring whether to buy Cadbury Schweppes' Snapple iced tea brand or build its own tea brand, a spokesman said Wednesday. "We're always looking at whether to build or buy," spokesman Dana Bolden said...

SOON AFTER, WE GOT A CALL FROM A NEW GROUP AT COKE CALLED VEB (VENTURING AND EMERGING BRANDS) TO SEE IF WE WERE OPEN TO A CONVERSATION ABOUT THEIR INVESTING IN HONEST TEA. THE BREAKDOWN WITH NESTLÉ HAD GIVEN US A BETTER SENSE OF WHAT KIND OF ARRANGEMENT WOULD WORK FOR US, SO WE AGREED TO MEET WITH VEB'S MIKE OHMSTEDE AND DERYCK VAN RENSBURG.

AND THIS IS THE KITCHEN, WHICH DOUBLES AS OUR R&D FACILITY.

WE DON'T NEED A LOT OF HIGH-TECH EQUIPMENT TO BREW TEA.

YOU DO ALL YOUR FORMULATIONS HERE?

AFTER THE OFFICE TOUR, WE DROVE TOGETHER TO EXPO EAST IN BALTIMORE.

VEB WAS CREATED TO HELP FIND AND DEVELOP COKE'S NEXT BILLION-DOLLAR BRAND.

AFTER SURVEYING 3,000 BEVERAGES, WE NARROWED IT DOWN TO THE 10 MOST PROMISING, WHICH LED US TO HONEST TEA.

WE'RE LOOKING FOR COMPANIES WITH A UNIQUE PRODUCT, AN AUTHENTIC BRAND, STRONG MANAGEMENT, PROVEN COMMERCIAL SUCCESS, AND GREAT TASTE.

I'VE BEEN BRINGING YOUR PRODUCTS HOME, AND THEY'RE THE FIRST THINGS MY KIDS TAKE FROM THE FRIDGE.

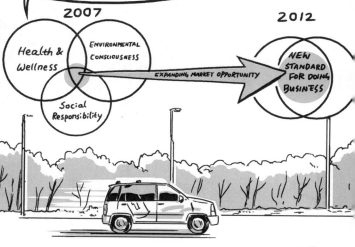

HONEST IS AT THE CONVERGENCE OF THREE MEGATRENDS. IT'S MORE THAN JUST A TEA BRAND. IT SETS THE NEW STANDARD FOR DOING BUSINESS, AND THAT'S WHAT WE WANT TO INVEST IN.

2007

Health & Wellness
ENVIRONMENTAL CONSCIOUSNESS
Social Responsibility

EXPANDING MARKET OPPORTUNITY

2012

NEW STANDARD FOR DOING BUSINESS

THAT SAID, YOU HAVE BOTH DANONE AND NESTLÉ AS INVESTORS AND A PEPSI DISTRIBUTOR ON YOUR BOARD. IT SEEMS THERE ARE A LOT OF BEARS WITH A HAND IN THE HONEYPOT.

THE PURPOSE OF HAVING MULTIPLE STRATEGIC INVESTORS WAS TO KEEP OUR OPTIONS OPEN. WE MADE SURE NO INVESTOR HAD PREEMPTIVE RIGHTS.

THAT'S GOOD TO HEAR. BY THE WAY, SETH, I UNDERSTAND YOU'RE A RED SOX FAN. WOULD YOU AND YOUR SONS LIKE TO JOIN MY FAMILY AT FENWAY FOR A PLAYOFF GAME?

MY KIDS WOULD SIGN A DEAL RIGHT NOW.

SO, SETH, WHAT ARE YOU HOPING FOR OUT OF THESE NEGOTIATIONS? ARE YOU LOOKING TO RETIRE? START SOMETHING ELSE?

NOT MANY FOUNDERS STAY ON AFTER THE COMPANY IS SOLD. IT CAN BE HARD TO GO FROM BEING THE BOSS, WITH A LOT OF EQUITY UPSIDE, TO BEING AN EMPLOYEE.

AND DEALING WITH CORPORATE BUREAUCRACY CAN BE FRUSTRATING WHEN YOU'RE USED TO ACTING QUICKLY.

I LOVE WHAT I'M DOING AND WANT TO KEEP DOING IT. I'M NOT A SERIAL ENTREPRENEUR—I WANT TO KEEP BUILDING HONEST TEA.

244

ON THE + SIDE:

1. THE TIMING IS GOOD.

- OUR INVESTORS HAVE BEEN PATIENT: 10 YEARS.

- WE'RE THE TOP-SELLING, AND FASTEST-GROWING, TEA BRAND IN NATURAL FOODS IN *EVERY* REGION OF THE U.S.

- SALES TREND LOOKS GREAT. WE GREW 70% TO $23M THIS YEAR.

- VALUATIONS ARE SKY-HIGH.

    JONES SODA HAS SALES OF $40M AND A MARKET CAP ABOVE $400M (DOWN FROM $800M, BUT STILL HUGE). VITAMIN WATER RECENTLY SOLD FOR $4.1B.

2. THIS IS THE BEST OPPORTUNITY TO TAKE THE BRAND TO A NEW LEVEL.

- COKE'S DISTRIBUTION SYSTEM IS THE MOST POWERFUL IN THE WORLD.

- WE'RE STARTING TO HIT ROADBLOCKS FOR SIGNING NEW DISTRIBUTORS.

3. OUR PERSONAL GUARANTEES HAVE GROWN TO $5M. YIKES! IF WE DON'T DO A DEAL, WE COULD LOSE EVERYTHING WE HAVE (AND MORE).

4. IF WE DON'T DO A DEAL, WE'LL HAVE TWO NEW COMPETITORS BACKED BY COKE AND NESTLÉ. YIKES! AGAIN.

5. BARRY IS ABOUT TO TURN 50. EXITING SOONER RATHER THAN LATER HAS PERSONAL ADVANTAGES.

ON THE – SIDE:

1. WE'RE STILL HAVING FUN.

2. WE'RE FINALLY SEEING REAL GROWTH FROM GROUNDWORK WE'VE DONE.

3. WE WANTED TO GROW SALES TO $100M BUT ARE ONLY AT $23M. THAT MAY NOT BE BIG ENOUGH TO SEND OFF INTO THE WORLD. COKE KNOWS HOW TO GROW A COMPANY FROM $100M TO $1B, BUT CAN TAKE $20M DOWN TO $0.

New York Times, January 13, 2001
COMPANY NEWS; COCA-COLA BUYS OWNER OF PLANET JAVA COFFEE

Brandweek, May 14, 2001
Following weeks of rumors, Coca-Cola finally announced the purchase of premium tea, juice and soft drink maker Mad River Traders for a reported $7 million....

Businessweek, May 16, 2004
Things Go Better with... Juice...
"We just didn't see the opportunity," says Ron Wilson, president of the Phila-delphia Coca-Cola Bottling Co. Given the apathy, Coke execs shelved both Planet Java and Mad River last year...

4. OUR LOYAL CUSTOMERS MAY BOYCOTT US BECAUSE THEY DON'T TRUST COCA-COLA.

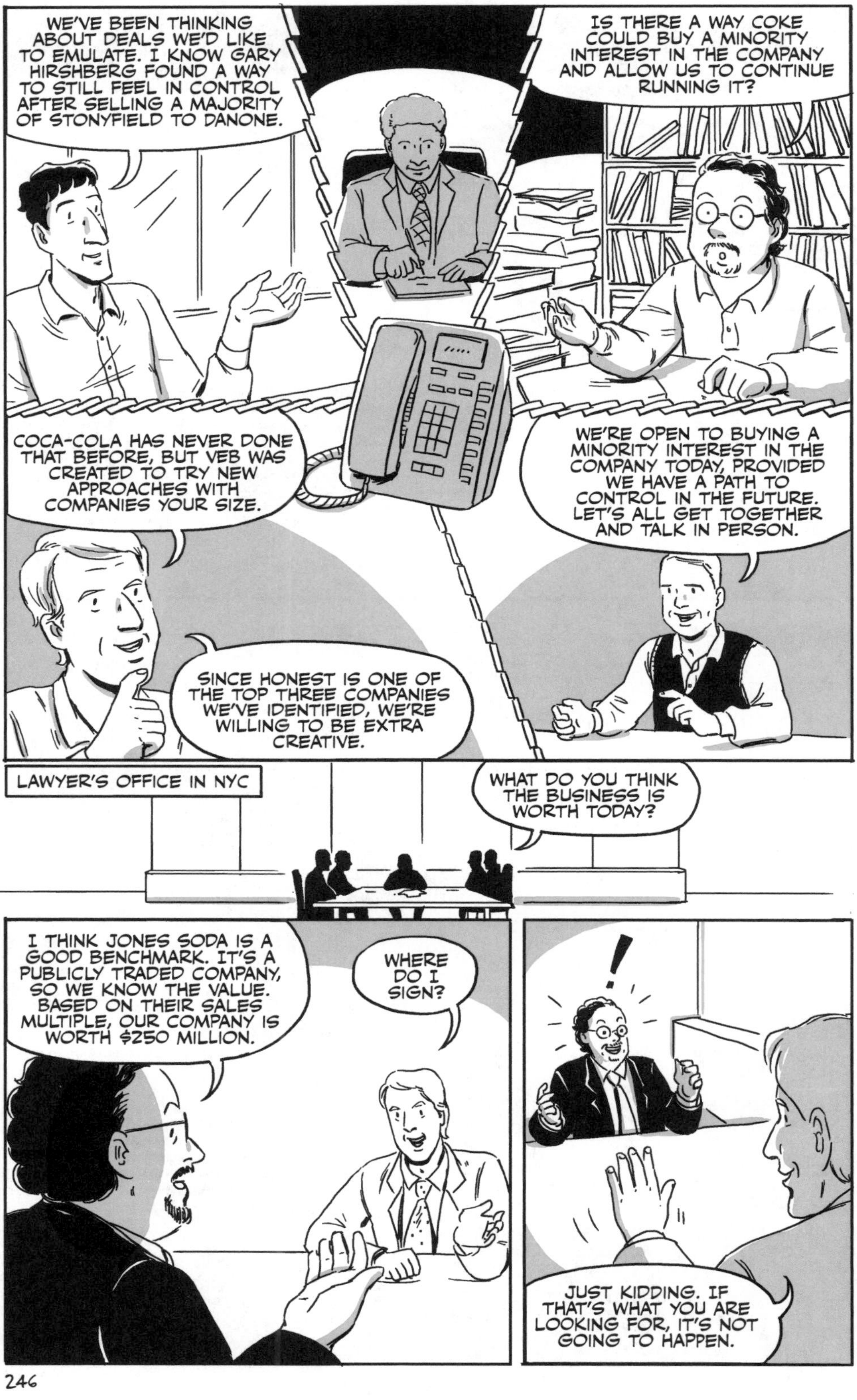
WE'VE BEEN THINKING ABOUT DEALS WE'D LIKE TO EMULATE. I KNOW GARY HIRSHBERG FOUND A WAY TO STILL FEEL IN CONTROL AFTER SELLING A MAJORITY OF STONYFIELD TO DANONE.
IS THERE A WAY COKE COULD BUY A MINORITY INTEREST IN THE COMPANY AND ALLOW US TO CONTINUE RUNNING IT?
COCA-COLA HAS NEVER DONE THAT BEFORE, BUT VEB WAS CREATED TO TRY NEW APPROACHES WITH COMPANIES YOUR SIZE.
SINCE HONEST IS ONE OF THE TOP THREE COMPANIES WE'VE IDENTIFIED, WE'RE WILLING TO BE EXTRA CREATIVE.
WE'RE OPEN TO BUYING A MINORITY INTEREST IN THE COMPANY TODAY, PROVIDED WE HAVE A PATH TO CONTROL IN THE FUTURE. LET'S ALL GET TOGETHER AND TALK IN PERSON.
LAWYER'S OFFICE IN NYC
WHAT DO YOU THINK THE BUSINESS IS WORTH TODAY?
I THINK JONES SODA IS A GOOD BENCHMARK. IT'S A PUBLICLY TRADED COMPANY, SO WE KNOW THE VALUE. BASED ON THEIR SALES MULTIPLE, OUR COMPANY IS WORTH $250 MILLION.
WHERE DO I SIGN?
!
JUST KIDDING. IF THAT'S WHAT YOU ARE LOOKING FOR, IT'S NOT GOING TO HAPPEN.

LET'S TAKE A STEP BACK FROM TALKING ABOUT PRICE. WHAT DO YOU HOPE TO ACCOMPLISH? WHAT DO YOU WANT THE FUTURE OF HONEST TEA TO BE?

I'M AS COMMITTED TO OUR MISSION AS I'VE EVER BEEN. IF WE CAN TAP INTO COKE'S DISTRIBUTION POWER, HONEST TEA COULD FINALLY MAKE THE SHIFT FROM BEING A MODEL FOR CHANGE TO BEING THE ONE MAKING THE CHANGE HAPPEN.

ARE YOU WORRIED HONEST TEA'S CORE CONSUMERS MAY REACT NEGATIVELY TO YOUR BEING AFFILIATED WITH COCA-COLA?

SHOULD WE TAKE THE INVESTMENT FROM AN LLC FUNDED BY COCA-COLA?

WE'VE ALWAYS BEEN TRANSPARENT WITH OUR CONSUMERS, SO DISGUISING A RELATIONSHIP WITH COKE WOULDN'T BE HONEST.

IF WE BELIEVE IN PARTNERING WITH COKE, AS I CERTAINLY DO, THEN IT'S OUR RESPONSIBILITY TO HELP CONSUMERS UNDERSTAND WHY IT WILL HELP TAKE OUR MISSION TO SCALE. AND THEN IT WILL BE UP TO US TO KEEP IT HONEST.

AS LONG AS WE DON'T COMPROMISE OUR PRODUCT, IF WE CAN SELL A BILLION BOTTLES RATHER THAN A HUNDRED MILLION, THEN WE'RE DOING MORE TO ACHIEVE OUR SOCIAL MISSION.

BARRY, WHAT ARE YOU LOOKING FOR?

I WANT HONEST TEA TO BECOME THE NEXT GREAT BRAND OF THE 21ST CENTURY. I WANT TO HELP IMPROVE THE AMERICAN DIET.

AND I WANT TO PROVE H. L. MENCKEN WRONG: YOU CAN SUCCEED WITHOUT UNDERESTIMATING YOUR CUSTOMERS.

THE GOOD NEWS IS WE SHARE THE EXACT SAME GOALS.

HOW CAN WE STRUCTURE A DEAL THAT HELPS EVERY-ONE ACHIEVE THIS?

IN BROAD TERMS, CONSIDER THE FOLLOWING:

YOU BUY 40% OF THE COMPANY TODAY AT SOME AGREED-UPON PRICE. YOU OPEN UP YOUR DISTRIBUTION NETWORK TO HONEST. THEN, AT SOME POINT IN THE FUTURE, YOU HAVE THE OPTION TO BUY THE REST OF THE BUSINESS AT AN AGREED-UPON FORMULA.

YOU UNDERSTAND WE DON'T OWN THE DISTRIBUTORS. WE CAN'T MAKE THEM CARRY HONEST TEA.

BUT YOU CAN GIVE THEM THE OK TO CARRY IT IF THEY WANT.

THAT WE CAN DO.

HOW WOULD YOU DO THE BUYOUT FORMULA?

FIRST, WE'D LIKE TO HAVE THREE YEARS WHERE WE HAVE FULL AUTONOMY.

IN THAT TIME FRAME, WE THINK WE COULD BRING HONEST TEA TO $100M IN SALES ON OUR OWN.

OUR FORECASTS ARE MORE LIKE $70M, BUT GO ON.

THUS, WE SHOULD GET REWARDED FOR DOING THAT AT A FAIR MARKET MULTIPLE.

WE DON'T WANT TO BE PENALIZED FOR HELPING YOU BUILD SALES AND THEN HAVE TO PAY MORE FOR THE COMPANY.

UNDERSTOOD. THAT'S WHY, FOR SALES OVER $100M, YOU'D PAY A LOWER MULTIPLE, SINCE YOUR HELP CONTRIBUTED TO THOSE EXTRA SALES.

WE LIKE THE STRUCTURE, THOUGH I'M NOT SURE WE AGREE WITH YOUR TARGETS AND MULTIPLES. LET US PROVIDE YOU WITH THE FINANCIAL DETAILS OF SOME OTHER DEALS WE'VE DONE, AND THEN WE'LL REGROUP.

I JUST GOT A VOICEMAIL FROM THE M&A TEAM AT PEPSI. THEY HEARD A RUMOR WE MIGHT BE DOING A DEAL, AND THEY WANT TO TALK WITH US.

DERYCK AND MIKE WERE CLEAR THEY WEREN'T WILLING TO PARTICIPATE IN AN AUCTION. NO INVESTMENT BANKERS. WE CAN'T PLAY THEM OFF AGAINST EACH OTHER.

OK, BUT WE'RE THINKING ABOUT GETTING MARRIED HERE. IS COKE THE BEST PARTNER FOR US, OR WOULD PEPSI BE BETTER?

I THINK WE OFFER MORE TO COKE. LIPTON ICED TEA IS WORKING FOR PEPSI, AND SOBE AND IZZE ARE HELPING THEIR NATURAL PRODUCT PORTFOLIO.

WE BRING COKE A TEA BRAND, A HEALTH BRAND, AND A BRAND WITH STRONG SUSTAINABILITY CREDENTIALS. AND I LIKE THAT THEY'VE CREATED A SPECIAL UNIT, VEB, TO INVEST IN AND INCUBATE EMERGING BRANDS.

SINCE WE'VE BEEN THE ONES NEGOTIATING, WE'VE GOTTEN TO KNOW MIKE AND DERYCK PRETTY WELL. I CAN WORK WITH THESE FOLKS.

ALSO, REMEMBER, THIS IS THE COMPANY THAT GOT BURNED BY NEW COKE—THEY LEARNED THE HARD WAY THAT IF IT AIN'T BROKE, DON'T FIX IT. I THINK THEY'LL BE LESS TEMPTED TO TRY AND REINVENT US.

I'M PERSUADED. LET'S NOT RISK EVERYTHING WITH A DETOUR.

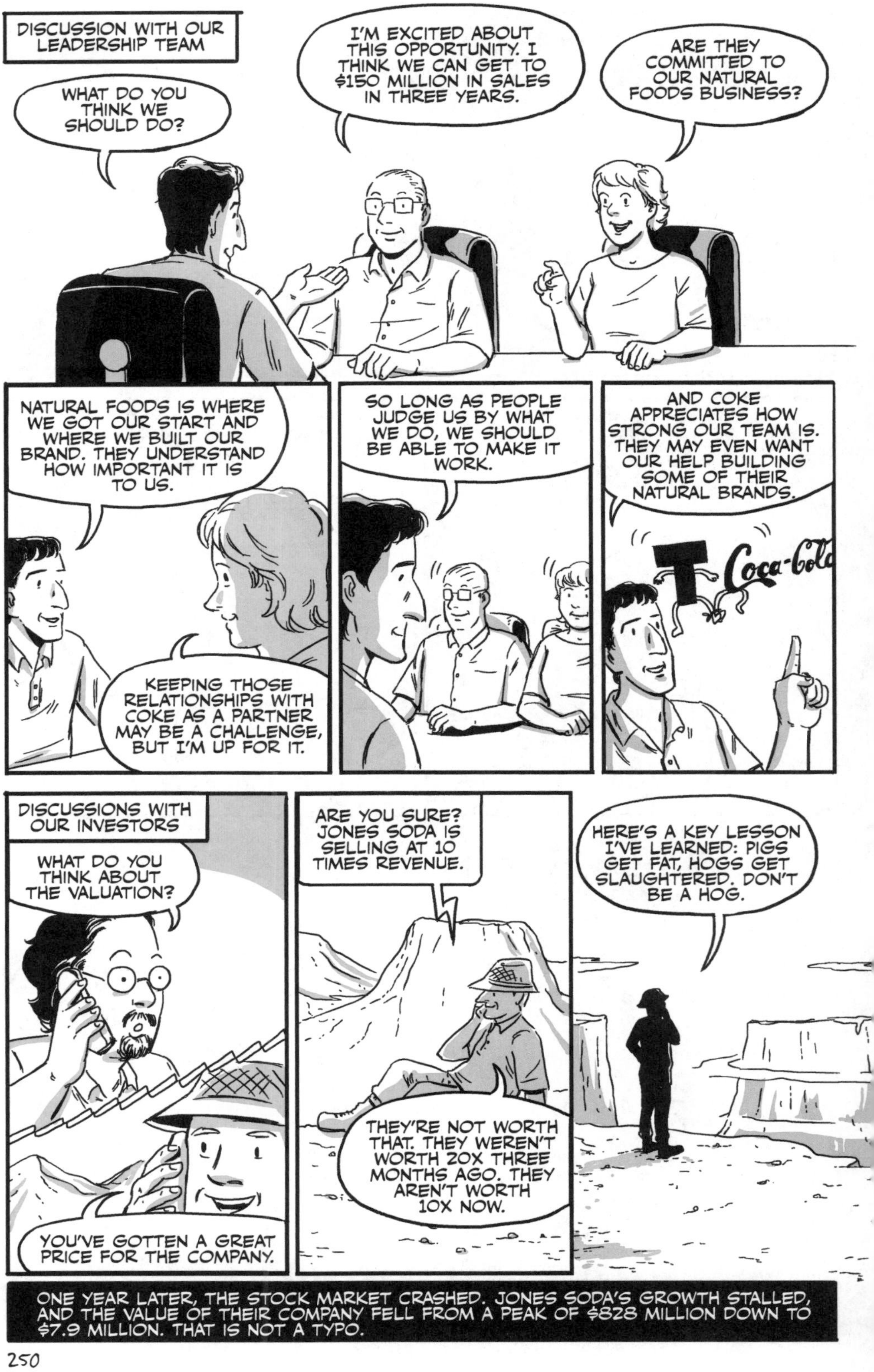
DISCUSSION WITH OUR LEADERSHIP TEAM
WHAT DO YOU THINK WE SHOULD DO?
I'M EXCITED ABOUT THIS OPPORTUNITY. I THINK WE CAN GET TO $150 MILLION IN SALES IN THREE YEARS.
ARE THEY COMMITTED TO OUR NATURAL FOODS BUSINESS?
NATURAL FOODS IS WHERE WE GOT OUR START AND WHERE WE BUILT OUR BRAND. THEY UNDERSTAND HOW IMPORTANT IT IS TO US.
KEEPING THOSE RELATIONSHIPS WITH COKE AS A PARTNER MAY BE A CHALLENGE, BUT I'M UP FOR IT.
SO LONG AS PEOPLE JUDGE US BY WHAT WE DO, WE SHOULD BE ABLE TO MAKE IT WORK.
AND COKE APPRECIATES HOW STRONG OUR TEAM IS. THEY MAY EVEN WANT OUR HELP BUILDING SOME OF THEIR NATURAL BRANDS.
T
Coca-Cola
DISCUSSIONS WITH OUR INVESTORS
WHAT DO YOU THINK ABOUT THE VALUATION?
YOU'VE GOTTEN A GREAT PRICE FOR THE COMPANY.
ARE YOU SURE? JONES SODA IS SELLING AT 10 TIMES REVENUE.
THEY'RE NOT WORTH THAT. THEY WEREN'T WORTH 20X THREE MONTHS AGO. THEY AREN'T WORTH 10X NOW.
HERE'S A KEY LESSON I'VE LEARNED: PIGS GET FAT, HOGS GET SLAUGHTERED. DON'T BE A HOG.
ONE YEAR LATER, THE STOCK MARKET CRASHED. JONES SODA'S GROWTH STALLED, AND THE VALUE OF THEIR COMPANY FELL FROM A PEAK OF $828 MILLION DOWN TO $7.9 MILLION. THAT IS NOT A TYPO.

THE PRICE IS GOOD—IT'S MORE THAN WHAT NESTLÉ REJECTED—BUT, AS ONE OF YOUR LARGEST INVESTORS, WE AREN'T IN FAVOR OF THIS DEAL IF WE CAN'T REQUIRE COKE TO BUY THE COMPANY IN THREE YEARS.

GUNNAR WEIKERT, INVENTAGES

...

DISCUSSIONS WITH OUR FAMILIES

HOW WILL OUR LIFE CHANGE?

I DON'T PLAN ON IT CHANGING. I GET TO KEEP DOING WHAT I LOVE.

IN FACT, I'VE SPENT SO MUCH TIME RAISING MONEY, BEGGING FOR DISTRIBUTION, AND STRUGGLING WITH PRODUCTION THAT IT WILL BE LIBERATING TO FOCUS ON BUILDING THE BRAND AND EXPANDING OUR MISSION.

BUT WHAT IF THEY MESS UP WHAT YOU'VE BUILT?

THAT'S WHY I WANT TO STAY ON. HONEST TEA IS ONLY 10 YEARS OLD. THAT'S THE SAME AGE AS ISAAC, AND WE KNOW HOW IMPRESSIONABLE HE IS.

I NEED TO KEEP PARENTING THE BRAND UNTIL IT'S MORE DEVELOPED.

WOULD WE HAVE TO MOVE TO ATLANTA?!

NO, WE GET TO STAY RIGHT HERE.

DO YOU THINK THIS IS A GOOD IDEA?

YES. I WANT TO SEE MORE OF YOU. SO DO THE KIDS.

BETWEEN TEACHING, WRITING BOOKS, CONSULTING, SERVING ON CORPORATE BOARDS, AND HONEST TEA, YOU'VE BEEN LIVING A CRAZY LIFE.

PRETTY SOON RACHEL AND ZOE WILL BE HEADING TO COLLEGE. DON'T MISS THIS OPPORTUNITY FOR US TO BE TOGETHER.

DISCUSSION WITH OUR BOARD

BASED ON OUR FORECASTS, THE PRICE WILL GIVE OUR EARLY INVESTORS A 30-TIMES RETURN ON THEIR MONEY, PLUS SOME LIQUIDITY TODAY.

MY BIGGEST CONCERN IS THAT COKE HAS AN OPTION TO BUY US, BUT WE CAN'T FORCE THEM TO USE IT. WE NEED A PUT.

THEY SAY THEY FULLY EXPECT TO EXERCISE THEIR OPTION.

THINGS CAN CHANGE.

THEY MAY LOVE YOU NOW, BUT IF THEY DON'T EXERCISE THEIR OPTION, YOU'LL BE IN AN IMPOSSIBLE POSITION. YOUR DISTRIBUTION WILL BE TIED UP WITH COKE, AND YOU'LL END UP AN ORPHAN.

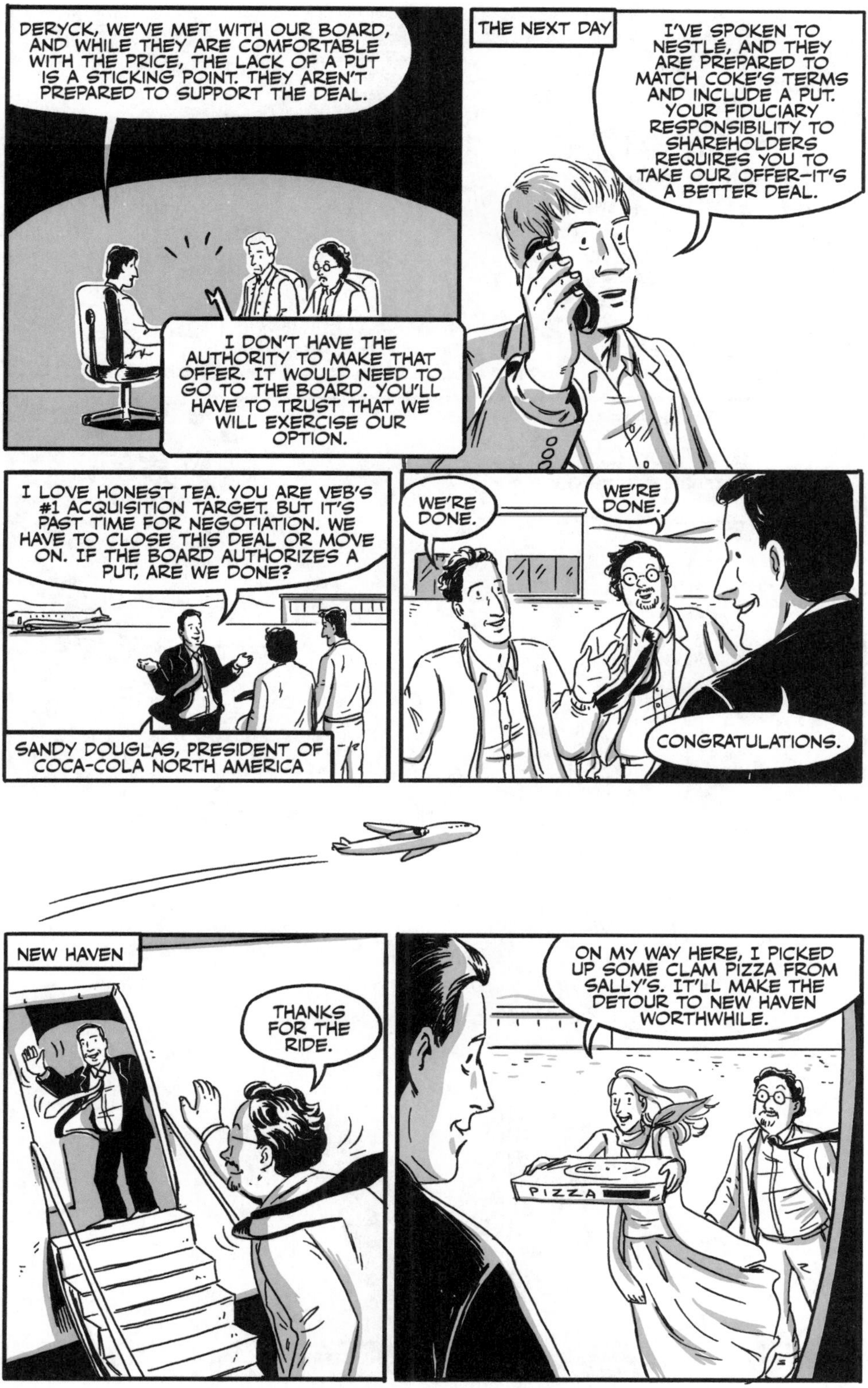
DERYCK, WE'VE MET WITH OUR BOARD, AND WHILE THEY ARE COMFORTABLE WITH THE PRICE, THE LACK OF A PUT IS A STICKING POINT. THEY AREN'T PREPARED TO SUPPORT THE DEAL.
I DON'T HAVE THE AUTHORITY TO MAKE THAT OFFER. IT WOULD NEED TO GO TO THE BOARD. YOU'LL HAVE TO TRUST THAT WE WILL EXERCISE OUR OPTION.
THE NEXT DAY
I'VE SPOKEN TO NESTLÉ, AND THEY ARE PREPARED TO MATCH COKE'S TERMS AND INCLUDE A PUT. YOUR FIDUCIARY RESPONSIBILITY TO SHAREHOLDERS REQUIRES YOU TO TAKE OUR OFFER—IT'S A BETTER DEAL.
I LOVE HONEST TEA. YOU ARE VEB'S #1 ACQUISITION TARGET. BUT IT'S PAST TIME FOR NEGOTIATION. WE HAVE TO CLOSE THIS DEAL OR MOVE ON. IF THE BOARD AUTHORIZES A PUT, ARE WE DONE?
SANDY DOUGLAS, PRESIDENT OF COCA-COLA NORTH AMERICA
WE'RE DONE.
WE'RE DONE.
CONGRATULATIONS.
NEW HAVEN
THANKS FOR THE RIDE.
ON MY WAY HERE, I PICKED UP SOME CLAM PIZZA FROM SALLY'S. IT'LL MAKE THE DETOUR TO NEW HAVEN WORTHWHILE.
PIZZA

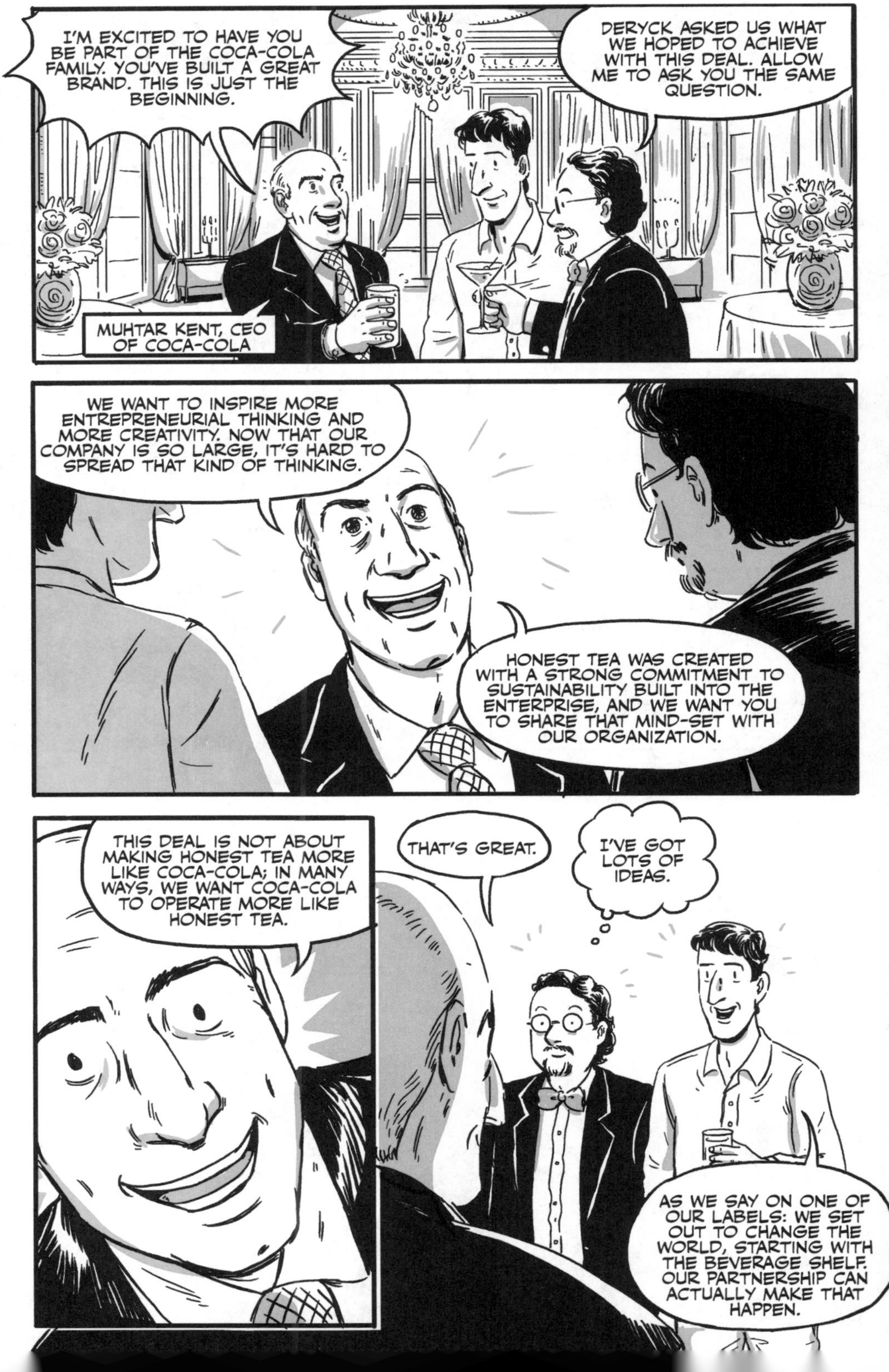
I'M EXCITED TO HAVE YOU BE PART OF THE COCA-COLA FAMILY. YOU'VE BUILT A GREAT BRAND. THIS IS JUST THE BEGINNING.
DERYCK ASKED US WHAT WE HOPED TO ACHIEVE WITH THIS DEAL. ALLOW ME TO ASK YOU THE SAME QUESTION.
MUHTAR KENT, CEO OF COCA-COLA
WE WANT TO INSPIRE MORE ENTREPRENEURIAL THINKING AND MORE CREATIVITY. NOW THAT OUR COMPANY IS SO LARGE, IT'S HARD TO SPREAD THAT KIND OF THINKING.
HONEST TEA WAS CREATED WITH A STRONG COMMITMENT TO SUSTAINABILITY BUILT INTO THE ENTERPRISE, AND WE WANT YOU TO SHARE THAT MIND-SET WITH OUR ORGANIZATION.
THIS DEAL IS NOT ABOUT MAKING HONEST TEA MORE LIKE COCA-COLA; IN MANY WAYS, WE WANT COCA-COLA TO OPERATE MORE LIKE HONEST TEA.
THAT'S GREAT.
I'VE GOT LOTS OF IDEAS.
AS WE SAY ON ONE OF OUR LABELS: WE SET OUT TO CHANGE THE WORLD, STARTING WITH THE BEVERAGE SHELF. OUR PARTNERSHIP CAN ACTUALLY MAKE THAT HAPPEN.

We were thirsty. And we were also very lucky.

It would be a mistake to think our fairy-tale ending was simply the result of hard work and the right strategy. The Whole Foods buyer might have gotten up on the wrong side of the bed, Elie's operation could have been less successful, the unusually shaped mold might have been in one of *our* bottles, Seth's car accident could have been fatal, Oprah could have gone to a different yoga retreat, Obama could have been a coffee drinker, etc.

Though we had plenty of good luck, our setbacks were bad enough to bring down many a similarly situated company. The big question is: How were we able to survive our mistakes and bad luck to still be around when the good fortune arose? Before revealing my thoughts, let me first explain why survival is such a challenge.

The business world can be unforgiving. On a math test, getting 9 out of 10 problems right earns you an A. But in a start-up, any one thing that goes wrong can bring everything else down with it. Fast growth can lead you to run out of cash. A global financial crisis can lead your bank to freeze your line of credit. Bad contracts can make your business toxic to an investor or acquirer. A wrong hire can kill your culture, your operations, a key sales relationship, or just about anything else.

The mistake that almost killed us was buying the bottling plant. By the time we sold Three Rivers in 2005, it had cost us more than $1 million and hundreds of hours of sleep. To put that in context, Seth wasn't sleeping much to begin with, and that $1 million meant we had to do an extra round of fundraising and suffer extra dilution. But the biggest scare was the risk to our customers: the glass shards in our bottles might have hurt someone. We could have had the right product, the right brand, the right leadership, the right timing, and lost it all due to the bottling plant.

Since you're not likely to get even 9 out of 10 right, how can you overcome those things that will inevitably go wrong, either self-inflicted mistakes or just bad luck?

SURVIVAL GUIDE

My first answer goes right back to the beginning: YOUR PRODUCT (OR SERVICE) HAS TO BE RADICALLY DIFFERENT AND BETTER.

If people truly care about what you are doing, they will be more forgiving. To get customers, buyers, and investors to care, you can't just be 10% better than what's already out there. Simply substituting cane sugar for high-fructose corn syrup isn't enough. Cutting calories by 70% and using real tea leaves is the kind of radical change that gets people's attention and builds loyalty.

As an early Apple adopter (going all the way back to the Lisa), I suffered through many detours and dead ends because on its good days the Mac was, indeed, insanely great. Finis Swimp3 headphones resonate sound through the cheekbones so you can listen to music underwater. Early versions of the product were buggy and clunky, yet I stuck with them and bought newer generations because the product provides a radical solution to an unmet need. For me, swimming is terminally boring. With the Swimp3s to distract me, I'm able to catch up on podcasts as I do laps. Sure, I want Swimp3s to work more swimmingly, and if someone else beats them there, Finis will be in trouble. In the meantime, I'm willing to cut them some slack.

Honest Tea's game-changing strategy was to meet the need for a much less sweet beverage. Water is boring, sodas and juices are too sweet, and diet drinks are artificially so. The big beverage companies thought customers like me and Seth, our spouses, our friends, and perhaps you, the reader, were only a niche market. Now it turns out this niche is becoming the mainstream, but back then our target customers had been ignored for so long that they truly appreciated our efforts and gave us the second and third chances we needed.

I wish being radically different and better was enough, but it isn't.

A second key to survival is access to capital. Money is crucial, but I want to focus on what economists call reputational capital. That's a fancy way of saying the value of your reputation.

INVEST IN YOUR REPUTATION. If you've built a reputation, it can buy you a second chance. The problem is, establishing credibility takes time. Initially, a start-up can leverage the reputation of its founders, leaders, and investors, but the company needs to establish its own reputational capital. They say bankers only lend you an umbrella when it's sunny. We take that to mean you can't wait until you need something to ask for it. The same goes for using your reputation. You have to build it before you can use it.

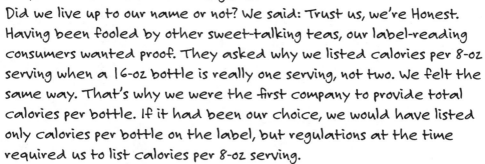

Here is where the name Honest came into play. Our name invited skeptical customers to challenge us. Did we live up to our name or not? We said: Trust us, we're Honest. Having been fooled by other sweet-talking teas, our label-reading consumers wanted proof. They asked why we listed calories per 8-oz serving when a 16-oz bottle is really one serving, not two. We felt the same way. That's why we were the first company to provide total calories per bottle. If it had been our choice, we would have listed only calories per bottle on the label, but regulations at the time required us to list calories per 8-oz serving.

Being Honest meant using real tea leaves, and honey, sugar, and agave for our sweeteners. It meant becoming organic, and then Fair Trade when that became feasible. Being Honest meant we wouldn't round five calories down to zero, even though that's legally permissible. When we messed up, we had "banked" enough trust to earn another chance with our customers. We sent our honest apologies along with lots of coupons.

With store buyers, we invested heavily in our reputational capital. When we discovered glass in a bottle, we did a voluntary product withdrawal before the situation escalated into the need for a recall. When stores needed someone to provide a demo, we always said yes. We invited buyers to try products during the development phase and took their input seriously.

Earning trust with our investors meant putting their financial return ahead of our own. It meant sharing good news and bad news. We wrote detailed quarterly newsletters and held annual shareholder meetings. It was time-consuming, but it meant our investors were never surprised.

Being radically different and better and having access to capital won't guarantee success, but at least they'll give you a fighting chance. That's why when students come to me for advice about launching a start-up, I generally try to talk them out of it.

ADVICE FROM THE PROFESSOR TO YOUNG ENTREPRENEURS

The young entrepreneur at my door may be full of passion, but that's not enough when his or her idea offers only a modest improvement on the status quo. Other times, the idea is plenty big, but it's something best done by an incumbent. The start-up would just be doing test marketing for an established player. Even when the stars are aligned, access to capital is almost always an issue. An entrepreneur may have enough funds to get started, but not enough to survive the inevitable storms. With too little capital, no reputation, and no experience, the odds of success, or even survival, are just too low.*

If you're concerned that I'm sounding negative, let me say that I don't think young entrepreneurs need encouragement. If anything, they tend to be overconfident and unable to imagine all the things that can go wrong or appreciate all the things that have to go right. If I can talk someone out of proceeding, then he or she likely didn't have the conviction and passion required to get them through. (Alas, now that I've revealed this ploy, it will be much less effective.)

* Of course, there are exceptions. While young entrepreneurs come with lots of disadvantages, web-based businesses, especially ones designed for their friends, is an arena where college students and recent grads are often uniquely qualified to understand the need and provide the solution. And there are some advantages to being young. You aren't yet responsible for someone else. You can sleep on a couch. Signing a personal guarantee is a lot less scary when there isn't anything behind the guarantee to lose.

What, then, is a young would-be entrepreneur to do? One option is to learn on someone else's dime. Join another start-up to see firsthand what they do right and wrong. In other words, learn from someone else's experience. Build your personal reputation. And make contacts, not just with regard to hiring people, but also with investors.

Be forewarned: having worked for a start-up, yours or someone else's, you may find it hard to ever go back to corporate America. It's not that employers don't value entrepreneurial experience—they usually see it as an asset—but after making things happen in a fast-paced start-up environment, you may not have the patience for the bureaucracy of a corporate setting.

There's no rush to pull the trigger. It took several years of noodling to transform the idea of mixing OJ with club soda into brewing a less sweet version of iced tea. For most entrepreneurs, the first idea is unlikely to be the best idea of your life. I've seen students give up a good portion of their bright college years building a catering business, a T-shirt printing company, and even a vending machine for umbrellas. This is a fine alternative to a campus job in the library. But don't lose perspective: think of it as a job, not something worth dropping out for, or even missing classes for.

In a world where Peter Thiel is bribing students to drop out of college to pursue their start-up dreams, allow me to make a shameless plug for my day job teaching MBA students. The normal course of education is to become increasingly specialized. An English major starts out reading fiction, nonfiction, poetry, and plays. Over time, he or she focuses on 20th-century literature, then Virginia Woolf, and finally Mrs. Dalloway and her flowers. Most graduate schools train you to be a specialist. Business school is just the opposite. We require our students to take classes in accounting, economics, finance, marketing, negotiation, operations, organizational behavior, and strategy. We force students to take courses outside their comfort zones.

The challenge in leading a start-up is you have to be a jack-of-all-trades and master of many. If you don't know enough about an area, you are bound to make mistakes. And by now you know the refrain: mistakes can be fatal. Sure, you can hire experts, but if you don't really understand the field, you'll have trouble hiring and managing the right talent. Witness our mistakes in operations.

Just as I encourage would-be entrepreneurs to enter the classroom, I encourage those who teach to gain real-world experience—the learning goes both ways. As I reflect on our real-world experiment, there are many practical lessons I'll take back to the classroom.

LESSONS I LEARNED

Through this journey, I came to appreciate the meaning and power of a brand. Creating a great brand means more than a snappy label. A great brand has to stand for something. Having seen countless mission statements, most of which seem indistinguishable from one another, I was skeptical that a name or a mission could be so influential, both externally and internally. And yet our brand guided everything we did and how people saw us. I'm a believer.

It's strange, looking back, that we initially failed to recognize what kind of brand we were really building. For the first five years, we  thought we were a tea company. That's why we added tea bags to the line. It wasn't until Honest Ade and Honest Kids took off that we appreciated the most important word in our name wasn't "Tea"—it was "Honest." Our brand meant authentic, healthier, organic products.

Knowing who you are creates opportunities to extend your success. In the first "Lessons Learned," I warned that others would copy you. The good news is that you can copy you, too. It's a bit like playing *Jeopardy*: you have a solution in search of a problem. Our solution was to create a less sweet, organic beverage that people could trust. Where else does that solution work? Fruit drinks and kids' drink pouches proved excellent opportunities to extend our brand. We didn't have this in mind when we started out. So now we're asking: Where else is there a need for a less sweet, honest alternative? Yogurt is one place. Breakfast cereal is another. How about a less sweet Gatorade? Soda? When we started out, I didn't think we could build a brand around club soda and OJ. But now that Honest is established and has access to world-class distribution, it might make sense. Stay tuned.

I'd also like to tidy up one loose end. We started the book asking the question, if this was such a good idea, why hadn't someone already done it? We trusted our gut, but we didn't really know the answer. Now that we better understand how the industry works, we can see why launching an Honest Tea would have been so hard for the established players.

First, they fall into a circular reasoning trap. If no one has done it, then it must be a niche market. The absence of data makes it hard to prove the size of the potential market. This leads everyone to go after the same established customer group. We'd rather have 10% of the market to ourselves than be one of 100 products competing for the well-defined 90%.

Big companies are designed to defend the mother ship. Imagine an established beverage company creates a new division to sell less sweet drinks. The newbie would want to knock the syrupy sweet competition. If that includes the company's own bestseller, the upstart's marketing would be muzzled in a hurry. But without making that type of stark comparison, the upstart brand would seem like more of the same.

A third explanation is that big companies set up hurdles that a fledgling Honest Tea can't clear. One global brand has a rule that "You have to beat the competition 60–40 in a blind taste test" before launching a new product. That seems reasonable at first look. Who would want to launch something that loses to the incumbent 60–40?

But a fledgling Honest Tea would never win this test, at least not the way they run it. In blind taste tests, sweeter usually wins. That's partly because samples are small (2 oz versus a whole bottle) and partly because the testers might be the wrong audience. Companies try to attract young consumers so as to develop a lifelong relationship. But tastes (and taste buds) change over time. Adults have less of a sweet tooth than teens. In running the taste test for Honest Tea, who would you put us up against? We'd surely lose with Snapple drinkers. We were looking for people who didn't like Snapple. The traditional market research test doesn't work well for creating a new category. That's why I think there's nothing so practical as a good theory.

Of course, it was Seth who would turn that theory into a reality. I had a simple job at Honest Tea: to help Seth be successful. That meant being a sounding board. That meant helping him avoid distractions. That also meant being the bad guy. People had to like Seth, and it helps that he's a naturally likable guy. But negotiations with suppliers, distributors, and partners can become contentious. If someone had to be blamed for us taking a hard line, it might as well have been me. At the end of the day, if Seth was successful, I would be, too.

Every week, Barry and I are approached by aspiring beverage and food entrepreneurs who want our advice on starting a company. The first piece of advice I give them is a line borrowed from *Monty Python and the Holy Grail*: "Run away! Run away!"

While it's easy to idealize the fun and rewarding aspects of building a company, the dangers are harder to imagine. You don't plan to get cheated out of money, lose sleep over meeting payroll, get copied by your competitors, or wake up in a cold sweat five out of seven nights because your life savings are on the line. I joke that, because of the wear and tear of the beverage industry, people should measure employment in dog years. Sometimes it feels as if a month goes by in a blur; other times a single day feels like a long week.

So why do it? Because it is a way to live out your passion. For me, Honest Tea is more than a great business opportunity and a way to quench my thirst—it's a way to improve the American diet by offering healthier drinks, help the ecosystem by reducing the amount of chemicals that go into it, and support communities in need of economic opportunities. Those broader missions are what motivate and inspire me. They are also what inspired many of our employees and investors. Naturally, some were more concerned with their financial return. The happy ending to our story is that we've been able to meet the goals of both our mission-driven and our financially driven stakeholders.

So, were we lucky? This won't be the first time I'm going to disagree with Barry. We were thirsty. We were lucky *enough*. And we worked our tails off.

We brought on Coca-Cola as an investor at a time when people were gravitating toward healthier diets and just before the Great Recession, which challenged our business, even with Coke's backing. But I reject the notion that we were lucky to be in the right place at the right time. It took us 10 years of hard work to end up in the right place at the right time—10 years in which several competitors with better access to resources arose and crashed. This was not an overnight success story.

One of my favorite bottle-cap quotes comes from UCLA basketball coach John Wooden. While we had our share of near-death experiences, we bounced back because we had enough of the Three Ps of Entrepreneurship: Passion, Persistence, and Perseverance.

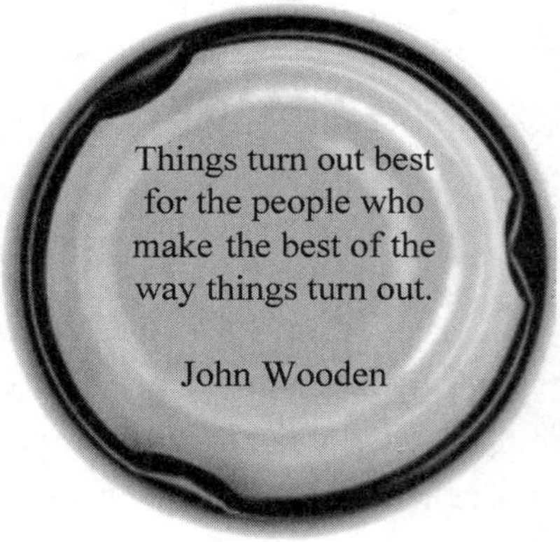
Things turn out best
for the people who
make the best of the
way things turn out.
John Wooden

Now that you've read our story, here are some lessons I hope you'll take with you.

THERE IS NO SILVER BULLET, ONLY THOUSANDS OF SMALL ONES. I've been asked if there were certain events or transition points when our growth really took off. It's easy to identify some pivotal moments:

- Getting a full-page write-up in Oprah's *O* magazine
- Stonyfield Farm investing and Gary Hirshberg joining our board

- Expanding our taste profile to "just a tad sweet"
- Making the entire line USDA Organic
- Dividing our product line and our distribution into glass and plastic
- Expanding beyond tea with Honest Ade
- Expanding to pouches with Honest Kids

I vividly remember the morning after we closed the transaction with Stonyfield. I was sitting in the office waiting for the phone to ring with all the great opportunities Gary would bring us. When I hadn't received a single call by 11 a.m., I realized we still had to go out and sell.

What made those moments pivotal were the opportunities they created for our team to make sales happen. It was the countless small things that added up, like each time an employee...

- got up a little earlier to perfect our placement in a beverage cooler;
- managed to smile after hours of standing at a sampling event and landed one more fan;
- tweaked a recipe or label design to make our drinks a little tastier and more eye-catching;
- convinced a supplier to extend a payment due date on a bill, thereby easing our cash crunch; or
- negotiated a better freight rate so that we had a little more money to hire another person.

These unheralded moments were what made the difference in our success. And those extra efforts represent the kind of behavior you can't buy—they are the result of dedicated people, inspired and united by a common mission and goal.

DOING A DEAL

If all goes well with your start-up, you may find yourself with one or more suitors. That can be a head-spinning trip. While I don't claim to be an expert when it comes to making deals, here are a few dos and don'ts I learned along the way.

DON'T FLIRT WITH STRATEGIC PARTNERS. In high school, I was extremely ineffective at asking girls out on dates. And while that meant my Saturday nights were usually spent at home watching *The Love Boat*, my inability to flirt became a useful trait as Honest Tea started being approached by potential acquirers. While it is flattering to be admired, we didn't enter into a conversation with a company unless we were genuinely interested in a long-term relationship. We may have turned away some good opportunities, but I also gained a reputation as a straight shooter who didn't play games. And by minimizing distractions, I managed to stay focused on building the long-term value of the brand by selling tea.

DO STAND BY YOUR MAN. When the conversation with Nestlé melted down, it would have been easy to point fingers, especially when I was told that Barry had screwed up my family's financial future. But Barry and I had worked together for 10 years as an effective team, and it was going to take more than one failed negotiation to derail our partnership. I knew that he had my back. I wouldn't trade Barry for all the tea in China—unless it was Fair Trade and came at a *really* good price.

DON'T DELEGATE YOUR MOST IMPORTANT WORK. Crafting the agreement with Coca-Cola was the most important negotiation we ever conducted. The process helped define the nature of the partnership and the tone of the relationship, not to mention the financial outcome for all our investors. Though investment bankers and lawyers typically conduct such transactions, Barry and I, along with our lawyer, actively participated in almost all of the discussions. As a result, we knew whom we were dealing with, how they operated under stress, how effective they were at solving problems, and ultimately, whether or not they were trustworthy.

At the same time, there is a reason why people turn to bankers and lawyers for negotiations: you can't be objective when you have so much skin in the game. Getting this wrong could have screwed up my dream job and my family's financial future. For the folks on the other side of the table, the result wasn't going to change their lives either way. That is why it was essential for us to have someone we trusted who could maintain objectivity. We had worked with our lawyer, George Lloyd, for many years, so he knew our strengths and weaknesses. He was a counselor in the truest sense of the word. You want to build that type of relationship early on. The middle of a high-stakes negotiation is not the time to start learning about one another.

DON'T NEGOTIATE YOURSELF OUT OF WHAT YOU WANT TO DO. The world of mission-driven business is littered with entrepreneurs whose companies lost their souls, or at least lost their leadership. Whether you talk to Ben Cohen from Ben & Jerry's or Steve Demos from Silk, they will tell you that, if they could do it over again, they would have done it differently. I am doing my best to make sure that never happens with Honest Tea. Our challenge was to find a partner who wanted to "buy in" to our mission rather than one who wanted us to "sell out." I had no interest in stepping away from the business—after all our years of struggle, finally, here was the chance to spread our mission to a wider audience.

Not all entrepreneurs will feel the same way. Some get bored once the business is more established and want to move on to the next start-up. Know what type of entrepreneur you are, and make sure you and your new partner understand each other's goals.

DO KEEP IT PERSONAL. I still read every email customers send to the company, and respond to many. When news of our transaction with Coca-Cola got out, some of our customers were none too thrilled. I personally responded to their concerns, explained our motivation, challenged their skepticism, and asked for their help in keeping us Honest.

I AM WRITING TO EXPRESS MY SURPRISE AND DISAPPOINT-MENT UPON HEARING THE RECENT NEWS THAT COCA-COLA WILL ACQUIRE A 40% STAKE IN HONEST TEA, MAKING IT THE COMPANY'S LARGEST STAKEHOLDER, AND THAT IT WILL HAVE THE OPTION TO PURCHASE A MAJORITY STAKE AFTER THREE YEARS. AS A BUSINESS THAT HAS BUILT ITS REPUTATION OVER THE PAST DECADE ON A COMMITMENT TO HEALTHY ORGANIC PRODUCTS, ENVIRONMENTAL QUALITY, AND SOCIAL JUSTICE FOR ITS PRODUCERS, HONEST TEA'S DECISION TO PARTNER WITH COCA-COLA—A MULTINATIONAL CORPORATION THAT HAS CONSISTENTLY VIOLATED ALL THREE OF THESE PRINCIPLES IN THEIR GLOBAL BUSINESS PRACTICES—CONFOUNDS ME.
—JULIE

You've got mail

HI JULIE,

THANKS FOR YOUR HONEST OPINION. BASED ON YOUR REMARKS I THINK IT'S FAIR TO SAY THAT YOU BELIEVE THE WORLD WOULD BE BETTER IF COKE SOLD PRODUCTS MORE LIKE OURS. SO THEN THE QUESTION IS WHETHER WE BELIEVE THAT HONEST TEA WILL BE CORRUPTED BY COKE. I'M CONFIDENT WE WILL CONTINUE TO SELL THE PRODUCTS WE'VE BEEN SELLING—WE PAINSTAKINGLY BUILT OUR BUSINESS OVER 10 YEARS IN A VERY DELIBERATE MANNER. WE WERE CONSTANTLY PRESENTED WITH THE OPTION OF MAKING THE PRODUCTS CHEAPER (E.G., USING HIGH-FRUCTOSE CORN SYRUP INSTEAD OF ORGANIC CANE SUGAR OR HONEY, OR TEA LEAVES WITHOUT FAIR TRADE CERTIFICATION) OR WITH MORE CALORIES BUT WE CONSISTENTLY CHOSE TO KEEP THE BRAND "HONEST." COKE FOUND VALUE IN WHAT WE'VE CREATED—IF THEY WANTED TO CHANGE US INTO A COMPANY LIKE THEIRS, THEY WOULD HAVE BUILT THEIR OWN BRAND RATHER THAN INVESTING IN HONEST TEA.

I HOPE YOU'LL JUDGE US BY OUR ACTIONS. LET ME KNOW IF YOU SEE US BACKING AWAY FROM OUR COMMITMENT TO ORGANICS, HEALTHIER PRODUCTS, AND SUSTAINABILITY.

HONESTLY YOURS,

SETH

PARTING THOUGHTS

Ten years ago, if someone had told me I would be engaged in a mission-driven career where I would...

- manage a team of passionate and diverse individuals;
- work to eliminate billions of calories from the American diet;
- support a more sustainable approach to agriculture; and
- create economic opportunity at a community level in the developing world

my first response would have been, "That's perfect. Those are all issues I care about deeply." My only question would have been, "What
nonprofit or government entity do I work for?" I would never have
predicted that the beverage industry would be my vehicle for
change, and occasionally I still wake up in the morning a bit surprised that I sell bottles (and pouches) of liquid for a living.

When I was growing up, I dreamed of work
that would empower people to improve one
another's lives. I used to think politics was
the best way to engage in that kind of
change. But Honest Tea has helped me
appreciate that consumers make decisions every day that can tilt the world
a little closer to the one we want, rather
than the one we live in.

If we don't
change the direction
we are headed, we
will end up where
we are going.

Chinese Proverb

A few years ago, John Mayer had a hit song, "Waiting for the World
to Change." Nice melody, wrong message. We won't change the world
by waiting. We will change it by making conscious choices every day
about what we wear; how we live, work, and move around; what we
eat; and, of course, what we drink.

At the center of Honest Tea's office is our sales board, where we
write down every order that comes in.

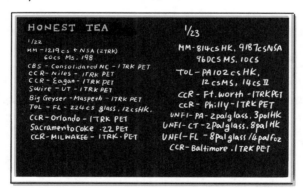

Ostensibly, the writing on the board tracks how many bottles we are
selling, but to me it represents something far more important—it is a

daily indicator of the impact of our mission. It is energizing to finish a day and see the board filled; it means we are playing a small role in taking things in a different direction.

But there are still days when the board is only partially full. On days like that we have to remind ourselves that, although we have come a long way, we are still offering products whose recipes and ingredients are a marked departure from what most Americans drink. Change is not supposed to be easy, but we are fueled by the challenge as well as our passion for a better future.

Those who say it cannot be done should not interrupt the people doing it.

Chinese Proverb

We've made a lot of progress since Barry and I poured tea into five thermoses in my kitchen (we still have the thermoses in our office). However, when we look at what's happening to the health of our population and of our planet, it's clear there is much more to do.

So, was Honest Tea in the right place at the right time? I've come to realize that even if you are building something you believe in, you still may not win. But if it is something worth fighting for—win or lose—you are in the right place at the right time.

Coca-Cola became a 40% owner of Honest Tea in March 2008, and full owner in 2011. Seth is still running the business from Bethesda. Barry is still teaching at Yale. Seth has been sleeping better, partly because there are no loan guarantees hanging over his head and partly because he and Julie bought a better mattress. Barry lost over 40 pounds and managed (with a lot of help) to sort through enough piles of paper in his office to find the desk.

As promised, Nestlé did buy a tea brand—indeed, they bought two: Tradewinds and Sweet Leaf. Pepsi took over the distribution of Tazo, further adding to the competitive landscape.

Even with Coke in our corner, there were plenty of challenges along the way. In the midst of the 2008 financial crisis, we were still growing rapidly, but our longtime bank wouldn't expand our line of credit. Thankfully, one of our investors provided us with the $10 million credit line we needed.

We entered the kombucha market in 2009 with an amazing product— and sales to match—and then had to withdraw it all after a store did a random test and found the alcohol content in bottles from all of our kombucha varieties exceeded the legal limit of 0.5%. No wonder they were so popular. (Our lawyers asked us to add that our products were in compliance when they left the production facility, but natural variation and poor handling may have led to the anomalous high reading.)

We haven't always been in total agreement with Coca-Cola, such as the time they asked us to remove the "No high-fructose corn syrup!"

message from the Honest Kids carton (we didn't). But we have made several exciting advances to-gether, including the installation of world-class tea brewing systems at two of Coca-Cola's certified organic bottling plants. Coke helped us improve the Honest Kids line so that it's now sweetened only with organic juice—something we had wanted to do but that wasn't practical without Coke's resources.

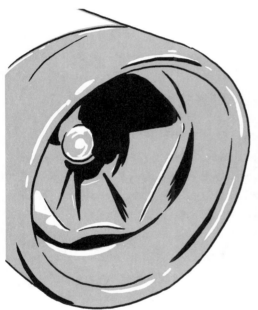

In order to reduce our plastic consumption, we came out with a lighter-weight PET bottle, but it dented too easily. To preserve the shape, our second design used pressure from a large inverted dome, but that caused some consumers to think we were employing a false bottom. We responded by temporarily adding a Post-it note explanation to our labels. Soon thereafter, we were able to fix the bottle.

In 2011, we launched a daring and tasty line of brewed cacao drinks, Honest Cocoanova, which failed brilliantly in a record-setting 12 months.

Just business as usual.

Throughout it all, Honest Tea continues to prosper. Our sales grew from $23 million in 2007 to $88.5 million in 2012. On July 11, 2012, the daily order board totaled $1.1 million, more than we sold during our first full year. We now have 112 employees, up from 52 in 2007. And you can find our beverages in over 100,000 outlets, compared to just 15,000 when Coke made its investment in 2008.

Along with increasing our sales volume, we've furthered our social mission. In 2011, we converted the last of our teas to Fair Trade Certified. We successfully lightweighted our PET bottle, reducing plastic usage by 22% (with no dents). To hold ourselves accountable, we started producing "Keeping It Honest," our annual mission report, which you can read at honesttea.com.

The beverage industry has evolved, too. While we can't claim credit for all the changes, consider the following:

• When we launched Honest Tea in 1998, the average 16-oz bottle of Snapple tea had 180 calories. In 2012, the average was closer to 140 calories.
• In 2007, when we launched Honest Kids, the typical Capri Sun pouch drink had 100 calories. In 2012, the calorie count was 60 (though they also shrunk their pouches by 12%). We like to think we helped demonstrate the viability of a lower-sugar kids' product, and with billions of Capri Sun pouches sold every year, that's tens of billions of calories eliminated from kids' lunches.
• Before we launched Honest Kids, all drink pouches ended up in landfills. Thanks to our partnership with TerraCycle, more than 140 million pouches have been taken out of the waste stream and upcycled.

Honest Tea's business model and market success may have helped pave the way for larger brands to follow, but there's so much more to do ourselves. By selling over 100 million bottles and pouches each year, we help cut billions of calories from the American diet. As we grow, we can cut even more calories and help lead a national shift toward healthier diets.

Sales of organic foods and beverages continue to grow, but still represent less than 5% of what Americans consume. We love natural foods stores—indeed, we couldn't have launched Honest Tea without them—but we need to extend the reach of organic, healthier food to all Americans. And now that Honest Tea is part of Coca-Cola, we have the chance to democratize organics. Our tea party is just getting started.

Honestly yours,

Seth + Barry

1. Build something you believe in—that's the first step to building a great brand.

2. Don't aim for 10% improvement. Make it radically better and different.

3. Prepare to be copied. Don't start unless you'll survive imitation.

4. Build up reserves of money and energy for bad luck and mistakes.

5. Never, ever give up control—until you sell.

6. Don't compromise on the big things—compromise on everything else.

7. Figure out how to achieve your goals on a tiny budget—then cut that number in half.

8. It's a marathon, not a sprint.

9. Take care of your family, personal, and spiritual health—if you aren't laughing or smiling on a regular basis, recalibrate.

10. Build the enterprise and the brand as if you'll own them forever.

11. Don't pay too much attention to the rules—as long as you're not breaking the law.

ACKNOWLEDGMENTS

Just as we could never have built Honest Tea by ourselves, this book is the result of the encouragement, ideas, criticism, and corrections of dozens of people.

We first want to thank all the book's "characters" for their roles in shaping Honest Tea. Some, like Melanie Knitzer, continue to build the brand today. Others, like George Scalf and Irving "H" Hershkowitz, have sadly passed away. We are also enormously grateful to Cheryl Newman (Honest Tea's Deputy Chief of Mission), Kelly Cardamone, and Lynette Taylor for all their help and support.

In addition to Honest Tea's employees, to whom we dedicate this book, we are indebted to the investors who placed their confidence (and money) in us. Along with sage advice, John MacBain provided a line of credit when banks wouldn't. And we are especially thankful to our parents, who invested in us from an early age and have never stopped.

When we decided to make this a visual story, Ric Gref, Executive Director of the American Institute of Graphic Arts, directed us to some of today's most promising artists. Although we couldn't describe what we wanted, once we saw Sungyoon Choi's work, we knew we had found it. We are exceptionally fortunate that she agreed to work with us. She has proved to have the patience, intuition, and thoughtfulness to match her talent.

We always struggle to keep our back-label messages under 87 words, so you can imagine how challenging it was for us to tell a 10-year history in word bubbles. Fortunately, we had Katie Pichotta as a passionate, straight-shooting, take-no-prisoners editor. Her painstaking attention to detail has been invaluable. More than anyone, she helped keep our tale concise, on track, and honest. We are also thankful to Ethan Kuperberg for helping us find humor and keep the dialogue natural and for drinking all the spare bottles of Honest Tea. Anne Fadiman, Judy Hansen, Timothy Young, Zach Greenwald, and Marcia Nalebuff also provided wise counsel. We tried to avoid scenes of people sitting around a conference table. There are still some in the book, but fewer thanks to Ethan, Katie, and Choi's creativity.

This book would never have happened if it weren't for our literary heroes, who believed a business book could be told in graphic form. We are grateful to our agent, Susan Ginsburg, who supported us from the start, and our editor, Roger Scholl, and his team at Crown Publishers, who have embraced and championed this book, which is not their usual cup of tea.

We are happily indebted to our wives and children. Seth's wife, Julie Far-kas, endured the Honest Tea journey from the passenger seat, and it was often a white-knuckle ride. The writing of this book has been a bit smooth-er, but her blunt advice and unflagging support have continued to be invaluable. Barry's wife, Helen Kauder, helped us connect with Sloan Wilson, our first graphic designer, and has been our secret focus group all along. Our kids—Jonah, Elie, and Isaac; Rachel and Zoe—have been never-ending sources of encouragement, diversion, and inspiration.

Finally, to our wonderful customers—without you, there would have been no story, or certainly not this one. Thank you!

T

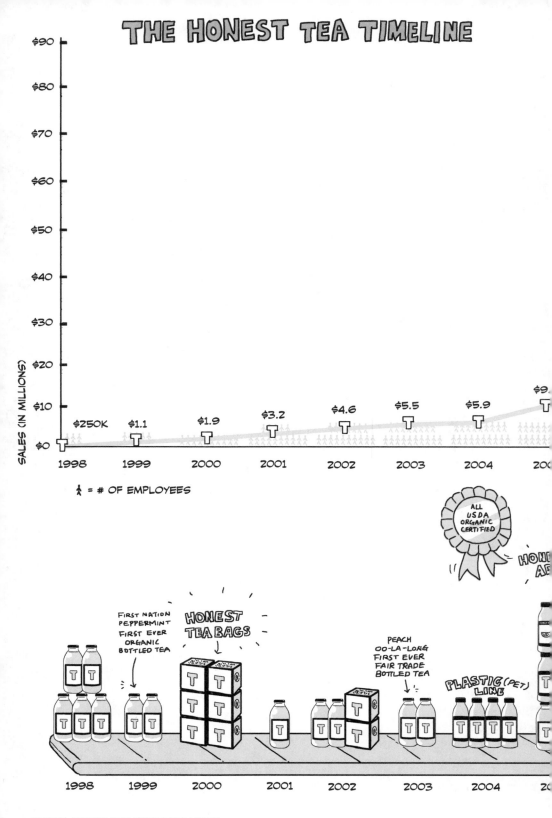

THE HONEST TEA TIMELINE

SALES (IN MILLIONS)

$250K $1.1 $1.9 $3.2 $4.6 $5.5 $5.9 $9.

1998   1999   2000   2001   2002   2003   2004   200

⌁ = # OF EMPLOYEES

ALL USDA ORGANIC CERTIFIED

HON AI

FIRST NATION PEPPERMINT FIRST EVER ORGANIC BOTTLED TEA

HONEST TEA BAGS

PEACH OO-LA-LONG FIRST EVER FAIR TRADE BOTTLED TEA

PLASTIC (PET) LINE

1998   1999   2000   2001   2002   2003   2004   20

NEW FLAVORS AND PRODUCT LINES

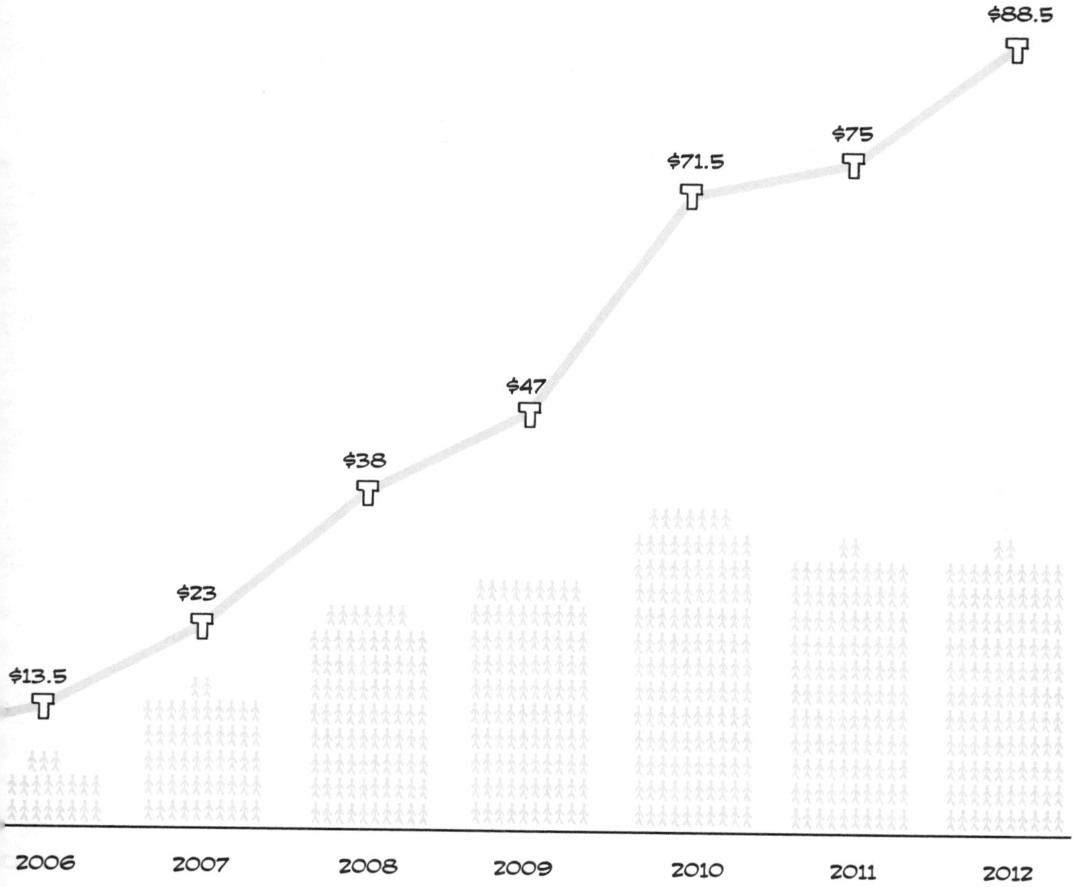
$88.5
$75
$71.5
$47
$38
$23
$13.5
2006
2007
2008
2009
2010
2011
2012

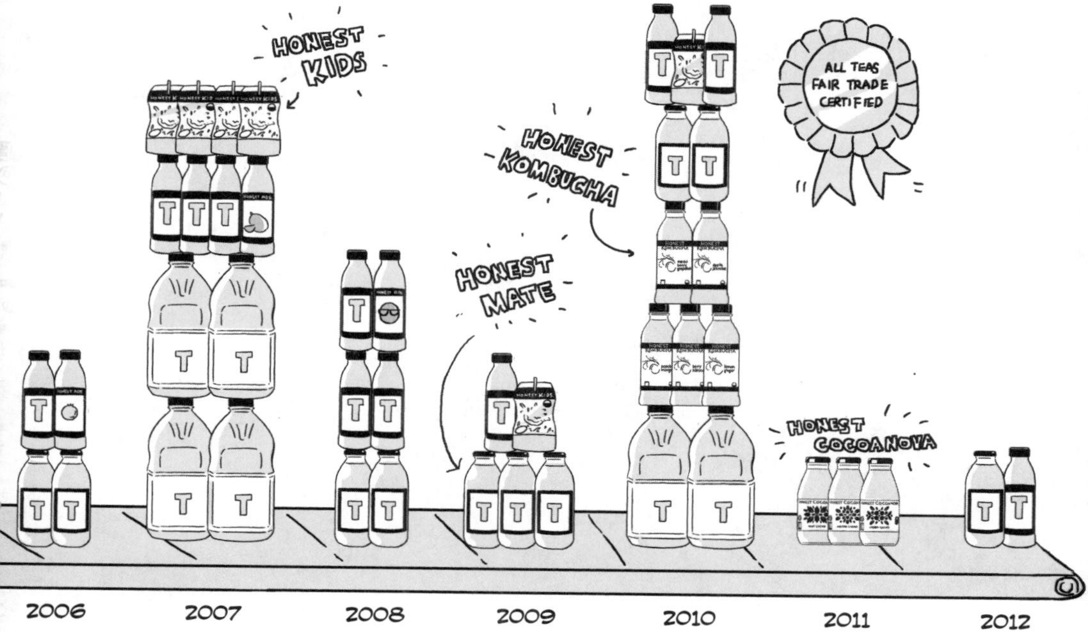
HONEST KIDS
ALL TEAS FAIR TRADE CERTIFIED
HONEST KOMBUCHA
HONEST MATE
HONEST COCOANOVA
2006
2007
2008
2009
2010
2011
2012